Candyland
S.I.N.S.

(Singles INternet-dating Services)
Mature Online Dating

Your Insider's Guide

male and female friendly

Welcome to My World

Joan Barrett

SINS member with over 22,000 views ... 1,000's of winks, flirts, favorites & emails

Numerous memorable dates ... and still counting

AuthorHouse™
1663 Liberty Drive
Bloomington, IN 47403
www.authorhouse.com
Phone: 1-800-839-8640

This book is a work of non-fiction. Unless otherwise noted, the author
and the publisher make no explicit guarantees as to the accuracy of
the information contained in this book and in some cases, names of
people and places have been altered to protect their privacy.

Cartoons by Randy Glasbergen
Author photos by Erik McNichol

Published by AuthorHouse 11/03/2014

ISBN: 978-1-4969-4011-7 (sc)
ISBN: 978-1-4969-4010-0 (hc)
ISBN: 978-1-4969-4009-4 (e)

Library of Congress Control Number: 2014916464

Any people depicted in stock imagery provided by Thinkstock are models,
and such images are being used for illustrative purposes only.
Certain stock imagery © Thinkstock.

This book is printed on acid-free paper.

Because of the dynamic nature of the Internet, any web addresses or
links contained in this book may have changed since publication and
may no longer be valid. The views expressed in this work are solely those
of the author and do not necessarily reflect the views of the publisher,
and the publisher hereby disclaims any responsibility for them.

Contents at a Glance

Contents

A Mature Single.

Where you are now and how you got here.

Most likely, you are in a vulnerable place, not there by choice
and want to move on.

Time to take control and take action.

SINS members ... Mature Singles in a range of decades.

Introducing you to your new community of friends and lovers.

How you fit right in.

As apropos a term as you wish it to be.

Singles INternet-dating Services offer tempting treats for
Mature Singles of all decades.

What such services provide their members.

Frequently asked questions answered for you.

Revealing statistics that lead you to ask yourself:
"What am I waiting for?"

Instructions for launching yourself and joining in.

Contact Joan at candylandsins@rogers.com
Visit Candyland S.I.N.S. at: www.candylandsins.com
Visit Candyland S.I.N.S. at: www.facebook.com/candylandsins

Candyland S.I.N.S.

What's It All About?

The *truths* and the *lies*

The *facts* and the *fiction*

The *preconceptions* and the *misconceptions*

The *expectations* and the *realities*

The *heartthrobs* and the *heartaches*

The *successes* and the *disappointments*

The *chills* and the *thrills*

Welcome to My World
To the Reader

You are alone ... and still very much alive. Missing companionship; and yes, admit it ... intimacy. When some of you think of how often you ignored earlier opportunities or did not appreciate them when you were contentedly married or in loving committed relationships, you could cry!! I mean for both the lost companionship and the sex! Others of you may never have had the chance of a relationship or marriage ... yet. Well, wipe those tears off your faces as you begin to make up for lost time and missed opportunities. An exciting social world awaits your participation if you are adventurous enough to enter the realm of online dating for Young and Seasoned Matures: **S**ingles **IN**ternet-dating **S**ervices. My reference for these online dating sites is **S.I.N.S.** or for ease of discussion: **SINS**! The latter could be as apropos a term as you desire.

SINS offer online dating site playgrounds filled with tempting potential partners for those of us who refuse to fade away. These dating sites are a candyland filled with delectable treats for us to savor. They call to mind the candy stores we remember from our childhoods ... visual feasts of sweets filling display cases. How could we possibly select just a few? That was candy; this is now. Your choices may be as plentiful and as tempting as those of long ago. *Candyland S.I.N.S.* can be your guide!

How many single Young and Seasoned Matures would have believed just a few years ago that SINS not only existed but also would now thrive ... teeming with many attractive (some no-longer-as-attractive on the surface) and lively Matures having the time of their lives? For many in their mature decades these dating sites have made the later years the best years of their lifetimes.

Candyland S.I.N.S. is based on this writer's firsthand experiences on various dating sites with over 22,000 'views', thousands of emails, winks, favorites, flirts, numerous mostly memorable dates ... and a few marvelous relationships. Within the pages of *Candyland S.I.N.S.* I give you a voyeur's view of what actually transpires in this electronic world that beckons to so many of us in our still-active years.

Many Singles, however, remain on the sidelines ... with a good deal of curiosity. They are hesitant to enter due to reasons such as caution about this unknown-to-them world and/or unawareness of *what actually goes on* in Candyland. They may also harbor personal anxieties or a self-perceived lack of sufficient electronic know-how. Perhaps they face insecurities as to how to handle the onsite interactions and possible relationships that might come their way ... while time marches on ... all too quickly for most of us.

No one must just hold back and wonder. All sorts of questions will be answered within *Candyland S.I.N.S.*, *the* insider's guide to Mature online dating. The compilation of staggering researched statistics, the author's actual experiences, factual member accounts and expert interview reports will shed light on Candyland and guide you through this new vibrant territory. What you will read will help you practically and emotionally in your new life adventure.

Pay attention and proceed at a comfortable pace. You will find much to absorb and understand in *this* guide to SINS. You will be on a real learning curve throughout the chapters of *Candyland S.I.N.S.* For many, your lost-but-not-forgotten dating skills will be re-energized and polished. For the hesitant, here is *the* guide to launch or re-launch a social life which just might lead to finding that someone who will take your breath away. For all, may your occasional *heart attacks* be smiling ones.

Read *Candyland S.I.N.S.* with an open mind and allow yourself to be motivated to act with anticipation of loads of fun and excitement. Never forget your attitude is *the game-changer*. At a time in your life when you find yourself wishing there were more time, the process can be stimulating and surprisingly invigorating because you will add *more life* to your life.

Let us begin our conversation

"You are only given one life, one chance at fully living it ...
take risks, believe in your dreams,
explore the world and her people,
live out loud!"
-Danell Lynn, *Philanthropic Wanderlust*-

To my dear daughters

Who have lived through the heartbreaks and the celebrations
of a mother who chose to live a life of passion.
A mother who has led a life blessed with opportunities ...
accompanied by their sometimes inevitable failures.
My daughters were brave to embrace
a mother who did not live
by the guidelines of a traditional community in which
they were trying to establish their own identities.
They loved a mother unlike their friends' mothers,
kindly masking from me
their odd moments of eye-rolling ... I am sure.
Whether secretly embarrassed or openly concerned,
my daughters were *always there* for me,
supportive of my efforts to broaden my world ...
and ultimately theirs and that of their children.
My dear girls somehow convinced
their wonderful husbands that
their mother was the real deal.
A mother who loves them all unconditionally.
They set the example ... their mother was to be loved
and to be respected for her right to be true to herself.
They have grown to be wise, loving, and nurturing
mothers to their own families.
My daughters have given me the most wonderful grandchildren
I could have ever imagined ...
each a gem with his or her own color, texture and sparkle.
My daughters have blessed me with
more than I ever dreamed.
I dedicate this to you both.
Hold on for another ride!

Disclaimer

The anecdotes I recount in *Candyland S.I.N.S.* are representative of the issues and situations I have encountered in my eight years of online dating. No real names are used. Nor are specific people or situations necessarily precisely portrayed. These accounts are a close depiction of occurrences commonly encountered in the massive online dating community. Many incidents represent the missteps and mistakes I have made. I share them with you to help you avoid the same common pitfalls.

The author and publisher do not offer professional advice; nothing in this book should be considered as such. You must seek such authoritative consultation from a reputable and educated professional in the fields you are querying. This author's advice is based on her experiences, research and the experiences of others. Her guidance is intended to be informative and helpful. You are solely responsible for how you utilize the information in *Candyland S.I.N.S.*

You are a unique individual with your own distinctive coping skills; you will be functioning in a unique set of circumstances. My situations, those of others and concepts discussed may not necessarily apply to you and your present or intended experiences in Internet-dating.

The dating websites I mention or discuss throughout *Candyland S.I.N.S.* are for informational purposes only. Their mention does not necessarily reflect my opinion or viewpoint. I receive no compensation from them for doing so. You should conduct your own investigation and apply due diligence as to the accuracy of my information before proceeding and/or joining various sites based on the information I have shared.

Candyland S.I.N.S.' mandate is to be informative, helpful and entertaining. It is intended to impart some insight into a subject so many are curious about and want to participate in but are reluctant to delve into. I hope I answer many questions. I have tried to be thorough, document all detailed research and do so honestly.

Enter

Candyland SINS

"Why not go out on a limb? That's where the fruit is."
-Will Rogers-

Here you are ... single ... maybe again!
Probably for the first time in decades ...
an inevitable ending or an enviable 'last act'?
What is your next step?

Are you going to cruise comfortably but unimaginatively to the standard inevitable ending *or* are you going to build a great 'last act' in the stage play of your life? *Candyland S.I.N.S.* offers you a guide and flexible template for crafting your coming years through participation in **SINS** (the author's playful and loose morph for **S**ingles **IN**ternet-dating **S**ervices). **SINS** are gateways to socially-focused adventures that serve Young and Seasoned Single Matures. Let's begin with a preview of things to come.

The author presents a sampling of true experiences of Internet-based daters along with her own. At times, you will laugh and you may feel a sympathetic tear in your eye. Most importantly, these accounts will take you deeper into the world of SINS. Warning ... some will surprise you. They will never bore you. *This* is Candyland and its SINS. *Candyland S.I.N.S.* was written by this suddenly Single Mature woman who navigates the tricky, exciting, and challenging Seasoned Singles (as in Definitely Mature) lifestyle in her chosen *modus vivendi.* So can you.

My SINS story began in my early 60's with my re-entry onto the Singles scene by proactively opening a cooking school for 'Seasoned' Singles. I saw the need to encourage social interaction in what could arguably have been described as an often socially marginalized segment of society. Then I discovered SINS ... a whole new exciting world that renewed my energy and love of life through social interaction with like-minded Mature Singles who were not about to roll over alone and be spectators of life.

I am still a member of SINS after eight years. I have logged more than 22,000 views and thousands of emails, favorites, flirts, and winks and numerous dates ... a long, active period of involvement and a deep enough engagement to know the game, how the game is played ... and how '*not to be played*'! I initially entered SINS with the intention to find '*the one*' and the one long-term relationship so many seek. I dipped into and out of various sites ... sometimes with my profile hidden ... something you can also do. At times, after disappointing or failed connections I had to pick myself up, dust myself off and start all over again. At other times I stepped away for happenings in my previous circles and for new, fun ventures in order to allow myself to heal and regain confidence.

Over the years, I have found that SINS continually percolate with activity ... always anything but boring.

I have never lost my fascination with SINS and how they function in Singles communities ... particularly communities dedicated to Mature Singles. I have seen SINS become the mainstay of Mature dating. Yes, SINS is *the only real game in town*. Seasoned Matures, especially, are generally neither hanging out at bars nor going to Singles socials to meet potential partners. SINS have provided me and *so* many Mature Singles a range of bounteous opportunities for smiles, laughs, good times and (to be honest) various causes for heartaches and tears. But, aren't all of these experiences how we know that we are still truly alive?

This is my story and I'm sticking to it ... your story may vary. *Candyland S.I.N.S.* is a compilation of researched information about, topical resources for and actual and truthful first-hand accounts of Mature online dating. It is based on my experiences and those of other Mature members of SINS communities. Interspersed with encouragement, at times funny and at times sad, *Candyland S.I.N.S.* will guide you through the interwoven aspects of this already massive and still burgeoning online venue ... its highways and roadways, its byways and pathways ... and its detours. It will entertain you and empower you ... no matter your decade of life. It will keep you looking with anticipation as to what is around the next corner *for me and for you*. Now, let us preview what this guide can do for you and how it can help you arrive at your next 'hurrah'.

A journey through Candyland is one you will always remember, just as you fondly recall entering as a child that old-fashioned candy shop filled with mouth-watering sweets. Similarly, SINS are new-fashioned sweet shops, a huge wonderland of opportunities filled with many wonderful members. You will find more than a few who will draw you, tempt you and beckon you ... just as in that childhood shop.

We Matures are no longer young adults. But, we do not have to move through these years oh-so quietly, waiting passively for the inevitable that every human being experiences. We still have the means to reshape our lives in small and larger ways. Here is your opportunity to do some of just that. Within SINS you will have the fun of relearning how to select, pursue, court and be courted. How to experience romance, have a revitalized sex life and, perhaps, even, settle down once again with a special someone for a spectacular 'next act'.

In *Candyland S.I.N.S.* you will find footings and steppingstones to make your journey safer, manageable and controllable, more fun, exciting and successful. You may very well relate to my experiences and those of other members later in your own journey, when you face some of the same yourself. Guiding hands will lead you through, to a certain extent. Every member's experience is personal and unique ... some stories of real events are offered to you for their entertainment value and others for their emotional support and learning opportunities.

You will have a bird's-eye view of what actually transpires in this unfamiliar world, one that beckons to so many in our mature years. When you enter this symbolic Candyland of delectable treats you will unearth a bit of your youth ... how overindulgence super-stimulated you or made you sick, how no treats left you with a sugar low, depressed and yearning for the satisfying feelings of their sweetness. Everyone has a different tolerance for sweets. You will find your levels as you travel through Candyland. Enter, enjoy and learn from your experiences, armed with the strengths of firsthand knowledge and researched information ... *and* with the all-important right *attitude*.

You are about to enter SINS, the very social world of online dating. It is a relatively new world phenomenon that is not merely growing but is flourishing. One study released in 2013 by the Pew Research Center's Internet and American Life Project[1] presented favorable growth figures. For example: the study reported the percentage of the American population who stated that they had used online dating websites grew from 3 percent in 2008 to 6 percent in 2009, and to 9 percent in 2013. [For additional figures see end of chapter Studies and Statistics, Item 1.]

In another initiative, a University of Chicago study commissioned by eHarmony.com found 35 percent of people who married between 2005 and 2012 met online. Forty-five percent of the 19,131 responders of a representative sample survey met on Internet dating sites.[2] [For additional figures see end of chapter Studies and Statistics, Item 2.]

The trending figures would suggest that Mature Singles better get with it! SINS are here to stay; they are dramatically changing not

---

[1] Aaron Smith and Maeve Duggan, Pew Research Center's Internet and American Life Project 2013, www.pewinternet.org, http://www.pewinternet.org/2013/10/21/online-dating-relationships/, accessed June 28, 2014.

[2] As quoted by William Harms, June 3 1013, http://news.uchicago.edu/article/2013/06/03/meeting-online-leads-happier-more-enduring-marriages, The survey of 19,131respondants was commissioned by eHarmony.com and followed procedures specified by JAMA, which included oversight by independent statisticians - See more at: http://news.uchicago.edu/article/2013/06/03/meeting-online-leads-happier-more-enduring-marriages#sthash.a2JSQi3a.dpuf, accessed June 28, 2014.

only the general dating scene but also the niche Matures dating scene. The Matures niche is the largest growth community on the dating sites. It is *the* still-emerging big weapon against the real or perceived isolation that besets many Mature Singles. Social media such as Facebook, Twitter, LinkedIn, etc. appear to be too techy and complex for some Matures to approach, handle and adapt to. And, perhaps, too publicly *personal* for many of them. But, most of us can handle SINS ... perhaps with only a little help from our friends. Great numbers of Mature Singles are finding they can readily navigate SINS without help because the clear and detailed instructions on the sites can be easily understood with little or no initial guidance. Also, be comfortable knowing that you are as anonymous as you want to be in SINS. Your privacy is of utmost importance to these sites, as it is to you. *We* like that security feature.

The majority of new members of dating sites, whatever their actual age and decade, share the same concerns and queries. Most chapters of this guide relate to any age group, particularly any decade within the 40's-80's. Yes. 80's. I have seen profiles online for members in their 80's *and* 90's. Since every one of us, given life's circumstances, has the freedom to live as appropriately as s/he feels, I address most important aspects of dating on SINS for all ages with special attention to Mature Daters.

Few experiences in this world can match the pinnacle of a truly passionate and broad-based healthy relationship ... at any age. I have had it. Gotta love it! We are all capable of achieving it with the right partner. Whether in youth or in later years, our hearts can flutter and sputter when seeking and entering new relationships. I will try to guide you ... female or male ... in any range of Mature online dating.

You may feel you are moving through the years too quickly and losing ground faster than you would like; but you have not lost your free will and spirit. Just picking up *Candyland S.I.N.S.* demonstrates you are ready to begin moving forward. You have already taken the first step to act upon the information I am about to share with you. You can live vicariously through my experiences and those of other members, and/or you can go on to create your own, better prepared than others before you who did not have the opportunity to read and benefit from the multi-faceted experiences within *Candyland S.I.N.S.* I recommend the latter action. Be proactive. Prepare first; create next!

If you want a guarantee, buy a toaster.
-Clint Eastwood-

The knowledge and skills I have learned through my acquaintances, new friends and interactions while on my own search have given me a valuable trove of worthwhile information to share that will help you learn to navigate SINS and avoid at least some of the mistakes I made along the way. I have made plenty; I don't want you to make the same. Follow along with me so you avoid some of the inevitable pitfalls and occasional disappointments, as well.

As a SINS member you can enjoy varying levels of interactions with people you choose or retreat from any activity you do not wish to engage in. Your online interplay is limited only by your degree of effort and your expectations ... if the latter are realistic or, perhaps, need to be better defined. Within the platforms of SINS exist nearly every type and status of companion, potential life partner or sexual encounter for you.

I encourage you to approach SINS with a sense of ease, with no feeling of dire need. You will meet new friends, have many good times and, I hope, meet your lifetime partner as the icing on the cake of your life. That is the goal for most of you, is it not? With a relaxed approach and *Candyland S.I.N.S.* as a guide to the inner workings of the online dating world, tips, important warnings and emotional support, you could very well become part of the aforementioned impressive successful relationship statistics that can be explored in this book.

I do stress that your attitude toward SINS should be one of *relaxed* adventure. Anxiety can project desperation, one of the most unattractive traits you can display when looking for possible partners. Lean back. Enjoy the journey. At times you will echo Goldilocks with her Three Bears ... this one is too tall (short), that one is too skinny (fat), this one is too needy (controlling), etc. Then, we have Prince Charming ... looking over all the eligible ladies in his father's realm. Oh, there's Princess May ... surveying possible suitors strolling by. Well. You won't be sitting back for too long. You are opening a new chapter in your life ... a chapter that could alter your life forever, as it did so for me. It was change you were seeking when you opened these pages. I offer you many keys to the opportunities that can bring that change.

"So many people our age are divorced and dating again, they're changing my class reunion to a prom!"

Here is your initial glimpse into the research that is one cornerstone of this guide.

The divorce rate has changed dramatically. In the U.S. it has doubled for people over 50 in the past 20 years compared with a slight decrease in divorce overall.[3] An interesting development, for sure. Many Matures are in their second, even third or more marriages. These marriages are less likely to survive according to Krista Kay Payne, researcher at the PEW Research Center for People & the Press. [4]One consequence of the increasing divorce rate among Matures is a greater number of individuals interested in a new relationship. Many will turn to SINS.

Now is when you come in. Seriously consider stepping into the realm of SINS and their abundant benefits. Research shows now is your time to enter the online dating world! Fifty-nine percent of Internet users agree: online dating is a good way to meet people. That figure is up from the 44 percent of 2005.[5] These numbers reflect overall increasingly positive experiences in SINS.

---

[3] As cited by Catey Hill, www.marketwatch.com, http://www.marketwatch.com/story/10-things-boomers-won't-tell-you-2013-07-12 THE AGING ME GENERATION IS STILL PUTTING ITSELF FIRST, The Burning Platform, July 12, 2013 from the National Center for Family and Marriage Research, Bowling Green University, 005 Williams Hall Bowling Green, Ohio 43403.

[4] Krista Kay Payne, PEW Research Center for People & the Press. Quoted in http://fellowshipoftheminds.com/tag/leftwing-boomers/, accessed June 28, 2014.

[5] Aaron Smith and Maeve Duggan, Pew Research Center's Internet and American Life Project 2013, www.pewinternet.org, accessed June 28, 2014.

"Here's our new retirement plan: at age 65, we'll get divorced then marry other people who planned better."

Please, never be embarrassed to say publicly that you are on a dating site or multiple dating sites. In fact, you quite often can make new acquaintances when speaking up! You should be pleasantly surprised at how many others come forth to affirm they are doing the same, after you 'come out'!!! Or, a number will often shyly share they are considering online dating; but, they don't really know how it works.

As a Single, be honest with yourself and others regarding your dating opportunities. And, be realistic about your chances within those options: bars, clubs, church, travel, the rare striking up a conversation, and the like. SINS really are *the only game in town* if you are truly looking for the most rewarding types of bonding and love ... for you.

The ever-rising numbers of others such as yourself looking for the same outcome on SINS, as well, give you a denser and larger pool to find and be found by potential partners. That's what SINS is all about, so jump in and enjoy the game. Be a participant, not a spectator. Be proactive. Finding the right partner and falling in love are not spectator sports. These hoped-for outcomes are why SINS exist. They are well-conceived, well-groomed and well-operated playing fields. *You* are about to begin playing on them ... perhaps the best game of your life!

Give yourself a mini-preview. If you are a Mature Single serious about finding a partner, open your computer and enter a search term such as *Mature or Senior dating sites*. Prepare to be amazed. You will find over 1,500 dating sites! Survey the types of sites in Candyland that suit you. Develop an idea of the diversity that awaits you. After some initial experience, most online daters are active in one or two or more SINS sites simultaneously. When the time comes for you, start with one and focus on it for a bit. Set up that first profile as perfectly as you can without torturing yourself. It will be all you can handle initially. [Use Chapter 7-How to Write a Profile.] Create your own but do not freeze it in time. Continue to touch it up as you move along ... maybe with the help of a friend or a for-a-fee profile writing service. Then, expand your horizons to other SINS sites ... perhaps selecting ones that will meet a variety of focuses. Often, variety *is* a spice of life.

Just setting up your profile can be intimidating; time and some thought are needed to formulate one properly and achieve your desired results ... especially if you are not a full-fledged member of the computer generation. (In which case you will be on a double adventure.) Most Matures now are computer literate to some degree ... certainly enough to maintain a profile on a SINS site. We will be previewing that later on.

Most members cut and paste their basic profiles onto the forms of the other sites they join. Then, they tweak a bit for each selected site. You may want to follow suit; doing so will save you a lot of time. Why totally reinvent the wheel?! You are the same person, are you not, whether you are on www.match.com, www.zoomersingles.com, http://dating.aarp.org, or www.SeniorPeopleMeet.com, etc. Just massage your template a bit to accommodate the focus of each site you choose.

Proceed with caution *and* the usual dose of positive *attitude*. As you enter the world of SINS your learning curve could resemble a rollercoaster track because you will encounter so much to take in. That's all right; that's okay. On the up rides many of your lost-but-not-forgotten courting skills should receive a sparkle and shine. Take the first steps forward now by nudging yourself into your best shape with anticipation of loads of excitement and fun. The process can be stimulating and surprisingly invigorating at a time in some lives that can be defined by anything but those descriptive words!!

Make the leap without fearing disapproval. What do you really have to lose? You are already alone and will most likely not meet that special *someone* in your present social circles. If you don't test SINS you might always wonder what could have developed if you had attempted even a short journey into Candyland.

The numbers are against you if you are sincerely looking for a future partner and you remain outside the SINS community. Here is another set of statistics some of you may want to read twice. As of June 2013 of the 54+million single people in the U.S., 40+ million of that number had tried online dating.[6] [For additional figures see end of chapter Studies and Statistics, Note 3.]

More interesting facts can be found in the 2013 compilation: Ten percent of online dating users left within their first three months ... not a bad dropout rate. Ninety percent must be enjoying some aspects of the SINS experience! Seventeen percent of all marriages reported were the happy outcomes of interactions that began online. Twenty percent of then-current committed relationships

---

[6] "Online Dating Statistics – Statistic Brain." 2013 Statistic Brain Research Institute, publishing as Statistic Brain. Research date 7/7/2014, http://www. statisticbrain.com/online-dating-statistics/, Reuters, Herald News, PC World, Washington Post, accessed June 30, 2014.

began online.[7] [See more interesting figures see end of chapter Studies and Statistics, Note 4.]

The above statistics make a very appealing case for you to consider enthusiastically online dating and possibly join this still-rising tide of potential. SINS make it very easy for you to join and proceed at a pace and financial commitment comfortable for you.

> *"People who don't take risks generally make*
> *about two big mistakes a year.*
> *People who do take risks generally make*
> *about two big mistakes a year."*
> - Peter F. Drucker-

As a SINS member, you can easily check in and out of your SINS sites at your will, as I have done over the past eight years. Your profile can be visible to the general membership or it can also be totally anonymous if you so choose to hide it ... for any period of time ... while you search discreetly for potential partners, check out your competition or just take a break. Seriously, you may want a break. SINS can be too much of a good thing at times ... offering so much attention and social interaction that you reach a point when you want to step back and catch your breath. I have put my profile into invisible status quite often. I must warn you, though, that a hidden profile takes you out of the game. No one can see you and, thus, be tempted to approach you as a possible romantic interest. In such a mode your hidden presence is more that of a voyeur ... seeing all around you but not being seen.

If you feel you have average attributes, take extra steps to create an appealing profile. [See Chapter 9.] You can become as popular as you want to be or have the time to be ... *if* you are realistic about your ability to attract potential dates suitable for you. We all do

---

[7] Ibid.

not possess top model looks or other obviously outstanding assets; but, we all have good attributes that we can enhance and utilize to their utmost. Once you create your profile you have the choice of proceeding as a social butterfly or a lazy sloth while you survey profiles looking for prospective love interests, respond to others' invitations ... and extend your own.

Reading *Candyland S.I.N.S.* at this point in your life brings you nearer to the gates of SINS. As we move through the book we will employ a set of terms applicable to life's journey throughout the decades. Let's establish the framework. Once folks move through the first two decades of life and roughly two decades of young adulthood, they arrive at their fortieth birthday. From there on, they are in the *Mature Adult* decades of life.

If in your 40's and 50's, most of you are tending to all the matters that occupy those years and more... paying your dues, dealing with life and moving forward. In this framework, 40-year-olds join 50-year olds in the *Young Matures* category. *Young Matures* certainly are not living the old concept of 'middle aged'. What happened to the term? It morphed. Or, totally disappeared! Beyond are what I call *Seasoned Matures*, those in their 60's and 70's. In the 60's most of life's demands have been completed and the next generation has gone its own ways. In the 60's and 70's, so many individuals are still active, young at heart and surprisingly adventurous. Now, extend *Seasoned Matures* into the upper decades. I am increasingly seeing profiles of members in their 80's ... and a few beyond. SINS is a happening place for all these age groups!

No matter what your decade, follow the directions each site clearly gives you. And, take to heart my guidance, advice, tips, and those of other experienced Candyland travelers. Enjoy the sweets, but beware of the nuts. A few are definitely mixed in among Candyland's delectable treats, just as in the other social communities around us. How important it is that you guard your safety because you are dealing with strangers within the anonymity and unaccountability of the Internet, not within a local church group, organization or club.

On a more upbeat note, Young and Seasoned *Mature dating* and *sex* are here to stay! Get used to it. Matures are once again breaking down barriers. Yes, these *three words ... Mature, Dating and sex ...* are now even mentioned ... in public ... a triad not common in polite conversation until the success of online dating. Our hearts can still skip a beat ... and, unfortunately, ache and break as well. May the happier sort of *heart condition* be in store for you as you venture through the Candyland of SINS. Be ready for rollercoaster rides that can place your heart in your throat ... a heart pumping with new life, exhilarated, re-generated ... a heart sometimes broken *if* you leap into SINS without sufficient guidance and controls in place.

Rejection can play a role in the broken heart syndrome. What is your sensitivity to rejection on a sliding scale of one to ten? Be prepared to have it tested in SINS. It likely will be. For your own sake, please, be open to attempting to move your sensitivity gauge in a direction more tolerable for you ... toward the end of the scale that is not too hard on you. If you at all can, emotionally step back a bit. Rejection in one form or another is a part of the journey for nearly everyone. Don't let your ego be a stumbling block. Know before you enter SINS that your ego *will* be dented and *perhaps* crushed at times ... quite often by your potential mates' issues and not your self-perceived inadequacies. Try to keep your list of the latter to a minimum. You *can* lift yourself up to begin again. Isn't doing so a better alternative to watching the world go by and only vicariously experiencing closeness and romance through movies, books and television?

So, go ahead. Enjoy the flirting, frolic and fun ... or the debauchery. Yes, I mention debauchery ... a possibility also available to you on Internet-dating sites. What is unacceptable to one of us may be just what another is seeking: casual consensual sex and nothing more. The popularity of these sites is proof of extended sexual boundaries at all ages. The more provocative adult sites are not discussed in this book. Many adult sites are available and a few are listed for you along with the mainstream and niche sites you will come upon here and in the results of a google/search for 'adult dating sites'.

Candyland S.I.N.S. has been written to clarify misconceptions and reveal the realities of Mature dating on SINS. My intention is to take you to the gates of Candyland, the astounding online venue teeming with millions of members interacting socially. My goal is to make Candyland easily understood and smoothly accessible by you. The sweet Candyland of SINS is just a click away ... if you allow yourself to take a well-calculated risk. SINS is a world full of interesting people who will broaden your life and, as has happened quite often, change it forever. It has mine.

> *But risk must be taken*
> *because the greatest hazard in life*
> *is to risk nothing.*
> *The person who*
> *risks nothing,*
> *does nothing,*
> *has nothing,*
> *is nothing.*
> *He may avoid suffering and sorrow,*
> *but he simply cannot learn,*
> *change,*
> *feel,*
> *grow,*
> *love,*
> *live.*
> *-Leo Buscaglia-*[8]

---

[8] Leo Buscaglia, http://www.abundance-and-happiness.com/leo-buscaglia-quotes.html, accessed August 12, 2014.

You have in your hands a guide to help you avoid the inevitable pitfalls, functional or emotional, you will encounter when you join an online dating service. Even though difficulties may surface, they can be most often sidestepped with caution and sound advice. *Candyland S.I.N.S.* is my sincere effort to make your new journey through a foreign territory one that is positive and fulfilling; your membership fees well spent. You will learn about the RED FLAGS you are likely to encounter as you weave your way along its paths ... moving through some of its many opportunities, experiencing interesting people from all walks of life. The accounts of some members will invite you to step out of your world and into theirs, to experience other slices of life that you may very well find stimulating, if you allow it.

I was born into this world enthusiastic about people. People are my joy. I appreciate them all and their individual journeys, some much more or less fortunate in worldly possessions and opportunities than others. I hope I always come across as an inclusive person, one automatically sensitive to and deeply compassionate about almost every person I meet. They ultimately broaden my life.

During the past eight years, my signature enthusiasm for life has led me to members I never would have met in a dozen years of dating within my traditional communities, the only communities I'd known ... those of family, friends, tennis, gyms, business and entrepreneurship. These arenas may appear broad, but they, along with the strictures of time, geographically limited my social options ... which after retirement seemed ever-shrinking into smaller and smaller social circles.

You, too, can expand those horizons. Join me! Let's begin by taking the first steps to your new and exciting life in Candyland. *Your best assets* are a positive attitude and a willingness to try something new. What you are about to learn will allow you to move forward and, I hope, savor life in a way you may have thought was all but lost to you. Reading the vast range of information, advice and tales I share should help you embark on your own new round of dynamic years.

To smoothly launch yourself, plan first to become familiar with pertinent aspects of Internet dating in SINS. Come prepared to the new table set before you. Candyland *is* a veritable feast, if you approach it with well-based expectations. You do not want to fumble your way through this new and very important endeavor in your life. To find someone to spend the rest of your life with, in whatever your arrangement may entail, is a goal that requires planning ... not potluck. My wish is to guide you closer to that future.

Delights and treats, happiness and perhaps, at times, not-so-much of each await your discovery. As you prepare yourself with *Candyland S.I.N.S.* and move through the necessary early segments of information you will access quite a spectrum of true experiences, both my own accounts and those of seasoned Internet daters. You may very well gasp, cringe, laugh and cry. Most importantly, you will learn from these all-too-human experiences. Warning: some will surprise you. None will bore you, for *this* is Candyland and its SINS!

The next two chapters discuss
who YOU are and who THEY are... in Candyland SINS.
Are you one and the same?

*"Don't be silly... you're much prettier than
anyone I dated before you!"*

STUDIES and STATISTICS
Additional Materials for ENTER

....

Item 1. More stats related the PEW study:
First: The study reported the percentage of the American population who stated they had used online dating websites grew from 3 percent in 2008, to 6 percent in 2009 and to 9 percent in 2013.

Second: Five percent of all Americans who were [then] currently married or in a long-term partnership met their partner somewhere online. Among those who had been together for 10 years or less, 11 percent met online.

Third: The number of American Internet users who believed that "online dating is a good way to meet people" would increase by 14 percent to 59 percent in the time lapse between the 2005 and 2013 studies.

Fourth: In 2013, 66 percent of responders had dated someone they met through a dating site or app whereas eight years earlier in 2005, 43 percent reported the same. [An astounding increase, don't you think?]

Fifth: One quarter of online daters (23 percent) in 2013 said they had entered into a marriage or long-term relationship with someone they met through a dating site or app. In 2005, 17 percent reported they had done the same.

Sixth: Thirty-eight percent of Americans who were "single and looking" reported they had utilized an online dating site or mobile dating app. This batch of statistics is a testament to the public's acceptance that online dating is no longer an act of desperation. That negative viewpoint diminished from 29 percent in 2005 to 21 percent in 2013.

Item 2. More findings related to the University of Chicago study:
The study also found these online couples have happier, longer marriages than couples who met traditionally. People who met online compared to those who met in traditional venues were more likely to be older, employed, enjoy higher incomes and be diverse racially and ethnically.

Item 3. More findings related to the *statisticsbrain* research:
With regard to 40+ million singles (out of a total of 54+ million U.S. singles) who had tried online dating, *two sites* shared the vast majority of that online number. Match.com tallied 21,275,000 members; eHarmony reached 15,500,000 members. The average spent on these sites by each member was $239.00 per year ... not a huge amount when you consider members were investing in making positive changes in their lives with strong potential to meet a heart-satisfying match.

Item 4: More findings related to the *statisticsbrain* research:
The average length of successful courtships begun *online* was 18.5 months ... compared to 42 months for the average length of successful courtships begun *offline*. 52.4 percent of online dating users were male and 47.6 percent were female. [Not a bad ratio, ladies.]

Item 1. Aaron Smith and Maeve Duggan, Pew Research Center's Internet and American Life Project 2013, www.pewinternet. org, http://www.pewinternet.org/2013/10/21/online-dating-relationships/, accessed June 28, 2014.

Item 2. As quoted by William Harms, June 3 1013, http://news. uchicago.edu/article/2013/06/03/meeting-online-leads-happier-more-enduring-marriages, The survey of 19,131respondants was commissioned by eHarmony.com and followed procedures specified by JAMA, which included oversight by independent statisticians - See more at: http://news.uchicago.edu/article/2013/06/03/meeting-online-leads-happier-more-enduring-marriages#sthash.a2JSQi3a.dpuf, accessed June 28, 2014.

Items 3 and 4. "Online Dating Statistics – Statistic Brain." 2013 Statistic Brain Research Institute, publishing as Statistic Brain. Research date 7/7/2014, http://www.statisticbrain.com/online-dating-statistics/, Reuters, Herald News, PC World, Washington Post, accessed June 30, 2014.

Chapter One

You

Who are YOU and why are YOU at the
entrance of Candyland SINS?
Are YOU sculpting your next act?
Where do YOU fit in?

Here you are ... a Young or Seasoned Mature and single. Probably single for the first time in decades. You ask yourself how you got to this state at this stage of your life. You may never have committed to a partnership or marriage. You may have lost your partner through death, divorce or breakup or you have chosen to be a committed Singleton. But, things can change, right?

*"I guess nobody stays together anymore. Peanut
butter and jelly are getting divorced."*

You bear your life's earlier successes and disappointments by yourself
as you approach or are in your later years ... possibly thinking about
seeking a meaningful personal attachment. You are grateful most of
the time that you still are so very much alive. You miss companionship
perhaps and, yes, admit it ... intimacy. When you think of how often
you passed by, passed on it or did not appreciate it when you were
married or engaged in meaningful previous relationships you could
cry! I mean, both for the companionship and the physical closeness!

You may be licking your wounds from relationship battle defeats.
You may be obsessing about a lost love; or worse ... because there
has been no love in your life to have lost. Now, you have *Candyland
S.I.N.S.* and are about to take control of your life and create options.
You may feel battered and beaten in love, romance and relationships
for the moment, but that situation is about to change. Whatever the
sad sweetness or lingering loss you still live with, your life could
take a new turn. Give yourself the chance.

"People who live life in fear of taking risks
die without living it."
-Fola, *The Seed*-

You have survived the first half of your adult life paying your dues along the way. You now stand at the gates of Candyland SINS, perhaps one of your last major entrances before those 'pearly gates'. Generally, it has taken you 20+ adult years to arrive here. Would you have dreamed you would be alone at this time of your life, having shared some or much of it with a partner? When life gives you lemons, make ...! It is so refreshing.

You are among the more than 50 percent of American adults who are single. Thirty-one million (roughly one out of every seven adults) live alone and make up 28 percent of all US households. Fifteen million of those solo dwellers are between the ages of 35 and 64; ten million of them are 65 and older.[9] These numbers are staggering but do not necessarily imply failures. Stop moping about, hiding in the fact that you are alone. Stand up straight and hold your head high. Be assured you are not an anomaly but part of a large and growing segment of our society.

Despite having borne the pain of love lost or love unattained, you can choose to face your future (be assured you have one) with courage, knowing that heart piercing pain need not be relived. Choose not to live *with* your past. Choose to move beyond it. Benefit from your mistakes and failures to utilize lessons learned and create a 'next act' that could very well be the most exciting and riveting one in the stage play of your life. After all, you are now an experienced Mature, one maybe about to draw back the curtain ... poised to begin the grandest adventure of your life before an exceedingly interactive audience ... inside Candyland SINS.

As you read this book, you may be a Single alone by choice or not by choice, among the mature segment of society which is often dismissed and labeled 'retired', essentially retired from a full

---

9   Eric Klinenberg, Going Solo: (New York, New York: the Penguin Press, 2012), p. 5.

romantic life; held back for whatever reasons from what could be a vibrant and even warm, sexily adventurous time of life. Mature Singles who express interest in finding romance, intimacy and love often are stifled by those around them. Some of their peers may brush off attempts at deeper sharing. Some married and non-married friends chuckle and smile uncomfortably when Mature Singles mention what they are considering ... their rebirth. Many of their children find a parent's intention difficult to discuss. And, their grandchildren can't fathom it.

Grandfathers may still take their grandchildren fishing and grandmothers may still bake them cookies. However, more is going on in grandparents' lives these days than in the not-too-distant past ... more than tackle boxes and ovens. I know it and you know it. It is time we let the world know it ... many Younger and Mature Singles are alive and kicking ... and plan to kick up more dust before they settle under it.

These later years are for many Matures the time of being a grandparent, a retired pillar of the community, an active member of various groups, etc. ... gasp, yawn!!! Society sees and relegates Matures' roles within their communities as such. In SINS, Mature Singles can cast off accumulated masks. Whether or not they feel their time is running short, some of them have dreams, even fantasies, to fulfill. Some may feel they have only one more real shot at finding and securing the elusive happiness of close and deep connection.

Let's review my terms in play in Candyland S.I.N.S.

Singles INternet-dating Services becomes the acronym S.I.N.S. That acronym I have playfully transposed into SINS. They are online dating sites. Most of them are very inclusive, opening to all comers their 'niche' doors to Candyland. Online dating services are not just for the younger generations anymore. Another name I use interchangeably with SINS is Candyland ... the colorful and lighthearted online world laden with never-ending (and continually replenished) tempting treats waiting to be sampled. Candyland is my affectionate and evocative term for SINS websites and their communities. These can become a fun-filled and fulfilling part of your life.

Enter when you are ready. You can participate at your own comfort level or time schedule and make your entrance as simple or as challenging as you please. Once you register with your selected site/s you will be spoon-fed the directions you are to follow. [But, before you leap into interactions with other members, you *absolutely must* read and internalize Chapter 12.] Always, always adhere to the rules of safety. Doing so could literally save your life.

You might consider why you have not found *'the one'* after possibly years and years of seriously searching and engaging in various social activities. Or, perhaps it is time for some self-examination. You may be just unlucky to this point. Perhaps you are emotionally unavailable, which is beyond the discussions in this book. Therapists, a great many books and other resources can be of help. Google/search for certified counselors and psychotherapists in your area to assure you are not interacting with someone who just decided to hang out a shingle and give advice on your deep life issues. Better yet, ask friends for a good referral. Since so many of us have undertaken therapy; it is not a shameful thing for others to ask about. In fact, it is a commendable approach to understanding how you tick ... or not! [A discussion you will come to in Chapter 16.]

GLASBERGEN

"I never realized how self-centered I am until ten online dating services matched me with myself!"

Your coming years can include a rebirth of sorts as you explore your inner and outer well-being and expand your community of friends and what they bring to your life. SINS members can be part of that enlarged community. On SINS I have met my best male friends and some of my best female friends, as well.

You have reached a point in life's journey where you can either coast along or choose adventure. The choices many Mature Singles are unaware they make can be conscious or subconscious, predetermined perhaps by their natures, their health or their finances. Or, even by chance; just picking up and browsing through a book such as *Candyland S.I.N.S.* can change your life. Believe it! The fact this book is in your hands and you are reading beyond its front and back outside covers demonstrate your interest in changing your status quo ... in modifying your life at a deeper level or just playing in the realm of Candyland S.I.N.S. Also, perhaps whatever happens is meant to be.

You can accept this stage of life and live much of it sitting in an armchair, waiting for the inevitable outcome. *Or,* you can literally hop on a motorcycle and start savoring life's adventures. You will decide how you will travel on this journey into new territory ... with the speed and enthusiasm of an easy-going coffee-sipping stroller ambling along or with the vim and vigor of a touring bike rider. Take control! Make choices!!

Here you are ... a Singleton. You are in your mature years ... deliberately considering or seeking a change in your sometimes too quiet, too lonely and possibly unwanted Single state. You do have the option to embrace its freedom and its other appealing benefits. [More of this option later in Chapter 16.] Either of these goals, to change your Solo state or embrace it, can be achieved successfully within the SINS community. Such members are just like you ... individuals who have found a new 'tribe' that celebrates the freedom to seek companions and/or partners or ... to happily fly Solo.

Whatever path you choose to pursue, Partnered or Solo, wipe the frown or blank stare off your face and begin to make up for lost time and missed opportunities. Start those endorphins flowing again! A vibrant dating world exists for Mature Singles ... and for you, if you are adventurous enough and prepared to successfully enter ... **S**ingles **IN**ternet-dating **S**ervices, aka SINS.

This phase of your life is akin to attending a costumed ball, for which you wear a heavy mask sculpted over many years to accommodate others' perceptions of who they want or expect you to be. So few people in your life know who you *really* are deep inside. Within SINS, your mask and its accompanying weight can be cast off to give you a fresh start. Sadly, some new members foolishly replace the old burdened masks with fresh false ones. Old masks were to please family and friends and encase self-perceived deficiencies; new false masks are perhaps creations of how a member wants to appear to his/her new communities of SINS. Here is my sincere advice: Remain true to yourself ... be as authentic as you can be or you will live a lie ... perhaps for the rest of your life. Seek to connect with someone who loves you for your most true self and not for the persona you want the world to perceive.

Persona originally referred to an actor's mask. Now, the word means more of a false front. One of my dear friends is someone I previously dated on SINS. He is now gloriously, happily settled with another Mature he met online. My friend had a marvelous idea: create masks with exteriors that portray the persona the wearers want to present to the world and interiors that represent the wearers' authentic selves. What incredible potential for self-study and artistic interpretation, don't you think?

The optimal choice is to sculpt such a mask as close to your true identity as possible ... inside and out. Very few individuals can live healthily the rest of their lives being someone they are not ... stress can cause emotional strain, disease and even death.

Please enter SINS presenting a true profile of yourself. Attempt to be as authentic and sincere as possible for the *special someone* you have not yet met. Give yourself the real potential to lead a genuine, happy and deeply-fulfilling life with the person waiting for you. Attempt to be as relaxed as you would with the family and friends who love and know the *real* you. If you enter SINS as your genuine self you will never slip-up or experience anxieties, failures or regrets because you were not truthful.

Your deep and very real desires can surface when you know time is running short in fulfilling your dreams and, in some cases, your fantasies. You have another real opportunity to find your happiness and fulfill your desires ... perhaps even those fantasies ... within SINS. Allow them to open their gates for you. Add your participation in SINS, if only for a trial, to *your* bucket list.

You may be shy or feel you do not want to be 'seen' online by others whom you do not want to know about your membership in SINS. No one has to know you are dating on the Internet, if you do not wish it. You simply do not include pictures in your profile. You have the option to be totally anonymous. Member profiles offer neither actual names nor personal contact information. Neither should be shared online with other members ... or the public. You simply select your own fantasy Username; you decide to post your picture ... or not.

Warning: Without a picture, you will receive very few approaches and very little response to your contact attempts. I never respond to anyone who does not present a profile picture unless he has good reason for not initially presenting one, such as being a public figure. The necessity to include photos in your profile is very important for you to grasp because both males and females are greatly influenced by what their eyes send to their brains. *No photos* translates into few views and even fewer responses to your flirts, winks, favorites, messages, etc. Thus, you would defeat the purpose of your participation in SINS ... and have wasted your time and effort for a poor quality return on your combined investment of fees, energy, time and initial hopes. Popular recipients of winks, flirts, etc. will seldom if ever answer members who do not have a picture on their profiles. Please embrace the fact that having your pictures on a dating site no longer carries the stigma it once did. Posting a picture to who knows how many members is very acceptable to the membership ... and almost mandatory if you anticipate positive results.

Once you have some results to act upon do not throw out the many potentially good matches because the '*chemistry*' just was not there. Thanks to SINS I have dated members who, although they were not to be romantic matches, have remained in my life as '*friends for life*' matches. These members have given me a second career, hobbies, interests, and self-expansion toward horizons I would have never dreamed of.

As I write, due to my ongoing positive healthy connection with *failed* romantic matches, my life is, in fact, the richer. I have made efforts to revitalize a career of a retired singer/songwriter who, after his wife's death, had thought his singing days were over. I add positive dimensions to 'living' for a member friend whose life is riddled with health issues. I also exchange a great deal of laughter with a wonderful, elegant and well-educated gentleman via telephone conversations and online connecting. I designed and executed beautiful gardens on a large property for a great guy ... who broke my heart (I got over him, as one must). And, continue to applaud a wonderful couple who not only found their life partner in each other but also their ideal dynamic business partner on SINS at a time in their lives when they each seemed to be winding down their separate personal and professional stories. We three maintain a beautiful friendship as a happy result of an initial SINS match that did not work in the romantic department. We all have kept the best part of our relationships and friendships ... and left the dead wood behind us.

Your life will be made richer as has mine due to the broad spectrum of members I have met who did not give up on living and, actually, are leading their remaining years quite to the contrary. You will find Mature Singles looking toward new horizons, seeing the rest of their lives lit with sunrises, not sunsets. These are the sort of people you want to meet ... and be fortunate to know because of SINS.

So much awaits you within the world of SINS ... with a few taps on the keyboard or keypad, exciting opportunities can develop to meet others that bypass the usual, generally inefficient, difficult and time-consuming routes to find a certain *someone* in the general population. To join clubs and teams, volunteer, and go to bars and large social events, etc. may be valid in their own right *but* they just are not well-aimed. In the past, to find an appropriate mate was akin to locating the proverbial needle in a haystack. Now as a savvy member of SINS you will become, you can use your time much more efficiently to meet potential partners online in the quiet comfort of your own home or cozily settled with a café latte in a coffee shop. No longer must you investigate venue after venue fruitlessly searching with disappointing results. Statistics support the customary lack of success in finding possible *someones* in those environments.

Not so in SINS! Picture yourself at an electronic dessert buffet ... many tempting treats placed before you on your computer screen. Although you may be anxious to dig in and chow down, you can begin to enjoy the delicacies only after you set your profile up to your best advantage and maintain it carefully. *Then* join the buffet line and begin savoring your new adventure.

Time waits for no one; we no longer have the larger part of our futures ahead of us. In fact, time flies before us more quickly with each year, month and day. At this point in our lives many of us want to share affection and be in love again before our days dwindle down. What is to stop you from pursuing such a dream? Fear of the unknown, fear of criticism, fear of rejection or being hurt, fear of looking foolish, etc.? It's time to talk about these demons and help clear yourself of them. If you are to share your remaining time with a new partner you must dump your baggage and jump on that speeding train ... while you are healthy enough to enjoy the ride. The experience can be exhilarating with the right attitude and a letting go of ego.

I'd like to share a favorite quote:

Every year that I live
I am more convinced that the waste of life
lies in the love we have not given,
the powers we have not used,
the selfish prudence that will risk nothing,
and which shirking pain,
missed happiness as well.
No one ever yet was poorer in the long run
having once in a lifetime
'let out all the length of the reins.'
- Mary Cholmondeley -

With SINS to support and embrace you, during your Mature Single state, you have no cause to remain alone if you yearn for more warm connection in your life. You can expand your circle of friends ... and lovers. You are only limited by your expectations. If those expectations are realistic and well-defined, every type and status of a potential partner or friend waits for you within SINS sites' structures.

Before you join the activity in SINS, you must move past the perception that joining SINS is a desperate move. I see it as quite the opposite. You are taking control of your life, making positive steps forward extending your hand to others with the same intentions ... sharing the common goal of meeting potential partners, companions and friends. Forty-six percent of people who use online dating sites claim finding someone long-term is a major reason they are on SINS. Twenty-five percent of online users 'just want to have fun' without being in a serious relationship.[10] (The latter is fine, too.) SINS offer at least one online home base for everyone and their differing goals

---

[10] Aaron Smith and Maeve Duggan, Pew Research Center's Internet and American Life Project 2013, www.pewinternet.org, http://www.pewinternet.org/2013/10/21/part-2-dating-apps-and-online-dating-sites/, accessed June 30, 2014.

in SINS. The memberships of the various sites are so vast and so diverse that most members can easily find others of like mind.

I encourage you to approach SINS with not a sense of dire need but one of ease; you will meet new friends, have many enjoyable experiences online and off and perhaps, as a bonus, link with your life-capping partner or even a soul mate. With a sunny relaxed approach and your *Candyland S.I.N.S.* guide to SINS' inner workings, including tips and important warnings, you could become part of the impressive successful couple statistics mentioned earlier. No matter your level of engagement, though, follow the tips and cautions to avoid at least some of the inevitable pitfalls and the occasional disappointments along the way.

Be sure to define your own goals and proceed with *diligence* when you meet prospective partners in order to discover what mindsets you are dealing with … theirs and yours. Do their goals mesh with yours? Are they seeking marriage, a long-term relationship, casual encounters, a travel companion … or an occasional but steady dating/special events partner, etc.? It is fairer play if each of you can be as truthful as possible about the real objectives of your SINS membership and voice them at the onset.

Once you establish mutual ground and after sincere introspection, try to leave yourself open to exploring a fresh perspective on how to lead your remaining years. … open to a possible alternative lifestyle you had never considered. Your potential mates can reciprocate by sharing their thoughts on other life paths and arrangements you may not have imagined. Discuss your objectives; be time efficient. Why waste your time or theirs in pursuit of a dishonest or unrealistic match? Don't you hope your dates will do likewise?

Early dates are very important. You must remain aware of what you want in a future partner. Listen carefully to your dates; what they don't say may be more important than what they do say. Always remain alert in your SINS experiences and apply the vetting processes that naturally narrow your choices ... of which there should be many. Do not let the procedure control you. Be prepared to reject people and to be rejected in the vetting process. After all, most of you want only one partner. Thoughtful elimination of those you meet and continue to meet is the only way to narrow down to three ... to two ... to one ... or possibly to none (for a particular go-round). Although the process can be painful, it is not terminal. You will survive to meet and explore with others until the right one comes along, if you are patient and realistic. When that special meeting happens or as it develops you will know there was a reason the others did not work out.

Now comes one of the many cautions you will come to. The Candyland of new found 'treats' that SINS offer can become addictive enough that you can lose sight of your goals and your safety. You must maintain self-awareness, your intended direction and always follow safety guidelines. Allow SINS to work for your benefit. If you do not do so consistently you can be hurt. Or, at the least, feel a bit dented and confused ... or worse.

© Randy Glasbergen
glasbergen.com

"They say the best place to meet women is the supermarket. The only women I met were Sara Lee, Betty Crocker and Aunt Jemima."

Are you now finished with floating about wistfully, now ready to chart a new course in your life's journey? You can start rather quickly ... at no financial cost to you. Many online dating sites are totally free or will give you free access with limited functions such as capability to perform searches without the ability to receive or send messages. You can join as many sites without cost as you want or feel you can easily handle. Most likely, you will eventually add a site or sites that have monthly fees. Of the plethora of sites for all tastes some are not worth a fee ... or the time and effort, even for free.

As we move along and continue setting out the foundation for your coming adventures, place the following question on your right shoulder and give it permission to whisper in your ear every now and then. Are you going to progress passively through the additional years of your life or are you going to create an enviable next chapter of your own? The choice is yours ... in the audience or on the stage?

"Better to put your heart on the line, risk everything,
and walk away with nothing than play it safe.
Love is a lot of things,
but 'safe' isn't one of them."
-Mandy Hale-
--The Single Woman: Life, Love, and a Dash of Sass--

Chapter Two

THEY

SINS MEMBERS
Who are THEY and why are THEY in Candyland SINS?
Are THEY sculpting their next acts?
Single and alone or ...
Single and loving it?

Many think the majority of *Matures* still live in the pen and paper world of communication. Far from the truth. While most of us are not quite as tech savvy as our grandchildren or even our children, AARP statistics reveal that 94 percent of AARP members use email on a monthly basis and at least 85 percent have broadband Internet access in their homes. Seventy-six percent of them own at least one cell phone and receive texts, pictures and instant messages.[11] Granted, as in my case, most IM's are with my grandchildren who

---

[11] Ibid. Aaron Smith and Maeve Duggan, Pew Research Center's Internet and American Life Project 2013, accessed June 30, 2014

communicate in this mode. It's great ... easy and non-intrusive instant access to connection with someone you care about.

Unfortunately, until the advent of SINS, our communities and social groups left many Mature Singles bobbing alone in the sea of what could be many remaining years ... with few attempts to throw us a lifeline. Seldom, if ever, is a friend's dinner invitation extended along with one to someone else who is appropriate and alone unless that person is a member of the same sex. Seldom are we offered an introduction at a party to another Single. Is it peers' fear of our criticism of their effort if we might be disappointed in their choices? Or, is it society's general lack of interest in non-couple 'others' and their situations? Perhaps a bit of both. In the past, the fall-out for Mature Singles has been versions of oblivion!

The following pair of extracts that fit so well here regarding marital status have been drawn from A Profile for Older Americans issued in 2012 by the U.S. Census bureau. The first set: Older men were much more likely to be married than older women—72 percent of men as opposed to 45 percent of women. And, widows accounted for 37 percent of *all* older women. Over four times as many widows were reported in this survey than widowers. The second set: Divorced and separated (including married/spouse absent) older persons represented approximately 56.3 percent of all older persons in the 1980 survey. However in the 2012 results, the same divorced and separated (married but spouse absent) category represented 12 percent of the population.[12] In thirty-two years, not quite one third of a century, the percentage more than doubled.

At least a few individuals in the above groups are your fellow and sister SINS members. You are part of those statistics, as well. You are not alone. The fact that many of you are included in the ever-increasing Single Matures' numbers contributed by the Baby

---

[12] *Based on online data from the U.S. Census Bureau's Current Population Survey, Annual Social and Economic Supplement. http://www.census.gov/cps/data/*

Boomer generation is a bonus. The dating pool will never diminish in your lifetime.

"*Here's our new retirement plan—*
At age 65, we'll get divorced then marry
other people who planned better."

The splitting of assets, alimony, lawyers' fees and the general costs of maintaining an accustomed-to lifestyle make it likely that many new Singles will seek another committed partner with whom to share life's financial demands ... as well as some of life's joys. These startling divorce statistics and their fallout, along with early deaths of partners and the steady increase in deaths as the years advance nudge a large segment of Matures onto the dating scene.

Single Matures are no longer side notes but people who are forging their own directions, meeting life's challenges as a Single while recognizing and seizing opportunities ... one of which is Mature dating, a practice almost non-existent in your parents' generation. Such strange behavior went on quietly and was discussed in hushed tones when the children weren't listening. In many small communities Mature dating was often considered almost immoral or an act of desperation by those actively searching for a new partner. Most of those who found themselves alone for whatever reason found it hard to move on from a spouse's death or divorce in small, tight-knit and judgmental communities, clubs, church groups and entire towns. Mature Singles were the outsiders; sadly left to the compassion of a few brave and well-meaning friends to take the initiative to introduce their mature single relatives, co-workers or acquaintances to someone they felt appropriate ... who most often were not. Even these pale attempts seldom occurred.

On to sunnier occurrences. Most of us have experienced it ... 'falling in love'. Mature daters newly in love exhibit the same telltale characteristics with those zany feelings and emotions of their teens and twenties. Falling in love at any age can bring out the teenager in most of us ... the best and the worst parts. Quite often we develop even better relationships ... less fleeting and with more depth. Most of us who have loved and lost are more appreciative of this glorious state in which we may come to find ourselves once more.

Young and Seasoned Mature Singles are suddenly 'hot' and 'cool' again. Yes, Mature Singles are again breaking new barriers, aging differently than their parents did. Matures in all age ranges are changing the complexion of what were almost taboo thoughts ... *mature romance, love* and *sex.*

Mature daters would not want to embarrass their family and friends, their children and grandchildren. But if the truth be known, many of them might risk that. Oh, well. Today, our families just have to deal with it, as they have every other step of our lives: our dysfunctional marriages, less-than-perfect parenting, hidden affairs, revealed affairs, debilitating breakdowns, tragic divorces, endless business demands, and punishing failures, etc. That's life!

So many Matures have weathered some, if not all of those flaws, foibles and tragedies. I wonder what our point totals would be if we weighted and combined all those life events in various appropriate columns: career accomplishments, personal achievements, celebrations, etc. as well as career failures, personal failures, grieving, etc. In this day and time, Mature daters observe their children deal with some of these very human milestones and conditions in their own lives. We watch, cheer on and try to help where we can.

The relatively benign stage most Matures are now in doesn't seem intolerable to those around us when put into perspective against our previous years. So. Embrace your life at this stage with good humor, passion, gusto and goals. Your family and friends will just have to go with your flow! Many Matures will not be deterred from living their remaining years and decades with enthusiasm ... and positive actions exploring and forging new paths for greater happiness.

Seasoned Matures may not be as firm, flat, hard and svelte as they once were. However, for many their hearts are still as soft and tender and as wide open to romance as they ever were, if not more so. The majority of Matures in this decades-range are now more and more free of the demands of their younger years ... raising families, holding jobs and advancing their careers. They have placed the cloak of their responsibilities on the shoulders of the next generation. Today's Matures are liberated ... if they wish to be *and* choose to be. The vehicle waiting for them to hop on and start moving is ... Candyland S.I.N.S.

A big plus for most Seasoned Matures is they now have practically full-time opportunities and nearly full attention to devote to the arts of searching, courting and romance ... to enter the realm of Candyland SINS, a new territory overflowing with tempting treats to be sampled and savored. SINS is a here-and-now world being explored and enjoyed by so many Matures. It has arrived. You are fortunate to have access and opportunity to participate in it if you so choose.

While the mission statements of most SINS inform you that they will help you find romantic relationships on their sites, more than just romance occurs quite naturally among the membership. Friendship and a sense of community mark the Mature age group. Matures have stretched society's boundaries once again, embracing and welcoming others into their dating world, a sphere of social/ romantic activity previously reserved for the *young*.

SINS members. Who are they? They are you. They are Matures a step or two or three ahead of you in your evolution from *'single and alone'* to *'single and loving it'*! Or, to *'partnered and loving it'*! You and SINS members share the common DNA described in this chapter, but they have already begun their search to broaden their lives and find fulfillment … in the Candyland of SINS.

During my own later years (my *now*) I have made some of my best friends through contacts and acquaintances found within the communities of SINS. We discovered that we may not have been *soul mates*, but we surely found we had much in common and much to like about each other. The resulting friendships proved we had written our profiles honestly and had done our vetting well. If we had not, we would not have stepped beyond the initial dating stage of the SINS process. We knew on those first dates, at the very least, we could be friends.

All the important criteria had been met, but the elusive *chemistry* was lacking. We wisely acknowledged the final pieces of our puzzle would not fit. Even so, some of us have cheered each other on and added to our own quests the task to be-on-the-lookout for potential partners for one other ... romantically, personally and professionally. We SINS members have met compatible *others* leading similar lives with the same challenges and the same joys. And, we take great pleasure in our new-found friendships.

I have been fortunate to remain close friends and participate in helpful exchanges with SINS members outside of our mutual dating world. SINS have broadened my life extensively and can do the same for yours ... with the right attitude. Seven years ago, I met one of my very closest and dearest friends through Match.com. We enjoyed travels to Mexico, Spain, the Caribbean and in many states. Those experiences and memories never would have occurred without SINS. They enriched my life. He is now happily settled with a SINS *perfect match* ... the one for him I could never be.

Discussions with this dear friend on life, values and ethics helped me discover what wealth and goodness were hidden below my surface. Previously, I was not consciously aware of how my life choices were so intertwined with my values, innate gifts, deeper long-standing issues, etc. Such conversations, going deep within my mind, emotions and soul, make me more grateful to this wonderful friend ... even more grateful for the inner journeys than for those marvelous travels we shared on land, sea and air. I hope you find someone in your SINS experience you can relate to on this level. Leave yourself open to that possibility when you read profiles. Some members are deeper thinkers and better communicators than others ... great sounding boards for a Single facing life's challenges. With other members, you may want just the sheer joy of riding on a motorcycle, going to concerts, playing tennis, traveling or going sailing ... all and more await.

Most members are on SINS for the same reason(s) you are. You should feel relaxed knowing that. So many new members begin their profiles apologetically explaining they are uncomfortable being on the site. They should have nothing to feel ashamed of or uncomfortable about. They should all actually revel in the fact they have found their tribe, so to speak ... with so much in common, a community in which to relax and have fun enjoying meeting each other. In fact, expressing your discomfort with your SINS efforts in your profile is not at all appealing and can be perceived as a judgment of others' participation in SINS, as well.

Many Matures serious about finding a partner belong to a few SINS. It is a personal preference and one that also reflects how much time you have to spend on such pursuits. Being a member of multiple sites casts your net farther and perhaps with a different focus on each site, widening your possibilities to find someone in a particular arena of life that is important to you. As examples, one site could be faith-based, another site focused on a particular interest such as sports or hobbies, some age-based, etc. I generally belong to three sites at once with different focuses. I find three as much as I can maintain time-wise. Unfortunately, every now and then, even just three call for more interactions than I can give proper attention to.

Allow me to alleviate at least some of your fears of the unknown while entering an exciting world that has been tarnished and sullied by a few unsavory members. The great majority of those 40 million people who have joined online dating services[13] are good trustworthy people such as you who are sincerely looking for a partner. However, each person decides how the outcome should evolve ... running the gamut from marriage, co-habitation, travel partners, event companions, casual dating, non-exclusive but intimate dating, etc. Be careful about the types of interactions

---

[13] William Harms, June 13, 2013,
http://news.uchicago.edu/article/2013/06/03/meeting-online-leads-happier-more-enduring-marriages, based on survey of 19,131 racially and ethnically diverse people, accessed June 30, 2014.

in which you choose to engage. [I have a strong suspicion you will not skip Chapter 15.] Perhaps your relationship will grow to be a committed but non-live-in relationship, or a committed and live-in relationship or even marriage. A myriad of options and their variations are available with different potential partners bringing their desired versions to the table. Your eyes will be opened at a time of life when they could have become heavy-lidded and perhaps closed. Give yourself a gift ... an exciting experience not to be missed ... SINS!

We'll close this chapter with one more set of numbers. Between 2005 and 2012, 35 percent of people who married met online in one forum or another while 45 percent of those met on Internet dating sites.[14] You can add yourself to these impressive and ever-growing stats for online dating when you join SINS. YOU and THEY (SINS members) are one and the same. SINS is *your* mutual community ....

---

[14] Ibid.

Chapter Three

SINS

What is Candyland SINS?
Why do SINS tempt so many of us?

Candyland SINS (my loose acronym for **S**ingles **IN**ternet-dating **S**ervices) is a seemingly murky, if not temptingly exotic, world to which so many Single Matures are drawn. Internet-dating is an ever expanding world-wide phenomenon that is more than flourishing. You can be part of and benefit from that growth because the dating pool for Matures is becoming increasingly larger. The 2013 E-Harmony study predicted that the age 55-64 bracket is expected to have the biggest online growth, with a 30 percent increase between 2013 and 2030 ... from 1.87 million to 2.41 million members in this age category. The study further foresees by 2031 half of all couples will have met online ... as will seven in ten couples by 2040.[15] The

---

[15] John Cacioppo, the University of Chicago, Department of Psychology led the survey sponsored by eHarmony, 2013, <u>Pew Research Center's Internet and American Life Project 2013</u>, accessed July 1, 2014.

sites within SINS await you to join other mature daters in their search for future partners and mates. Isn't it great to think not of inevitable endings but of expectant beginnings?

As a member of SINS, you are limited only by your expectations; they should be realistic and may need to be better defined. With SINS to support you as you take steps to move beyond the personal life you now live, you should have little reason to feel or be alone. Every form of a potential partner awaits you within SINS' online communities.

Changing times and their mores have expanded the somewhat clearly-defined and traditional Singles states ... 'married' or 'on the trail to being so'. Now we have a plethora of choices ... encompassing every shade of relationship, allowing us to meld into a compatible and happy union with a like-minded and like-hearted person. SINS allow you to explore options with countless potential partners whom you would not meet in your traditional social spheres. You will be introduced to others with similar goals and, interestingly, to those with alternative goals that might lead to new definitions of your *intended relationship*.

Again, never feel uncomfortable to say publicly you are on a dating site or dating sites. You will be pleasantly surprised at how many others come forth to affirm they are doing the same!!! Or, are considering it ... held back from joining by the unknown mechanics of something vast and new to them and by their own fears. Add to those reasons, a perceived lack of trusted and truly helpful information. Pew Research Center's Internet and American Life Project shows evidence attitudes toward online dating "have progressed in a clearly positive direction."[16] The stigma of online dating in its earlier years is rapidly being erased. Thirty-eight

---

[16] Aaron Smith and Maeve Duggan, <u>Pew Research Center's Internet and American Life Project 2013</u>, accessed June 30, 2014.

percent of Americans who are "single and looking" say they've utilized an online dating site or mobile dating app.[17]

In fact ... I repeat for your reassurance ... Single Matures serious about finding a partner belong to multiple SINS. And, being a member of more than one site allows you to search wider and farther ... possibly into unexpected focuses. Each additional site widens your possibility to find someone in particular areas of interest important to you. One site, for example, could be sexual orientation-based and another sports-related dating for fans of a particular sports team. Perhaps add a SINS community site centered about a type of pet ... even breed ... or hobbies and the niches therein. Some sites are age-span based, May/December scenarios ... both males and females defined as either the May or December part of the combo.

Here is a need-to-say that I continuously stress: Safety *must* take precedence over every aspect of your Candyland experience. As you tend to your on-site activities, you *must* take care of your safety. [The focus of Chapter 12.] You will have plenty of opportunities to enjoy all the treats available. If you miss a few because you should nix initial connections, you must feel confident that it was for the best. Do not regret saying "no" to someone you are uncomfortable about or skeptical of. If someone pressures you to step outside your comfort zone or outside the guidelines set here, be assured that individual is most likely not for you. (That's not to say that as a relationship progresses you shouldn't allow yourself to be nudged by a trusted someone to take on new experiences that might expand your lifetime tally of adventures.)

In today's highly technological world, online dating has become the most popular strategy for finding a date. Thousands of dating sites meet the

---

[17] Ibid.

differing inclinations of their members. Whether you are just looking for a casual encounter or for serious love, dating online is certain to offer you options ... maybe more options than you ever thought existed.

Below are some of the most frequently asked questions about online dating:

1. **Is online dating safe?**

   Yes, SINS is a world filled predominantly with goodwill and hope. The great majority of members are involved for the same reasons you are ... to find love, companionship, interesting dates, friendships, travel partners, dance partners, dining partners, concert partners, life partners, etc. Just as in other social communities, odd or deceptive types are mixed in among Candyland's delectable treats. Once again I impress upon you: It is most important that you guard your safety because you are dealing with the anonymity and unaccountability of the Internet, not the familiar setting of a local group.

   With that said, if you follow common sense and the safety procedures [Chapter 12] you should be as safe as you would be in a traditional dating situation and certainly safer percentage-wise than randomly meeting strangers in a bar, a large impersonal social gathering, while shopping, waiting in a line or when attending an entertainment event, etc. Within SINS you do most of your vetting before you actually meet someone.

2. **Would anyone be interested in me?**

   Yes, generally. Of course, you have to be realistic in your expectations of how many might be interested in you. Also, you may not find those contacting you acceptable. In which case, you must do more searches, extend yourself, truthfully re-work your profile and approach those whom you want to meet because you sense something special about them in their profiles. Expect to *strike out* sometimes ... at other times you will *hit it out of the park*. Your appearance, lifestyle, interests, background and, certainly, how well you present yourself and express your personality in your profile all come into play.

3. **Can You Join Multiple Services?**

Yes. Many online dating services offer free memberships, so you should take advantage and join as many as you think suit you and you have the time to manage. Being a member of SINS does take some time ... and attention. You must remember individuals who contact you are looking for responses ... unless these are "no". In which case, most often they prefer no response. Silence is an acceptable protocol in online dating especially when the contact is just an automated compliment or question.

4. **How Much Does Online Dating Membership Cost?**

The monthly cost differs with each site. Many SINS have no fees; some have free limited access and fees for more communication privileges. All-inclusive dating site fees generally range from $25.00 to $60.00 per month. However, you can also join for 6 or 12 months and thereby receive a substantial discount.

5. **How Many Dating Services Are There?**

Hundreds and hundreds ... well over 1,500 sites! Although, not all sites are good value for what they charge (if they do) or worth your time. Some of the smaller sites have very few members, which limits your selection ... maybe in a good way, maybe not. Ask folks you know who are online dating members for their recommendations. And, read the overview later of some of the best dating sites and the most popular trusted services.

Some readers may have noticed recurring mentions of key ideas. These are offered to help the very tentative create an ever larger and solid understanding of the scope of SINS.

As you launch into this new online world be truthful with yourself and others. And, be realistic ... SINS truly is *the only game in town* if you are earnestly looking for love. Life might bring someone to you; SINS is just about a sure thing to bring many possible candidates to you. Since that's what it is all about, jump in and enjoy the game, the dance, the play ... be a participant and not a spectator. Finding the right partner and falling in love is not a spectator sport. The search is an engagement on your part that just may lead to another type of engagement.

> *"We can't be in survival mode.*
> *We have to be in growth mode."*
> -Jeff Bezos-

As you progress through your search in SINS, you can easily check in and out of the action at your will, as I have done over the past eight years. You can also be totally anonymous if you so choose by hiding your profile ... permanently, or temporarily while searching for potential partners, checking out your competition, just taking a break from all the communications or from dating itself. Seriously, you may want a break. SINS can be too much of a good thing at times ... offering so much attention and social interaction that you want to step back and catch your breath.

SINS processes can be stimulating and surprisingly invigorating at a time in your life that can be defined by some as anything but those descriptive words. Now may be the time to take the leap … without fear or disapproval. What do you have to lose? You are already alone. If you don't try, you will most likely never meet that special *someone* in your present social circles … you might always wonder what could have possibly developed if you had attempted even a short journey through Candyland. The numbers are against you if you are looking for a future partner and you remain outside the SINS community. As of June, 2013 the population of the U.S. included 54 million Singles. *Forty million* of these Singles had tried online dating.[18] Those numbers obviously translate into a high percentage of Singles having utilized SINS.

In fact if you are truly are serious about joining SINS, finding a match and have not checked out Candyland, take five minutes to open your computer, begin a search and be wowed by the diversity of sites available for your perusal and choosing. Survey a focus appealing to you. Too many temptations, possibly? Merely dip your toes into the water. Choose just one to quickly scan and give yourself a preview of a typical site configuration. Don't let yourself be drawn in just yet, though. Come back to your reading! You have so much more to learn!

> *"Risk comes from not knowing what you're doing."*
> -Warren Buffett-

Once more I mention RED FLAGS… be wary of them. They exist, and can most often be sidestepped with caution and attention to sound advice. Discussed further on are the danger signs [the darker side of SINS, in Chapters 10, 11 and 12] … the RED FLAGS that you should be aware of as you

---

[18] http://www.statisticbrain.com/online-dating-statistics/, Reuters, Herald News, PC World, Washington Post, research date: 1/1/2014, accessed June 30, 2014.

weave your way through many opportunities to introduce yourself to interesting people from all walks of life. Vigilance is not only a good thing but *imperative* when you will be invited to step out of your comfortable world to experience other slices of life... ones you just might find enjoyable and more, even find intriguing and stimulating.

As you continue reading, you should inform yourself about truly important aspects of Internet dating on SINS so you come prepared to the glittering tables of treats set before you. If you approach Candyland wisely you will find a veritable feast. You do not want to fumble your way through this unfamiliar and very important endeavor in your life. To find someone with whom to spend a life segment or the rest of your life, in whatever your arrangement may entail, is a journey that requires planning and effort and awareness ... not luck.

"So you think we might have a lot in common, do you?"

You are learning about SINS from someone who has gained a new life because of them and has happily lived to tell her tales and those of others. This chapter should have helped you to understand and accept you are not alone *and* you are not an anomaly in today's society. You are part of the main stream, so you'd do well to jump in and start swimming ... enjoy the frolic and fun. Happily thrash about or dreamily float along its natural flow. Whatever your style or pace, SINS allows for flexibility. The sheer numbers of others who are looking for a partner online give you a sizeable pool in which to swim your strokes *to find* and *be found* by potential partners. Those two purposes are the dual foundation of SINS.

You now know *attitudes towards online dating are becoming more positive over time.* The PEW 2013 report states nearly one quarter of online daters (23 percent) say they themselves have entered into a marriage or long-term relationship with someone they met through a dating site or app. That number is statistically a bit higher than the 17 percent of online daters who said that the same outcome had happened for them when they were first asked this question in 2005.[19] And remember, millions more joined between 2005 and 2013. Thus, the actual number of successful unions increased significantly.

To this point, most of you have spent your lives involved in family and work ... whether you were martyrs or not, it is the truth. Now it's time to REFOCUS and CREATE a new truth for you via a spirited adventure, a truth that would be the center of the best act in the stage play of your life.

What is next for you to best live your new truth is to become a new *best you* ... exercise yourself into physical shape, deepen your self-awareness, actively pursue interests and expand your mind. SINS

[19] Aaron Smith and Maeve Duggan, Pew Research Center's Internet and American Life Project 2013, accessed June 30, 2014.

are a great motivator! Their possibilities bring you into an active and proactive life. I love it. I swear I would not be in as good a shape or in as youthful a state of mind if it were not for SINS. Participation in it keeps me on my toes … whether in the gym, in a classroom, on a trip or on the front porch for a goodnight hug and kiss. SINS propel me to be the best me possible. Let's turn our attention to your becoming *The Best You*.

Chapter Four

FROM  **TO**

The Best YOU

Discipline, sweat, attitude and ...
a little help from some friends

Becoming the best you. Wow! You might be thinking this is a major demanding undertaking. Well, in truth it does require focus, consistency, dedication, gumption, perseverance ... and attitude. Mental traits that you MAY THINK have dropped away with time. NOT TRUE!!!

As many of us moved through life, some of its tolls appear to have darkened positive self-image and drive. Perhaps the *'humbler'* is life itself. We faced so many struggles and did not always win. Many of us can still resemble that once-achiever with seemingly endless goals and a boundless unforced energy infused with a youthful, forward-looking mindset. For some, the goals mechanism has been in hibernation. Many Matures now have the time, the will and the reasons to resurrect and revitalize themselves. In addition, science can help.

Presently, an unprecedented amount of information is available about slowing up or even preventing some aging processes. Our bodies and how they age continue to be the subject of a multitude of widely ranging studies with many interesting findings. Dietary aids and cosmetic enhancements previously only available to a privileged class are now accessible to you depending on your budget constraints ... or not. Two of the consistent highly important aids to aging gracefully are exercise and diet. Both need not cost you much money. Discipline and consistency are the keys to their success. Most of us make attempts to meet doctors' recommendations for us in these areas. Start doing your own homework and apply yourself. Find what will work for you.

If you are reading this book, you already are interested in taking control of your life, making some substantial moves to select a few of the many options available to you. Perhaps the next biggest option is committing yourself to becoming, over time, the best you that you can be. Perhaps your next biggest option is becoming an active member of SINS. Some of you are aware you really should get yourself into better shape. To make the decision to do so is a positive step all by itself ... just the realization and acceptance that things cannot remain the same. Decide to fine-tune or, if needed, greatly improve your appearance, health and attitude ... all necessary to live a more fulfilling life *and* to attract someone new and worthwhile into your life. Do not turn your back on renewing yourself in various ways ... even if you take on only what limited finances will allow. Your daily life and remaining years will be enhanced and, in some cases, the healthier for it whether or not someone special comes into your life.

The phrase *dealing with aging and dating enthusiastically* in SINS (my recommendation for maintaining some level of youthfulness) almost sounds like an oxymoron, doesn't it? But, it is not ... believe me. The key words are *'dealing with'* aging, which you already are or will soon be doing, and '*enthusiastically*' dating, which you aspire to. Both will happen naturally when you begin dating, along with some intentional input by you as you move forward at a pace comfortable for you ... consciously and with purpose along your path through *Candyland S.I.N.S.*, following its suggestions, *getting out there*, and enjoying your progress.

Let's begin. I look forward to knowing you will take flight and leave this SINS veteran to cheer you on. Make a note to yourself, one that I cannot emphasize too much: your *attitude* will make the whole difference in your outcome. Work on it daily.

"Your *doctor can only do so much. The rest is up to you. Stop getting older.*"

Our own aging and that of family, friends and prospective partners is a tough reality to accept but one that we must acknowledge (and, weirdly, honor) if we are going to *deal with it*. This awareness will be addressed by me ... and then by you. We are a team, one which will take a polished you to the finish line.

It is normal to revisit occasionally that rosy mental film of what we were like when dating in our teens and twenties and, perhaps, thirties... all before our bodies had reached their peaks and started the slide to the Antarctic. Everything about our bodies began to head south, literally and figuratively, from our hair on down. Where did the shiny thick hair, the sparkling eyes, the vibrant bouncing steps go? Into where did the muscular torsos and the shapely waists, calves and ankles disappear?

Those questions are for other books to discuss in greater detail. Let it suffice for us to admit that the loss of physical vibrancy to one degree or another is very real for most of us. Enough so that some of us attempt what we can to put the brakes on and perhaps slow down the drop ... in order to regain and re-energize as much of what has been lost as is possible within our means, both physically and financially. All is not irretrievably lost. But, I know very well how it is to feel that way. I felt no hope about having any relationship after I was left *suddenly single* at age 62, much overweight and feeling very unlovable. Nothing was farther from the truth ... and proven so after I committed myself to positive steps forward. That can be your path, as well.

Let's start your journey back ... with enthusiasm.

"Years may wrinkle the skin,
but to give up enthusiasm wrinkles the soul."
-Samuel Ullman[20] -

Both lack of enthusiasm and aging skin have a major impact on our appearance. I cannot think of any natural contributor better than exercise to lift your spirits and make your skin glow. [Except maybe one. ;-D] As well, antidepressants when deemed necessary by

---

[20] Sam Ullman, wwww.brainyquotes.com, http://www.brainyquote.com/quotes/quotes/s/samuelullm103893.html, accessed June 30, 2014.

a physician can create a huge turn around for some people. And, so much is available to help us restore some of our youthfulness that the array is mind-boggling. Let us begin with the simplest, the cheapest and the absolute 'musts' ... exercise and healthy eating.

In fact, exercise has been proven to be an effective treatment for Major Depressive Disorder (MDD). Many of you may have experienced or now have mild to severe depression after losses in your lives and while facing life alone. Now, sufficient research helps doctors prescribe the proper doses of exercise for depressed patients. Interesting, huh? According to a new report in the *Journal of Psychiatric Practice*, protocols for successfully addressing many forms of depression include aerobic exercise ... along with some resistance training. Researchers recommend three to five exercise sessions, 45 to 60 minutes long per week, and to bring the heart rate up 50 to 85 percent of your maximum heart rate. If you truly want to feel better physically and emotionally, commit to a weekly schedule. Not only will your body thank you but also you should experience relief from your depression in as little as four weeks. The greatest antidepressant effect will develop after ten to twelve weeks. In one study the dropout rates for exercisers were comparable to those in medication-based and psychotherapy studies. Such a comparison, if repeated, confirms the psychological effectiveness of a commitment to an exercise regimen.[21] I encourage you to do some regular exercise, even if your weekly program cannot meet the above guidelines and you are not depressed. Following through with any amount of regular exercise will help you feel and look better.

I have observed the Matures who frequent the gym I belong to are noticeably trimmer or shapelier and far more energetic and enthusiastic about life than most of those I meet in the general population. It was slow to dawn on me, but it is true: Those of us who maintain a regular exercise program definitely display suspicious traits of liveliness ... skin that is pinker and tauter ... steps that are bouncier. We are quicker to smile than the average Joe and Josie. ;-D All are signs associated with youthfulness. Keeping our blood flowing, our heart rate up and our muscles more or less firm make the above traits more noticeable in us than in most people in our age range.

Nowadays, multiple options for exercise exist at home, in your neighborhood or elsewhere. Go online for incremental exercise routines or search your closet for those old CD's. Start with your local YMCA or YWCA[22]. These facilities are excellent and offer a variety of options and levels from the most basic beginner level to super fit. The local YMCA has been my choice for many years. Local Y's provide a wide range of programs for everyone in state-

---

[21] PsychCentral,   http://psychcentral.com,   http://psychcentral.com/news/2013/05/11/new-guidelines-for-using-exercise-as-an-antidepressant/54728.html referencing *The Journal of Psychiatric Practice*, accessed June 30, 2014.

[22] http://www.YWCA.org, YWCAcanada.ca, YMCA.ca, YMCA.net, http://www.ymca.int/

of-the-art-facilities with well-trained staffs. Mine has swimming facilities that include (at no extra cost) in-water exercises as well as age-targeted floor exercise programs, great workout machines with TV's attached and computer-tracked results for individual members. My Y also promotes social interaction with pickleball (a form of modified indoor tennis), Zumba dance classes, bike spinning, group floor classes, etc. Check with your Y and private gyms for a healthy and effective start on your path to fitness. A costlier option, available at the gyms or privately, is springing for a personal trainer to create a custom program for you, work with you and keep you on track.

Commit yourself to an exercise program that suits you. Occasionally, move up the intensity a notch. Attempt to be consistent and dedicated. You will need emotional, mental and physical energy to travel through Candyland. Prepare yourself! If you pay heed to the experience of SINS members and their tips within this guide, you will be busy.

"Of course I think about death. I'd like
to die young at a very old age."

Of course, participation in your local sports activity clubs is a social route to becoming fit in uplifting outdoor environments. Play tennis, golf, hike, walk, ski, snowshoe, take nature walks, learn karate or yoga, etc. Tennis is my game of choice. The courts have given me my local community of friends. All the above and other personal choices will do the same for you. They will affect your spirit, your mental alertness and your all-important attitude. You will gift yourself with a more positive persona that should be most effective when you meet your prospective partners in SINS. You cannot arrive on the scene as a 'deadhead'. Get with the uplift program as soon as possible. No one wants just to entertain you. SINS members who contact you want to relate to you, appreciate and bask in your energy, conversation and enthusiasm ... as you do in theirs. Heed the law of attraction: You attract what you radiate.

Beauty aids and cosmetic treatments for both men and women are endless topics. Men are an increasing segment of the mushrooming interest in anti-aging products and procedures; more are paying greater attention to their faces, bodies and personal hygiene. Even though self-enhancement is no longer a women's domain, we'll proceed ladies first.

Speak to people whose appearance you admire, people who take good care of themselves ... who always seem to have a spark and a sparkle. They must be doing something right. Ask what they might be doing differently than you. How do they decide what products to use? What tricks do they use? And, if your situation allows for something dramatic, what procedures and surgeries have they had and by whom?

We are so fortunate to live in a time of effective over-the-counter treatments that can diminish tell-tale signs of aging ... thinning hair, lips and eyelashes. I will mention a few of the products that my friends and I have used with good results. What follows is not in any way professional endorsements of the products but is an expression of enthusiasm for items that helped us and just may do the same for you.

One important-to-many concern is thinning hair and what can be done to thicken it. Some think it is a major-enough issue to invest in treatments and products that have a track record of good results. I have seen two products on the market that produce noticeable results: Anacaps by Ducray yields thicker hair; Nioxin has a great line of hair thickeners, as well. Both are available on Amazon.com and at beauty outlets and dermatologists in the USA and Canada. Other proven lines are out there, I am sure. I encourage you to investigate and try them. Hair extensions also can be a boon for thinning hair. The Joan Rivers Beauty line has a very interesting hair fill-in powder available to the public that is also used by professional makeup artists to improve the appearance of exposed shiny scalp due to thinning hair. A full head of thick, shiny hair takes years off your appearance. Also, use a shine product either as a shampoo, a conditioner, a treatment or a spray. Hair that is shiny (but not greased down) is more attractive *and* healthier.

"They regrew your hair with stem cells?"

We'll focus on gals here.

Numerous eyelash enhancers are on the market that you apply topically to the base of your eyelids. In a few weeks time, lashes that have seemingly disappeared over the years thicken and lengthen. Three effective products are Latisse, Rapid Lash and CityLash. Also, a thin strip of darker liner or pencil color lightly applied to the outside corners of your eyes adds a very subtle interest. Enhanced lashes highlight the sparkle in your eyes and make them stand out to whatever degree you wish. We definitely want that!

Topically applied lip plumpers are painless and give you back luscious lips that may have unfortunately receded with age. City Lips is one of many plumpers that seem to do the trick. Too, lip glosses in beautiful colors make your lips appear very kissable. Sometimes current shades of lipstick can be very flattering and a nice update.

If God had to give a woman wrinkles,
he might at least have put them on the soles of her feet.
-Ninin de L'Enclos-

If your budget can take the costs, consider the plethora of procedures and surgeries that will contour your body as well as your face. Several simple and painless procedures can take many years off your face. Their popularity and resulting affordability for us non-celebrities is both exciting and mind-boggling. Where to begin and end? I have spoken with two experts who own clinics in Ontario to ask their recommendations and opinions on aging and their patients' experiences with them. I have attended the clinics of both over the years and admire their expertise and their dedication to their professions. And, have researched and judiciously tried some of the procedures and products that they offer ... with a limited budget. Do not turn your back on youth enhancing aids ... if you can afford to do so. Your self-image and remaining years will be all the sunnier for it. If you cannot see a cosmetic professional, find an over-the-counter skin treatment product (maybe on the advice of friends) and follow suit. Here is a face-care tip: Once you apply that specialty product, allow it to soak in and then overlay some moisturizer to seal in the product for full effect. Do so twice daily. Enjoy the gradual changes.

"After you confirm my appointment with the cosmetic surgery team, I'd like you to file restraining orders against Father Time, Mother Nature, and the Flab Fairy."

Gentlemen, we shall consider your self-care items later. Now, onto something gender-free.

A healthy diet is all-important, along with your exercise. They go hand-in-hand. To eat properly when you live alone is a tall order. I know. I struggle with that ... and I love to cook! Somehow cooking for oneself is not half the fun as cooking for or with others. When I cook something special, I generally prepare large amounts and freeze meal-size portions for later use. When I serve them to myself at a later date I add salads and fresh vegetables. In that way, I have good nutritious dinners most of the time. I sit alone evenings with a lovely meal, a glass of wine and a beautiful view outside my windows. That works for me. You will settle into what suits you if you take the time to think about it and do what is necessary to implement it, i.e. to check out what daily diet regimen is right for you, meal planning, easy but mouth-watering recipes, grocery shopping routine, etc. You might create a pleasant setting for your meals as well. Pleasing surroundings and music can only enhance our feelings of wellbeing.

"It's made from seaweed, bee pollen, fish oil and organic dirt, but the magazine says it tastes exactly like chocolate cake!"

I can't imagine what someone does when s/he cannot or does not like to cook. To eat regularly in restaurants and to consume re-heated processed food for your regular fare cannot be healthy. Perhaps you take vitamin supplements. You are what you put into your body … and it shows … on your skin, your torso and elsewhere. Do your best to create nutritious meals as often as possible and make their prep fun, even if you are alone. So many guides exist online and off to move you into modern, tasty, health supporting eating. If you establish your mindset correctly and are determined, you should be able to bring yourself back to some level of shape after years of slacking off or pretty near total neglect. I had to do the same.

"I want you to keep eating pizza and cheeseburgers. At this point, a salad might shock your system and kill you."

Don't forget to stimulate your mind. You may not have always had time for this while you were raising a family and/or working throughout your younger years. Now is the opportunity to sweep out those mental cobwebs. So much is out there to stimulate and extend you. Feed your mental acuity with books, new magazines, informative television, courses, travel, cultural events, new friends and new experiences, etc. The list might be endless. Only you can fill in the blanks. You want to be as interesting to yourself as to anyone you meet in SINS. You may also meet someone on all those self-improvement ventures. They are win/win additions to your life. You may even find you enjoy your own company ... not always needy for others' attention ... as you develop your mind, body, spirit.

And, your all-important self-esteem. As I write this, I realize why I am so busy. So much still to do and enjoy; so little time left!

Even though I do not have a reference for the following, I came across it in my recent reading. Documented research into the effects of smiling states that if someone smiles softly into a mirror for a few minutes a day, in a fairly short time changes happen ... good ones. Regular gentle smiling-back-at-yourself sessions relax the head and face muscles, release more of the happiness chemicals and affect the blood-pressure, etc. I dare you to try it for a month! You should find more specifics online.

Wear a smile and have friends; wear a scowl and have wrinkles.
-George Eliot[23]-

Of course, your most effective beauty treatment is your smile. It costs you nothing. Who does not look their best when they smile? With a smile, even those who feel the most unattractive among us can appear approachable, open to interaction. How many of you would be drawn to hug someone who has a smile that radiates from the inside out? Do so when you speak on the phone to potential dates ... others can *hear* your smile! Practice when you prepare for your dates. They might not notice what you are wearing or what you consider the less attractive elements of your appearance when you smile ... a sincere smile.

;-D

Here is another hint to maintain a pleasant demeanor: if you lightly hum at times as you go through your day your face will become more and more relaxed. You will appear pleasant, content, and more appealing ... and others likely will sense you are at ease with them.

---

[23] George Eliot, www.brainyquote.com http://www.brainyquote.com/quotes/quotes/g/georgeelio107837.html, accessed June 30, 2014.

"*Actually, I'm 57 years old! Would you like the name of my plastic surgeon?*"

To become The Best You ...

add a healthy dose of the *game changer 'attitude'.*

Attitude
Excerpt from Charles Swindoll[24]

"The longer I live, the more I realize the impact of attitude on life.
Attitude, to me, is more important than facts.
It is more important than the past, than education,
than money, than circumstances,
than failure, than successes, than what
other people think or say or do.

...

We cannot change the inevitable.
The only thing we can do is play on the one string
we have, and that is our attitude ....

---

[24] Charles Swindoll, www.goodreads.com, http://www.goodreads.com/quotes/267482-the-longer-i-live-the-more-i-realize-the-impact, accessed June 30, 2014.

Chapter Five

Feelings of Fear, Rejection, Mistrust, Hurt, and Anger ... dump them ...

What a gruesome picture!
These 'thieves' rob you of your potential
for happiness and/or contentment.
How can you rid yourself of such ballast?

FEAR

Time waits for no one. Many Matures no longer have most of our lives ahead of us. In fact, time flies faster with each year, month and day ... and takes us with it. Many of us want to share joy and affection and to be in love again before it is too late. What is stopping us? Fear of the unknown? Fear of rejection? Fear of being hurt? Fear of looking foolish? Or, whatever? It is time to talk about such emotional blockages and help clear ourselves of them. If we are to wondrously share our remaining time with new partners we must begin to rid ourselves of our baggage and step onto the carousels of Candyland ... while we are active and healthy enough to enjoy the ride.

You may have fear of the unknown, particularly at this time in your life, when you find yourself in the world of Solo living; possibly feeling very vulnerable, hesitant to open yourself up to hurt, disappointment and abandonment once again. Perhaps you even feel quite worn down and unequipped to deal with the usual or new-to-you daily mundane challenges in your life; afraid to trust *new* people, deal with *new* rules, and act to bring about *new* relationships. Some of you may believe your time for meaningful connection has come and gone and prefer not to invite complication into your life.

© Randy Glasbergen
www.glasbergen.com

"I'm free-range, but I still feel caged in by my doubts and fears."

Whether your fears, deeper dreads or lighter insecurities are many or few, you are like the majority of us. Fear certainly seems to be one word that comes up time and again when discussing Mature dating ... fear of peer reaction, financial security fears, safety fears, fear of failure and fear of not pleasing your new date interest or your new partner as your relationship continues. Or, fears related to sexual intimacy and performance. The list might be endless. I am sure each of you could add a good number of other ones, as well.

If you want to enjoy your time in SINS, you should bite the bullet and begin to deal with insecurities. Begin! You might address one or two of the smaller ones at a time so you will not be overwhelmed. You *can* move through them ... as many do, with or without professional help. Each fear on its own is not unconquerable. Sometimes you just have to set your jaw and make a leap of faith. Lo and behold, before you know it, fears previously endured will have been erased by each success you have in SINS. Yes, you are likely to have setbacks, as with anything in life. Just expect them; deal with them; move through them. Remember the bit about *attitude*?

FINANCES

One major set of fears for some relates to finances. As you move along through the bonding process with a selected someone, you should refrain from sharing your financial life. However, before you make your decision to settle definitely on a new partner or mate, have that other talk ... the financial one. Before you settle down together, have that talk again. Financial fears and practicalities have to be addressed by both partners. What if s/he has little or no money? What if both of you are lacking sufficient financial resources to really enjoy your remaining years? What if one is *after* the other's money? If either one of you is so inclined, the other should agree to meet with an advisor or a financial professional. Be proactive ... eliminate your fear about this sensitive subject.

INVESTMENTS AND
RETIREMENT PLANNING

GLASBERGEN

*"Many people like to start a new hobby when they retire.
Hunting and gathering might be a good choice for you."*

If you two share similar economic backgrounds, you generally can easily set up equitable and agreeable financial arrangements. But even then, family members can insert themselves if they attempt to 'protect' their parent's interests ... or perhaps attempt to protect their inheritances. The latter scenario brings with it yet another fear, one now harbored about people we hope love us and care more about our happiness and security than what we may leave behind.

Wow. How brave and exhilarating to meet and slay even just a few of those fears! Isn't it great to have challenges to sharpen your mind and your senses at a time when many Matures see themselves on a downward slope? Bored, with little energy or interest in changing the slow drawing-in of their lives. Some are, quite frankly, in what might be termed depressing circumstances. Yes, have compassion for them as I do ... but seize the opportunity to confront your own fears, move through them and prepare to enter a future that will be brighter whether or not your initial set of interactions on SINS leads to something grand.

At a difficult juncture in my life I moved to a new town two hours away from my family and friends, not knowing one soul ... at age 66. It was an invigorating adventure ... although I was totally alone. I then proceeded to build a home with no one to share the responsibilities of all my negotiations, deal with the trades and make the endless decisions necessary to create my dream home in my little paradise. I was able to meet the challenges and progress toward my vision pleased with and even proud of both the results and myself. You, too, likely can meet some variation of fulfilling your dream or your heart's desire ... in spite of whatever gauntlets are cast before you. Don't let age and your Single status fill you with fear or deter you from pushing your boundaries.

The challenges you could face in SINS should re-invigorate you, open up new areas of thinking, bring you to stimulating and unforgettable people and open doorways to energizing and memorable experiences. These potentials are all available to you if you can overcome some of your basic fears ... most of which, if not totally unfounded, can be circumvented or dealt with in a healthy manner.

Don't confuse *fear* with a rational combination of caution and common sense that will protect you from danger and heartbreak. Precautions and rational behavior are important when strangers approach you, a new arrival in unknown territory. Because anyone can write an appealing profile, be very careful and call upon your natural instincts, as well. [You will learn how to examine profiles in coming chapters.]

Entering *Candyland* has very little downside when you begin with the right tools. With them you have the potential to add many happy fulfilling years to your life's calendar. I joined SINS at age 63 and since have delighted in some of the most interesting, enlivening and fun-filled years of my life ... much to my surprise. I, as some of you, was unsure of myself and how I would cope as a *suddenly single* gal dating at a mature age. I also found shades of love along the way. Even the pains of rejection or a broken heart let you know you have *lived* more and *ventured* more ... and *expanded* your life. Many Matures experience those sensations only vicariously through reading or watching TV or a movie. You are different.

REJECTION

You will most surely fail in your quest to find a partner or mate if you are unable to shelve or deal positively with your fear of rejection. You must realize that you will almost certainly experience some form of rejection and sense of failure in this new dating process. Always keep in mind, though, you have control of the larger picture. For most SINS members discovering a new partner is an elimination process ... you narrow candidates down to three ... two... one. The magical exception is when you meet someone and immediately feel that *shimmer* and that *click.*

Your likely unrecognized fear of rejection and how you cope with it affects how successful you are in so many aspects of your life ... from learning a new skill to searching for a job to finding a partner. If you can put fear of rejection in the back of your mind (along with fear of failure) and take the risk to continue through Candyland, you are much closer to finding someone special in your life.

You truly must understand that not everyone you connect with online will find you appealing enough to meet with you after the first set of email exchanges or phone calls ... or go beyond meeting over a coffee/glass of wine/etc. ... or want a second date. That is a reality that you must accept and cope with as painlessly as possible. Find something positive in the encounter(s) and move on. Terminations do not mean you are unattractive or unlovable; only that you are not the person who more or less fits the criteria important to the member you met.

Conversely, you know that not every person you will meet is meant to be *the one* for you ... just as you logically realize that you do not fit everyone else's ideal range for a potential partner. Allow everyone you encounter the right to make their decisions without your feeling hurt. You will be hoping for the same courtesy when you tell someone you just do not see a relatively complete match with him or her. Treat each one as gently as possible while being firm; some very nice people do feel hurt and do not like to let go. Such experiences can be difficult for both of you. You can come out of the experience a better person for the way in which you consciously treat others.

"Every time I thought I was being rejected from something good,
I was actually being re-directed to something better."

-Steve Maraboli-
--Unapologetically You: Reflections of Life and the Human Experience--

While we are speaking of 'rejection', take to heart and remember the following little known fact: Sometimes you can be rejected because your date does not feel worthy of you! Your interested potential mates can be afraid you will eventually reject them when you learn to know them. The fear can be based on their pasts, in memories and subconscious insecurities that prevent them from taking that young relationship with you any further. I have had that happen to me and, admittedly, found the experiences very frustrating and difficult to leave behind. You are told you are loved, that you are everything s/he wants. Yet, s/he cannot commit, even to non-marital exclusivity. Deep down, s/he is too afraid of abandonment. (I suspect that nearly everyone has some level of issues, shadows and deep darkness.) Do not always take someone's lack of enthusiasm for you at face value. Each individual, within the normal ranges, is a complex human being with personal unrealized wish lists and accumulated issues that can prevent the furthering of an inter-personal connection. In such cases, better to know sooner rather than later.

On the other hand, if you are repeatedly rejected, be sure to evaluate yourself. But, not from the intention to find everything wrong with you. Rather, with the intention to consider how you might reshape, improve, grow and even expand. Re-evaluate how you act on your dates ... your demeanor, your manners, your appearance, your conversational skills or lacks thereof, etc. Use 'rejection' as an opportunity to improve yourself. Do not wallow in it. Change what caused it. Check with truthful and caring friends for some feedback; do the work needed to correct or at the least minimize your flaws in order to better yourself. SINS experiences give you good reality checks on yourself. Pay attention to them. Work on your weaknesses and on personal growth and development. Eventually, you *will* come out a winner... and certainly at least a bit better version of who you were before you entered Candyland.

If you cannot take these initial steps to diminish the fear of rejection and the fear of failure, you will have a very short journey in Candyland. Because, likely, you will give up too soon. You must overcome your fears and take some risks. Think of all the opportunities you have missed in your life because you did not allow yourself to take sufficient chances outside your various comfort zones. Variations of risk-taking are a requirement if you wish to explore new territories successfully ... whether a job opportunity across the country, a new career move, an investigation into a new religion or life philosophy, new friends from different cultures, non-traditional travel choices, etc. Growth opportunities lost.

"I like the wings, but now I have this fear of being eaten by a cat!"

GOING DEEP

I have gone through a good deal of soul searching both alone and with professional help. I've found each venture to be enlightening and in the end ... after much, much work ... both very positive experiences. You may have to address painful memories and realizations, but you will emerge a better human being because you have some understanding of your fears and issues ... and your resultant actions and defense mechanisms. You will then be able to attempt some strategic changes, changes that will affect your general wellbeing, and allow you to be more at ease with those with whom you interact. Even small changes can make a big difference in life's responses to your aspirations. You might be pleasantly surprised. If you have the good fortune to discover a masterful therapist as I did and *do your homework*, most likely you will arrive at an emotionally healthy place. Such a small miracle will allow you to welcome a near-if-not-perfect new partner into your life ... or, alternatively, allow you to enjoy life as a deliberate Singleton.

Candyland SINS is a new territory for you; you must be willing to take a few emotional risks. But, I stress that I do not recommend ignoring safety risks. [More about such risks coming up.]

MISTRUST

Trust is a frequently discussed issue in budding relationships ... due to either no relationship history or the previous relationship and breakup history of one or both of the partners. For some of you, the fear of trust being broken is literally very close to the heart because of the pain caused due to past betrayal of your faith in another person. This issue actually became a personal one because of some of my experiences in SINS. But, ever the eternal optimist, me! Lack of trust can destroy potentially great relationships, so you must tread a very fine line. While you move forward with the relationship you must, early in your involvement, be alert to a potentially cheating partner and the ensuing issues ... while at the same time you relax into the delight of your new romantic interest. A tough balancing act, for sure.

"The affair saved my marriage. When his girlfriend ran off with my boyfriend, we suddenly had something in common again!"

Always be mindful that trust *must be* earned, never naïvely granted without being deserved ... over an extended time period. You must protect yourself from potential heartbreak due to the inherent anonymity of online dating when in a new relationship with a relatively unknown person, so very new in your life, one whom you met in SINS. If more whole and secure in themselves than not, your new interests should understand and respect your caution, as they should do in reverse as well, if legitimately looking for a deeply committed love in SINS.

HURT AND ANGER

When I say you must let go of hurt and anger, I speak from experience. I have lived with both. At present I am finally and gratefully without them. As you make your decision to move forward with your life, I cannot stress enough the need to shed old hurt and anger. Anger can be a manifestation of extreme hurt. Let it go. Don't allow your past to hinder you from living today. You will be more successful in achieving what you are seeking in your quest on SINS ... as well as in life. Hurt and anger serve no positive purpose ... in fact, no purpose at all in any aspect of your life. They are ballast; they do not allow you to buoy yourself to meet the new challenges that life inevitably presents.

> *Holding on to anger is like grasping a hot coal*
> *with the intent of throwing it at someone else;*
> *you are the one who gets burned.*
> -Buddha-

Letting go of hurt and anger is a beautiful achievement, one well worth striving for. When you are free of such baggage you can be whole and no longer need anyone to complete you. You are at peace. You can be a complete human being, one secure in yourself. One full of interesting thoughts and activities, secure in your love for self, family, friends, and your surroundings ... grateful for your life. Now you can be ready to find love ... and that may be in a far different form than you had imagined.

Your journey through Candyland will be one of discovery. You will have a mind-boggling multitude of initial choices the likes of which you never imagined. Freeing yourself of feelings of Fear, Rejection, Mistrust, Hurt and Anger will allow you to see and accept the possibilities offered to you in the new-to-you world of SINS.

> *"Let go of old anger and stop the past from letting you live today living today...."*
> -Patti Lomax-
> --a real character in "The Railway Man" --

Make every effort to unload the emotional baggage you carry from past relationships. They were *then*. You are living *now*, free to change and move forward. Enjoy your freedom ... even revel in it! How many people do you know fortunate enough to have the opportunity to step into a new life, meet all sorts of people and make friends, all the while awaiting that new partner or mate with a fresh outlook and a compatible approach to life?

"It was a painful divorce. Somehow I got custody of her lawyer's teenage children!"

Most likely you are reading *Candyland S.I.N.S.* because you are considering how you might expand your life or because you want to move beyond the negatives of unfortunate events ... perhaps a death, divorce or a painful breakup. I must be tough here. Deal with it! You cannot change the losses and failures of the past, but you can successfully sculpt the future you desire. *Do not* let the nay-sayers get you down. *Do not* be dragged down and held back by people who do not know your pain; who have lived a different reality than yours. No two lives can be expected to proceed exactly in tandem according to someone else's assessment of how they should have been or should be lead ... too many variables exist among human beings. Be your own person, your own rock. Face your demons and leave them behind ... a real self-help project for you.

LETTING GO

Letting go of the past and its residue is necessary to *move on* to a healthy relationship ... however you can accomplish it. Replace it with your *now*, accompanied by all your positive inner and outer work and their increasingly growing and appealing results. You can only *emerge* a better person ... one you like better and have learned to love. Perhaps a special someone will come into your life and feel the same way about you ... the authentic best you. You will be *ready*.

"You're allowed one small carry-on, but each additional piece of emotional baggage is an extra $10."

Freeing yourself of your past will definitely require you to take a really good look at yourself ... from the inside out. Please respect and do not skip this step as you enter Candyland. You want to be free of a past that can negatively affect your ability to handle some of the interesting opportunities that will present themselves on SINS. You want to be emotionally strong for your travel through Candyland, wisely able to manage the new experiences and people you will meet!! Remember: When you free yourself from the heavy weight of the past, you can carry yourself forward with the important lessons you have learned.

> *"Forgiveness is a gift you give yourself."*
> -Tony Robbins-

The reason why *letting go* of the past is so crucial is that doing so makes you less vulnerable to pitfalls and potholes and frees you of the drama of your past while you navigate the paths you will take through Candyland. You want to enjoy the journey and emerge happier than when you entered, perhaps even happier than you have ever been in your life.

In preparation for your Candyland adventure, you might try self-healing on your own by locating relevant material easily accessible for free on the Internet or by acquiring some excellent books on the subject of *letting go*, such as *Emotionally Free: Letting Go of the Past to Live in the Moment* by David Viscott, M.D. For other helpful reading try a google/search term such as "books on letting go of your past".

If, after several rounds of false starts, you cannot find your *one special person* perhaps it is time to self-examine. Perhaps you are emotionally unavailable. I repeat, many articles free on the Internet and a great number of books are available to help you in this regard. Invest in yourself; delve into some of them. You *can* create a self-help plan that is suitable and within your budget if you truly want to free yourself in preparation for your new life.

I must say emphatically I am not a psychologist, *but* I have truly lived a life heavily punctuated with lessons. Because I strongly recommend the educated, listening ear of a good therapist, here are a few more thoughts on the topic. Therapeutic conversations can be very helpful for your purposes. Perhaps you are still living in the aftermaths of difficulty or loss and are too close to the pain, its blockages and their causes. An appropriate therapist can help you sort yourself out. Seek good referrals from your doctors, acquaintances in the medical fields or reference services. Otherwise, finding the right therapist for you can be hit or miss. The wrong one can be costly and do more harm than good. I leave that mission in your hands and the guidance of others. I recommend this approach because I believe it is worth pursuing to take you to a better place at this time in your life... a time to invest in you.

Next, learn what awaits you online.

Chapter Six

Picking Your Site/s...

Like a child in Candyland ... choose
whatever site/s you like.
Yes, you probably will want more than one.
What sites are right for your 'sightings'?[25]

When you are ready to enter SINS, that question will be foremost in your search. As you begin to sift through likely dating sites for the few that will best serve your purpose and your vision, identifying sites that best suit you may seem an overwhelming challenge. After

---

[25] Reminder: The dating websites I have chosen to mention or discuss throughout *Candyland S.I.N.S.* are for informational purposes only. Their mention is not a recommendation and does not necessarily reflect my opinion or viewpoint. I receive no compensation for doing so. You should conduct your own investigation and self-verify the accuracy of my information before proceeding and/or joining various sights based on the information I have shared. Individuals are unique; so are their experiences.

you investigate a number of them and prepare to select your first one, two or three, consider what dating sites will be the best fit for you and be cost-effective.

Matchmaking services in the U.S. are a $2.1 billion per year business and continually growing, in 2014 at or near a predicted rate of 7.5 percent, even as the online dating market becomes seemingly saturated with 1,500+ websites that account for 52 percent of all matchmaking services in total.[26]

Match.com released the following impressive figures, as reported in 2014 by Marketdata Enterprises. The numbers demonstrate the strength and growth of online dating ... and how mainstream it has become. Almost 50 percent of Singles have tried online dating (of 107 million Singles in the U.S.). For these Singles, meeting online is the number one way for them to connect with people they might date (27.5 percent).[27] [For additional figures see end of chapter Studies and Statistics, Item 1.]

The number of members on the larger established sites is staggering. http://www.Match.com, a paid site available in 8 languages in 25 countries, has reported over 20+ million users and $350 million in revenues. Thirty percent of its membership is age 50+. (How about that?!) The Mature segment is the company's fastest growing demographic. Interestingly, within the Mature membership 84 percent have some college credits or a college degree. Match.com says it is responsible for more dates, relationships and marriages than any other site ... 2x's more relationships/marriages than the next competitor. It claims people who join Match are 3x's more likely to meet and develop a relationship than those who don't

---

[26] www.marketresearch.com, http://www.marketresearch.com/Marketdata-Enterprises-Inc-v416/Dating-Services-6773764/, accessed June 30, 2014.

[27] www.match.com, http://match.mediaroom.com/index.php?s=30440, Match Fact sheet 2014, accessed June 30, 2014.

join. [28] Match.com is part of a stable of dating sites owned by IAC/InterActiveCorp.

Plenty of Fish is a free site available in five languages. POF claims to be the largest dating site worldwide, with over 70 million members around the globe and accepting 50,000 signups every day. I have noticed when I sign into POF close to .5 million users are usually online. 3.5 million POF Singles log on each day and send 200 million messages a week. POF claims to create 1 million relationships every year with a couple confirming every two minutes that they met on POF.[29]

http://www.Zoosk.com is another top dating site. It claims over 27 million searchable members with users in 80 countries. Translated into 25 languages, Zoosk utilizes The SmartPick™ Behavioral Matchmaking engine that tracks a user's patterns ... as to whom s/he contacts and to whom s/he responds. [30] Another established site, http://www.eHarmony.com, claims 15.5 million users. It asks newly signed-on members approximately 400 questions in order to create successful matches. And, it has stated it is growing with new end-of-period subscribers at a rate of 20,000 to 30,000 per month.[31] Natalie Jarvey reported these numbers for eHarmony.com. OKCupid.com[32] claims to be the fastest growing and best free online dating site. Of its over 30 million active users, a million members log in every day.[33]

---

[28] Ibid.

[29] www.pof.com, Press Center, http://www.pof.com/en/press/, accessed June 30, 2014.

[30] www.zoosk.com, https://about.zoosk.com/en/about/, accessed June 30, 2014.

[31] www.statisticbrain.com, http://www.statisticbrain.com/online-dating-statistics/, accessed June 30, 2014.

[32] Natalie Jarvey, November 4, 2013, http://labusinessjournal.com/news/2013/nov/04/re-engaged/?page=2, accessed June 30, 2014.

[33] www.OKCupid.com, http://www.okcupid.com/about, accessed June 30, 2014.

When you combine such mindboggling membership numbers for these few sites alone with the combined membership numbers of all the other sites you can reasonably expect many of the people with whom you come in contact in your community are SINS members. Does it now make sense to *come out of your closet*, step into the sunlight and speak freely of your participation in SINS? You just might discover your exercise buddy, tennis partner, or work colleague, etc. is part of your online dating community. Your sharing may reveal an appealing common interest and create a spark with someone you didn't even know was single and/or looking!

In the early years, dating online carried a stigma; in some circles many Matures who admitted to dating on SINS were seen through a veil of despair or as bit crazy, at the least. That perception has changed significantly and rapidly continues to do so because of the online dating world's astonishing membership size and industry growth rate that includes ever-increasing numbers of Mature Singles actively seeking partners online. Until the year 2,000 or so, Mature online dating was not widely discussed publicly, like an embarrassing secret kept under wraps even within its own age group. The question used to be, "*Why* would you go to online dating sites to find someone?" Desperation implied. Now the question is: "*Why* would you *not* go to online dating sites to find someone?" Popular acceptance understood.

Two types of matching methods are generally used by the majority of the SINS dating sites. One pairing method is a matchmaking service that does all the work for you after you fill out a very detailed profile in order to help the matchmakers' computer-based protocols work their magic. A second pairing method is applied by www.Chemistry.com and www.eHarmony.com, two of the top SINS sites utilizing matchmakers *and* proprietary algorithms to help you connect with potential partners and mates. These sites offer scientifically-based compatibility matching services that help their members find mates with whom they can relate on many levels and offer a guided communication and dating process. These services do the searching for you and present your ideal potential partners to you. You then take the wheel and follow up via emails, phone conversations and meetings with the individuals specifically matched with you. Such services are traditional matchmakers with a technological twist ... and are highly successful at what they do.

© Randy Glasbergen.
www.glasbergen.com

"I said I'm looking for a date who is soft, sweet and a little bit nutty. They matched me with a loaf of banana bread."

www.Match.com, one of the largest and most successful sites, along with a plethora of other sites, utilizes your registration answers and your activity patterns which, by the way, are very revealing and may even contradict your conscious profile preferences. (Mmmmm.) What you say you want in your wish list for an ideal partner can differ surprisingly from your reality. Through application of successful algorithms active members receive contact information notices for likely compatible matches almost daily. I particularly like their auxiliary search features, whereby you do your own searches, as well, and open additional options farther afield than you had previously considered ... or dreamed of. You can approach anyone your mind or heart desires on these sites. SINS is a whole new world waiting for you to discover and explore its interesting and diverse memberships. Step into SINS! Enjoy!

Some clever SINS sites are linked to social media sites such as www.AreYouInterested.com and www.Zoosk.com through www. Facebook.com. One unique site is www.HowAboutWe.com. It matches its members by creating pairings in somewhat close geographical areas who suggest or express an interest in you. You communicate with someone who likes the same activity ... you rendezvous for any number of fun dates.

Each SINS site tries to be unique. Innovative niche sites can work very well for you. Through their specialized approaches they can help you meet like-minded people with similar interests, values, lifestyles, religious beliefs, etc. You select the playing fields within SINS on which you want to play. You more or less sculpt your dating scene for the near future. Your participation on SINS sites is flexible, not carved in stone. You can join for just a month or try only free sites to start. My experience has been the free sites, while opening a portion of their world to you, are not free if you want to interact meaningfully with their members. You are able to look at profiles and receive approaches but not send or reply to messages. If you want to interact with their members you must upgrade for a relatively small fee of $5 to $20 per month to gain communication privileges. Joining *for free* can serve you well, though. You can derive first hand insight into the content and quality of the sites ... a sort of test drive.

If you choose to try multiple sites simultaneously, you may want to test one "general" top-ranked dating site with a monthly fee, along with a "free" pet-based site if that focus is important to you, as well as another "free" site, which might center about a hobby. Or, consider slowly joining (as in not all in the same day or even the same week) a small combination of sites that might be appropriate and *for free* in order to get your feet wet and give yourself some experience. Doing so would allow you to explore varying pathways at little cost and simultaneously play the different fields just as some of you once did socially in your own traditional communities. SINS *is* your new community ... and a wide open one it is.

Please, be aware that the free sites tend to be more heavily populated with unsavory characters. Always practice safe 'singling'. Follow the safety guidelines you will soon learn of; stay in control of your communications and interactions.

You can join any combination of focuses with any number of sites, free or not. You can skip periodically around different sites and return to your favorites, as well. Doing so insures you will be the new kid on the block ... more than once. Newbies attract more attention in SINS.

Remember to be considerate and engaged: interact! SINS sites require your time and attention if you take them seriously, as you should. Other members take their time to sincerely contact you hoping for a response, as will you. If you follow the Golden Rule and treat other members of these sites as you want to be treated, you should be kept busy and happy.

I have compiled a list of many niche sites for you in this chapter which present a good overview of SINS world. My run-down is by no means complete. A full list of sites would seem to stretch toward infinity on these pages. You may want to investigate further on your own. [34]

---

[34] Reminder: The dating websites I have chosen to mention or discuss throughout *Candyland S.I.N.S.* are for informational purposes only. Their mention is not a recommendation nor does it necessarily reflect my opinion or viewpoint. I receive no compensation for doing so. You should conduct your own investigation and self-verify the accuracy of my information before proceeding

To find your perfect SINS site or combination of sites is quite simple. If you want to explore beyond the lists on these pages, google/ search your interest, hobby, religion, sexual preference, etc. place whatever word best describes your chosen focus in your google/ search box and add "dating sites" to the word. Two examples are "golf dating sites" and "big and beautiful dating sites". Pages of dating sites targeted to *your interest keyword* will appear in most search results. With this site-gathering method you could collect almost more SINS sites related to your interests and desires than you could reasonably process.

If you can find the website for your 'keyword dating site review' on the initial keyword google/search result pages, go to it immediately. Or, you can fast-track finding a review site (one of strong importance to you) by googling/searching your keyword followed by "*dating site reviews*" to learn if any review sites for your focus are available. Example: "*pet lovers dating site reviews*". Assessment sites review, compare and often rank the top sites in that category. The reviews and comparisons make your mission to find the best sites for you more manageable. Someone has done your homework for you … whew!!! Now, carry out the same procedure with any other niche category in which you wish to find your future partner or spouse.

The prismatic aspect of SINS' different matchmaking techniques and focuses can offer the newcomer too broad of a spectrum. Begin your adventures guided by *your* interests, style and goals. *Common interests* is stated repeatedly as the most important factor for most members looking for a mate. If your dog is a very important part of your life, you may want to join a site for dog lovers. If your religion is an integral part of your life, you may want to check out a Singles site for your path of faith.

---

and/or joining various sights based on the information I have used. Individuals are unique; so are their experiences.

To find a religion-based site such as Jdate.com/ or BigChurch. com, google/search your religion's or denomination's keyword plus "dating sites" for a bounty of like-minded popular sites. For example, if you are seeking a Christian partner, google/search "Christian dating sites". You will receive so many results that you might not know which one to use as your springboard. As a prime exercise to help you learn the most popular Christian-based dating sites enter http://christian-dating-websites.no1reviews. com . The well-organized and information-packed reviews of Christian-based sites you will find there will be of great help if this is an area of interest for you. You can perform a similar search for Jewish, Muslim, etc. faiths. Review sites can be found for most major categories of interest ... making your work load much lighter and less stress-inducing. If your first results for a category do not satisfy you, just play around with the terminology to see what else might come up.

Now, carry out the initial procedure with other important criteria you wish as you begin your search for your future partner in SINS. Google/search your key word plus "dating sites". The range of the results that pop up will depend upon your keyword's popularity with searchers. From these dating sites, make your own list of sites that catch your interest and explore them online. After some perusing, join one. Make the leap. Once settled into it, you might decide to add another site or even more.

Let's begin my lists of various interest sites ... below is the lightest of lists drawn from the full range of faith-based sites available to you.

www.jdate.com/
www.ldssingles.com/
www.christiansciencesingles.com/
www.muslima.com/
www.atheistpassions.com/

www.singlebaptists.com/
www.Presbyteriansingles.net

The following is my list of some of the top general dating sites. They rule … along with a few others. Take a close look at them. They are at the top of my list of over fifteen hundred dating sites for a dual reason … a combination of their high membership numbers and their dating site reviews. Once again, I would recommend you start with only one site for a trial period. Most paid sites offer a single month. At the time of this writing, the cost can range from *free* to approximately $60 per month. Many are in the $20-$29 range. The heavily discounted 3-month and 6-month deals are quite tempting, as well. The savings can be substantial. Whatever the costs, they are small investments when you consider you are searching for an important partner for your life. The costs of the super-elite sites are another story.

On to the next list. Here are my topnotch general dating sites for Mature daters.

www.OKCupid.com/
www.PlentyofFish.com/
www.Match.com/
www.EHarmony.com/
www.Zoosk.com/
www.SeniorPeopleMeet.com/
www.Mate1.com/
www.Ourtime.com/
www.zoomersingles.com/

The latest flurry of activity and growth involves sites' expansions into dating applications on smartphones and tablets. These dating apps are very dynamic and offer a good deal of action via instant chatting. Some facilitate spur-of-the-moment dates near your location. The technology is available in the relevant app stores. Some vendors supply their app "for free". Seventy percent of usage on Plenty Of Fish takes place via a mobile phone[35], which most likely is not the case for the Mature membership. The POF app and other sites offer further similar functions. Many give you instant access to these great features:

- Send and receive messages *on-the-go* for free.
- Go online and use their apps to message people nearby.
- Upload images and edit your profile.
- Flirt with local members via a fun *let's get together* feature, similar to the Why Don't We.
- Invite a site-matched member to meet for a mutually appealing date.
- See who viewed your profile.
- Peruse your site's suggested matches. Even more features differentiate the sites.

I understand how very confusing it is for most newbies as they stand at the gates of Candyland poised to begin their search. Relax and remember you will register on a free site, or for a month's free or paid trial or at a discounted rate for just a few months. The latter is likely a small financial investment. Enter starry-eyed if that's your nature, but be realistic. Unless the stars align perfectly you are not likely to find the perfect match on your first attempt ... or your first few ... or in your first round of selections. Do not be anxious. You are on a journey, not a day trip. As you move along the paths in SINS you can explore more options as you feel necessary.

In review: you can begin by trying some of the free sites and/or join another for a month or more. The free sites, while they open their little corners of Candyland to you, generally will not allow you to

---

[35] POF Media, www.pof.com, Press Center, http://www.pof.com/en/press/, accessed June 30, 2014.

completely interact with their members if you want to do so. Your status is akin to *look but don't touch*. You are generally restricted as a free-entry member. The free sites offer what might be called *freemiums*. To enjoy communication privileges you must upgrade for a relatively small fee, $5 to $20 per month.

Again, use the "free" level to start; it is a very valuable way to test a site to see if it is a good fit for you. Doing so allows you to scope out the quality and depth of the site's membership and experiment with the bells and whistles before you invest in a full membership. Different sites offer varying combinations of features. Many provide instant messaging, audio capability and video profile creation. They also might include options for sex compatibility reports, personality tests, chemistry tests, and star sign harmony reports, etc.

As you begin your adventures, each time you settle in to a site selection session talk to yourself. Tell yourself that you'll have more fun if you relax as you compile your site choices because you know A) some sites will come to suit you better than others and B) you can easily change your sites at any time as you move into and explore the Candyland that is SINS.

In order to make your registrations easier and save you time, I recommend that you type a template for your mini-essay responses to such prompts as *About Me, About You* and *About Our Relationship*, as well as your answers to most of the more thought provoking registration questions. Save your writings on the computer in a document file or to a SINS-designated thumb drive for use on other sites. Once your responses are appropriately transferred to other locations, you can massage them to suit the focus of each site. You do not have to rewrite your profile each time you join a new site, as you will be asked to supply most of the same search criteria, history and wish list you addressed when you created your first profile.

Since you can revise your profile at any time you do not have to become anxious that you might forget something important to you. You can rework it as often as you like as you evolve. If you give thoughtful attention and spend quality time crafting your template you should enjoy plenty of mileage out of it.

"Surrounded by wingmen and I still have trouble meeting women!"

Now, do some homework. Depending on the amount of time you can devote to your early efforts, select one to three sites ... or more ... that you feel may give you a well-rounded variety of dating options. You likely want to consider sites whose central subjects encompass what is important to you. You might add a site that specializes in hobbies or sports activities.

Consider tennis:
www.tennispassions.com/
www.tennismadandlookingforlove.com/
dating.canada.tennismadandlookingforlove.com

Golf:
www.golfmates.com/
www.dateagolfer.com/
www.singlegolfersclub.com/

Sports fans:
www.sportspassions.com/
www.mvpdate.com/
www.greenbaypackerslovers.com/

"Foodies', dieters, good cooks, etc.:
www.sameplate.com/
www.cookanddate.com/
www.veganpassions.com/
www.veggiedate.org/

STD and/or HIV Positives:
www.hivdatingservice.com/
www.positivesingles.com/
www.thepositiveconnection.com/
www.herpesdatingsites.us/
www.std-dating-websites.no1reviews.com/

Career professionals:
www.professionalsinglesover40.com
www.elitesingleswithkids.com/

GLASBERGEN

"I'm dating a werewolf. I met him on Monster.com!"

Are your pets most important to you? Why not select a site with members who are like-minded people? You would eliminate wasting time searching for that someone who might be near perfect for you but who, due to allergies, phobias or preferences, will not or cannot tolerate animals in the home. You increase your chances of meeting someone compatible who enjoys the same interests and lifestyle as yours in interest-related sites, as well. Some of the top pet lover sites are:

www.DateMyPet.com
www.TheRightBreed.com
www.PetPeopleMeet.com
www.LoveMeLoveMyPets.com

Focus totally on fellow cat lovers:
www.catster.com
www.felidate.com/

Or, focus on dogs:
www.youmustlovedogsdating.com/
www.loveunleashed.co.uk/about/

Or, equestrian pursuits:
www.equestriancupid.com/
www.horseloversconnection.com/
www.horsepeopledating.com/

Still another niche option exists that borders on the unusual. You might investigate becoming a pen pal with a prison inmate! These members often enjoy a variety of interests and hobbies that could be shared. Although inmates cannot take you out on a date many … both male and female … enjoy having pen pals, on-site visits and conjugal interludes. In addition to a likely unusual social connection, you may be helping a fellow human being in more ways than one. A very strong caution, though: Always remember these are convicted felons, so practice safe involvement and do not share everything about yourself. What you share with your correspondent may have unintended consequences. Inmates certainly have interesting, often dramatic and often tragic personal histories. Many have life stories that most of us would find hard to imagine.

www.meet-an-inmate.com/
www.loveaprisoner.com/
www.inmate.com/
www.prisonpenpals.net/

Perhaps you are intrigued by age gap dating:
www.agematch.com/
www.agelesshookup.com/
www.agedating.net/
www.agemeet.com/
www.agelessdating.com/
www.cougarlife.com/

Or, BBW dating:
www.thebigandthebeautiful.com/
www.bbpeoplemeet.com/
www.largeandlovely.com/
www.bbwromance.com/

Or, disabled dating:
www.disabledpassions.com/
www.disabledsinglesdating.com/
www.dating4disabled.com/

Or, garden lovers dating:
www.greenfingerdating.com/
www.compostdating.com/

Or, particular height preference connecting:
www.tallscene.com/
http://www.tallfriends.com
www.shortpassions.com/
www.shortpeopleclub.com/

Or, adult pursuits:
www.adultfriendfinder.com
www.benaughty.com/
www.flirt.com/

Or, sexual preferences:
www.transdate.com/
www.lesbianpersonals.com/
www.gaydargirls.com/
www.gaygirlnet.com
www.zoosk.com
www.gaycupid.com/
www.gayxxxdates.com/

www.mennation.com/

For married cheaters:
www.AshleyMadison.com
www.heatedaffairs.com
www.datingforcheaters.com

To catch a cheater:
www.cheaterville.com
www.catchyourcheatingspouse.com

For sci fi fans:
www.trekpassions.com
www.soulgeek.com/

The list is about endless! Just type your preference keyword and add "dating sites" in your google/search browser. You likely will find whatever dating opportunities your heart desires.

And, of course, you will want to view the sites dedicated to Mature Singles of all varieties. That's where you and I and millions of others are cozily on the same pages.

Mature Singles looking for other Mature Singles:
www.SeniorMatch.com
www.50plus-club.ca/
www.olderdatingagency.com/
www.ourtime.com/
www.SeniorPeopleMeet.com
www.BabyBoomerPeopleMeet.com/
www.widowsdatingonline.com/ca
www.zoomersingles.com
http://dating.aarp.org

I find the sites dedicated to Mature Singles very productive for our age group because the younger crowd usually stays away from them. These Mature dating sites are generally for the over 40's. While the attention of young members on other sites is very flattering, unless you are looking for a May/December relationship these contacts are usually timewasters and can be frequent happy hunting grounds for Scammers. Some of you may want to access those sites listed above, which concentrate on this style of dating ... both male and female older partners in a dating relationship. Actually, such a relationship could easily begin on any one of the Mature dating sites because of the decades-wide range of Matures.

You will quite often find review sites on the search results pages for particular niches that compare and rate the different sites. These assessment sites are extremely helpful in narrowing your candidates for your home site(s). For example:

http://en.wikipedia.org/wiki/Comparison of online dating websites
http://www.datingsitesreviews.com/

Interestingly, some 'traditional' dating sites have spawned offshoots such as TheJMom.com for parents of unsuccessful Jewish members of the usual sites. These clever and well-meaning Jewish mothers attempt to help the perhaps constrictive or unrealistic expectations of their offspring. These moms attempt to find partners whom they see as the most appropriate for their children. Who is likely to know an individual better than his or her *own mother*? Now, this is frighteningly true! Wow!! How history repeats itself!!! Marriages arranged by parents looking for eligible Singles to become possible suitable partners for their children. Many of us outside of certain traditions looked askance at the mention of such a cultural practice for a number of reasons. Yet, here we are in the 21st century resurrecting and updating this millennia-old concept on the Internet! (Hmmm ... there just may be a Broadway show in this development.) Our world can be a surprising and funny place.

**"I registered my dad with an online dating service.
They matched him with a recliner and TV."**

Let's take that concept one step further and imagine a site where children attempt to find someone for their single reticent or socially inept parents (at least perceived as such) entering the dating scene after decades of some version of marital bliss. Don't sigh. Our offspring's participation could be a blessing ... they quite often can maneuver all the latest technology much better than most of us. I have known many Mature daters whose children encouraged them to join the online dating world of SINS. They also helped their parents with the technical side. And, they actually know us very well if not better than anyone in our lives. They have spent most of their lives sharing celebrations and sorrows with us ... seeing us at our best and at our worst. They know our strengths and weaknesses, and our attributes and faults. And, most important of all ... most of our children want the very best for us. In general, we could not find better people to vet potential partners for us (except our previous partners ... perhaps).

Previous partners certainly know your standard operating procedures, too. The vast majority, however, may not feel that generosity of spirit you might require in order to make a great catch. They may possibly not want the new relationship to outshine what you had shared. I have long harbored a secret wish to be allowed to interview the previous partner of a potential love interest.

Yes, I do believe your children are a good bet to help you. By the time this guide is published, one or more such sites may appear that encourage you to involve your children in your search. You can make them part of the process of finding a partner for you ... a task that can be especially daunting when alone maybe too long and still vulnerable after a death, divorce or *suddenly single* event.

I can foresee sites emerging that allow you to give your friends and your immediate communities permission to join the hunt for the perfect partner for you ... good grief, what a relief!! You would no longer be alone out there in cyberspace looking for your first, second or last significant other. You would be the center of a niche community with your best interests at heart ... you would hope! You will have adapted your communities to the new world of technology in what could be the most intimate and important choice of your final years. My, oh, my. What next?

In early 2014, Match.com presented a wonderful survey of 5,300 singles. It is very comprehensive, covering many aspects of Singles dating. The good news in it is 'respect' is key for both genders and 'marriage' is in. And, 89 percent believe in living happily ever after. Gay/Lesbian marriages are cool ... as is having children out of wedlock ... but sexually open marriages are not. Go to www. SinglesinAmerica.com[36] to get the full scoop on this very interesting and revealing survey from Match.com.

---

[36] Match.com, http://www.SinglesinAmerica.com, accessed August 6, 2014.

By now, you understand that you will have to decide which sites initially suit you. Keep a list of the remaining possibilities, and perhaps switch after a trial period to sample a variety of sites in succession. I have set out for you an overview of some of the available sites for you to wade into, their focuses, their costs and how to choose a combination that might suit you. I now let go of your hand. I release you at the door of the candy store ... to survey, to choose and sample your favorite treats. Enjoy!

STUDIES and STATISTICS

Additional materials for Chapter 6 – Picking Your Sites

Item 1. More stats related to the Match.com figures:

The second most frequent scenario for meeting someone is through a friend (22 percent). Other ways to meet someone interesting have decreased over the last 3 years. For example, the rate for meeting at bars or clubs was 13 percent (2010), 8 percent (2011), and 7 percent (2012). 1 in 5 relationships begin online, and 1 in 6 new marriages are a result of a connection made on an online dating site.

Source reference first appeared on www.Match.com, http://match.mediaroom.com/index.php?s=30440, Match Fact Sheet 2014, accessed June 30, 2014.

Chapter Seven

How to Write a Profile...

You will be contacted or passed-over by SINS members
based on the strength of your profile.
The best advice I can give you is: *honesty is the best policy.*

The majority of the profiles remind me of ducklings paddling
along in a perfect line, so adorable but no noticeable individuality.
On closer look though, some do stand out from the rest. To earn
a closer look, you must present an outstanding primary photo
with a catchy Username and an interesting Headline to create a
memorable profile ... along with a story that SINS members will
find interesting, possibly even intriguing, like a good book they
don't want to put down. Write a story with descriptive words and
scenarios that serve as witness to your character, values and good
traits. Present a page of eye-catching photos that you incorporate
into your profile. Try to make yours a bit unique and memorable ... a
profile other Candyland travelers will want to follow up on. Examine
a few profiles already on a selected site. Pick up a technique or two.

Google/search 'how to take flattering photos of yourself' ... very helpful. Do not freeze! Begin!! Create a first-effort profile page to get yourself started. You do not have to activate it for public viewing until you are somewhat satisfied with it. What you will have is something of your own to evaluate against others on the site. Check out other profiles in your gender if the site allows, depending on your membership level, to see what the more appealing profiles offer. Grow with your adventure ... return occasionally to your profile ... allow you and your profile to evolve as you continue your journey through SINS. You are a work in progress ... your profile and your photos will reflect the same.

You want to show who you are. To formulate your profile, ask yourself interesting questions and answer them in ways that bring out your uniqueness. Avoid too much of the cookie cutter lists of what you are looking for; let viewers imagine what you would bring to the relationship and also what you are looking for in a potential mate. You want them to daydream, to imagine if or how they could comfortably fit into your story and vice versa.

Let's start with Usernames ... these are the online names you create and display at the top of your profiles. Your real name never appears on your profiles. You are anonymous. Usernames are important and should have some relevance to who you are.

Sometimes Usernames can be a dead giveaway for what to expect if you bought into the self-designations. Be prepared for these, everyone. The following are variations of some of the actual names under which I have received contact approaches. Dictator30a... hmmm, he would be a challenge. HotBunnyHopper270v... sorry, I'll pass. I'm not good at standing in line!

Many profiles are not opened a great number of times just because the Usernames turn off their viewers immediately. Some are actually offensive, as you will see below. Usernames should be descriptive of you or of your life in some way, perhaps tied to how you look at life. Have fun, be whimsical in creating your moniker ... one that should not be even close to the names you will soon see that I want you to read and forget. Some are actually insulting to the intelligence and sensibilities of those who read them. Others may draw a *what?!* or a humorous gasp. I cannot believe that the proud owners of these names could seriously think a self-respecting person would want to read further about who they are, never mind go out with them. If the Username owners were just joking and having their own sort of warped fun they are guilty of unfortunate taste and more ... as they offer a hint of what is to come.

The following are on my Username Wall of Shame. (They are not the actual Usernames but variations of ones that have visited my site profiles.) You *will* get their gist. I have cringed and/or laughed when they appeared. How can any adult, never mind an adult seeking to attract a potential mate, think someone would sincerely respond to winks, flirts, favorites, emails, etc.? associated with names such as these! But then, sincerity is likely not what such jokers are looking for.

Joan's Username Wall of Shame --Too Crazy To Be True, but they are, with slight variations...

Dictator30a Animal 402c FunSlickStick750z HotBunnyHopper270v SuckSonnie23s JuicyFun67n MrTasty89b Quickdraw94k GoldanRod23m Hammer69Wild753h Viagra44d TrickyDicky46x WillyMaker84c NiceSexyOldMan888c VictoriousNeedy003n Boink435b Peckerhead870s Potentate795v HotLegend704b Sniffer759v Guppy847x ShyBadLegs943z FastFreddie796c CharlieHorse8879w NoFriends4433m FruitofGod3376l RickyRatster7694f

DryStoneWall256v Buzzard7864m SmoothMuffins598z
Beast1987r ToBe6Xs
Hot69Mustang96v TummyRoofer6598h WidRetiredMan3267m
PropaneHank7390x
LoserYetAgain20 TooLonely286 WhatWentWrong8693
Spottedlung2869x WellHung24v
Loupy694z NeedYurMercy9621x QTip2709k UglynShy1686d
TenderCueBall962m
BigFunFoot851f GrandOpaqueGronk2665s ManGroomer5533y
DoughyDonut7775b
LastOnePlease8856m MagicWandGenie2245p Upgrades763v
FallingoffaCliff872p LeadFoot6336h
WildBronco8899a SoftHands3821x PurityofHeart2887x
Dany69 GoodBoy79v
Alkalizedsam3355q LouistheBookie9987z Exhausted7734 v
Leaky0105k HopeAndPray98
Forgiven1951 Pickled 298 TeddieBares372 TrapperMel376
HungryNWild764 Picky649
Enough said.

On your profile, your Username is followed by a Headline. It is similar to the headlines you see at the top of magazine and newspaper articles. They grab your attention and tell you succinctly what lies within the article ... just as your Headline tells someone what lies within you in just a very few words. When SINS members do a search and stop at your outstanding photo, they see your intriguing (in a good way) Username and your absolutely right-on Headline. Your Photo, your Username and your Headline are important, in that order. Make your Headline a teaser, a hint of what lies within your profile, an inkling of what you have to offer. It is your opportunity to stand out from the many common or boring profiles. One example is 'OntheGo365' (Username)...and 'let's go together' (related Headline). Together they give the viewer a picture of a very active you who wants someone to join you.

The good profiles, while stating what the member is searching for, put more emphasize on what he or she is bringing to the table. When SINS members search they are looking to spot someone who fits their criteria. So, show a good dose of openness. Openness is appealing. Lack of effort generally translates into lack of success in finding a partner who might become your loving, companionable mate. Must you attempt all of the above by yourself? Not at all. Many sites offer a service for a fee, under $50, to write a profile for you with the information you provide.

You are hand-fed the registration, and can always change any mistakes as you fill it out as well as anytime after you join. The process is a very forgiving one. Just follow the directions. This prelude to the search is a great opportunity for you to seriously consider who you are and what you are looking for. You have probably never had to encapsulate and express such self-awareness in so few short pages. Even so, try to have fun presenting yourself. Be prepared to spend a bit of time at it; do not leave many blanks in your profile information. If possible do not leave any item blank. A no-input item generally illustrates a lack of effort or interest in doing what is required to give your SINS viewers a full picture of yourself and your life. A blank item can imply you are a poor communicator. Too, an incomplete profile demonstrates lack of recognition of the process necessary for a SINS viewer to decide who s/he wants to take the time and effort to pursue. An incomplete presentation can easily translate into an unsuccessful and short journey through and out of Candyland.

The Personal Details portion is easy to fill in … and important. Most likely, you will navigate and successfully complete it yourself. As you do, make every effort to *not* misrepresent yourself. Doing so is a poor start to any potential relationship. Don't agonize over the questions … just answer them as honestly as possible. You can make any changes necessary due to oversights or lack of finding just the right wording at any time later. Your profile is alive and evolving, as are you.

Whether you create your profile alone or have someone (a friend or an employee of a for-a-fee site) help you with all or parts of it, a good profile is crucial to attract the person right for you. What you write may create interesting dating options you never would have considered for yourself even if you knew they existed. What you write gives the *matchmakers* on the SINS pairing sites data for the pairing possibilities they frequently will send you. What you write will help the sites' programs select the best available possible candidates for you. Supply the sites with more than minimum information ... truthful and authentic information. Your details, major and minor, attract certain potential partners who are on their own searches ... so be honest.

Someone who stresses he likes to hunt and fish to appear 'manly' will most likely not attract a woman who is into theater and opera ... her greatest passions. You must be realistic; what you say about your interests will attract like-mindeds. Each other's *interests* and *likes/dislikes* are very important and part of the vetting process. Commonality is not all about appearance and chemistry, although certainly do not underestimate their importance.

On the same tack, do not pursue someone whose interests are quite divergent from yours. Yes, a bit of variety does add some spice to a relationship. But, if she likes going on cruises and ballroom dancing and you like snowshoeing and kayaking, beauty and handsomeness will not be enough. Such a pair is unlikely to be a match ... for long. Be honest for yourself and others when writing your profile and when reading others' profiles. Your incompatibility will eventually surface and, perhaps, so far along in the relationship that one of you will be bruised if not deeply hurt.

Your essay-type questions are a good forum to express your uniqueness. What makes you different from all the other ducks in the lineup? Expect your free form essays (*About Me, About the One I Am Looking For, About Our Relationship*) to morph as your new experiences in SINS change some of your thoughts on dating, relationships and what you want to do with the rest of your life. My essays did. Likely you, too, you will find yourself becoming a better expresser than *the you* of pre-SINS.

Oh yes, the last line of your personal story should be something to pique interest, a zinger to reel them in ... or at least get them to bite the hook, to want to *favorite* you, and to return to your page for a second look. I also think it a good idea to ask your viewers to contact you if they agree with your thoughts or find your profile of interest. Prompt them to respond. Ask for their order!

Nothing you write is carved in stone, so complete your registration form with a relaxed attitude. Those who leave a number of blank spots do receive very little attention. I never read the rest of a profile of any men who respond with just a *tell you later* on the important questions. I don't care how attractive they seem in their photos. If they are not interested enough or are so guarded that they cannot tell their viewers what they are about, then why should SINS members take the time to pry it out of them? Just how self-enclosed and secretive would such a person be in a relationship? So many other members offer open, interesting profiles, the kind that are keen and respectful of their viewers, the kind presented by someone most members want to enthusiastically contact.

"If I want to impress a woman online, what font should I use? Aristocrat Bold so she'll think I'm rich or Comic Sans so she'll think I'm funny."

I hope you know how to spell or use the 'spell check' feature on your computer. Spelling errors and poor grammar make a very bad impression. Please check your profile for them very thoroughly. Have someone check it for you, as well ... you do not want to appear too lazy to present the best version of *you*. Even though few people know all the writing rules, punctuation is important; a comma in the wrong place can tell a totally different story. Please pay attention to them. An excellent example is:

> *A woman, without her man, is nothing.*
> *A woman: without her, man is nothing.*[37]

Be sure to be positive. One way to do that is to avoid negative words such as, *no, never,* and *not.* Such words send out a resistant, possibly judgmental vibe and might create an undertone in a viewers' mind that will subconsciously be applied to you. With a little inventiveness, most ideas can be phrased positively. Sentences such as "I am not into mind games." and "I don't want any drama." seem

---

[37] Lynne Truss, Eats Shoots & Leaves (New York, New York: Gotham Books), 2004. P.9.

to set up a viewer for rejection at the first difference of opinions. I never read beyond those statements ... and I have seen them many times. I feel they come from individuals who probably have been part of or, perhaps, damaged by such scenarios; perhaps they see mind games where they do not even exist. And probably, such people have been involved in earlier immersions of high drama due to what they or their other(s) brought out of previous relationships into new ones. The residue will most likely be brought into yours. Resistant statements are a no-brainer start on the wrong foot because they set up early barriers to the positive expectations we all take for granted. They create a readiness on the part of the writer to spring into action at any misstep on your part. Whoa, someone way too negative to think about as a possible mate.

Many new members try to be glib about why they are on the site ... they are "just taking a look around" or "they never thought they would be trying such a mode of dating". Don't unintentionally insult the people you are trying to attract. Such dismissive comments can be interpreted as negative and can be real turnoffs to some cool people you may want to meet. Be careful how you state why you are presenting yourself on SINS and what you are trying to accomplish ... which, if you are honest with yourself, is probably the same as most of the others on the sites. Do not portray yourself as superior or inferior to other members.

And PLEASE be truthful about your age, height, body type, education, and career! Ongoing communication with your contacts will uncover the truth eventually. Little lies in the beginning will destroy the trust they very much wanted to place in you when they approached you. Height and weight are pretty obvious when you meet; your approximate age will soon be more or less evident. Now, it *is* true that you will not look your age if you have had some *work* done. More sooner than later you are likely to trip yourself up talking about a singer popular when you were in high school or a movie you saw as a kid, the favorite car you owned, etc. The belier usually stumbles on the first date. Deception is definitely a bad start, and the moment of truth is at the least ... awkward. Heed my warning about lying on your profiles. Doing so could damage your prospects more than help them.

Both men and women, it seems, fib about different things because of the social understanding of what the opposite sex typically finds attractive in a potential mate. But you don't want to wave any RED FLAGS by fudging on your profile, either.

Although giving an age on a dating site seems a necessary evil, doing so is nevertheless generally mandatory. It is one of the main filters everyone has in mind when looking for a potential companion or life-mate. And, it is a critical filter by which we are either accepted or rejected. The age issue is especially difficult for women, because society is not as kind to women with regard to age as it is to men. So, the dilemma exists ... one by which we are judged ... whether we tell our real age and receive fewer views or lie about it and face the embarrassment of being found out when the time arrives to come clean. It's a tough one to win. So, be careful here.

To fib or not to fib about your age is a bit of a conundrum. You want to be appreciated for who and what you are ... not for your chronological clock. And, in fact, many of you can appear 15 years off the mark in calendar years ... in both directions!!! I have seen many who look and act 15 years younger, as well as those who project an image of 15 years older than their actual age. You will see profiles of two members who state the same age but one appears to be the parent of the other.

My philosophy on aging is that we should regard our age not by the number of birthdays we have had but by our life experiences and our growth from those experiences ... and, of course, our health. Our maturity attained through all those years of joys and sorrows should be worn as a cloak of honor in glorious living color, its fabric interwoven with all those who entered our lives. The strongest threads being our family and longtime friends; the frayed areas revealing perhaps too much wear and conflict that could not be borne, presented to us by those who entered and faded from our lives. Portions of the pattern in vibrant color represent the highlights of our lives that have given us great joy and pleasure. The more somber colored areas are life's inevitable lows interspersed throughout the pattern to make the highlights even more brilliant and precious, some remembered in their jeweled tones.

"Tell her you like long walks in the country and snuggling on the sofa, but don't mention anything about drinking from the toilet."

Some SINS members lie about their age for a variety of credible reasons. One reason relates to the age parameters entered into members' searches. If you are just outside the commonly used search parameters, like '40 to 50', '50 to 60' or '55 to 65', you can miss a good number of potential partners.

For a very short period, I actually gave a younger age in the personal information point form profile. It was an experiment. Though, I must admit, I did feel guilty about lowering my age to under 65 (I was 66) to accommodate more initial views of my profile and for the search engines. I found the answer to my dilemma thanks to another SINS member who helpfully pointed out the contradiction. Well, more accurately, reprimanded me. If people are going to fib on the age item in the personal information section to accommodate common search parameters, then they should have the decency to give their correct ages within the text of their profiles. He gave me a good solution I could live with that was fair to my profile viewers. His solution offers a hidden benefit: if someone has not bothered to read my self-description before asking for a first date, he might just have to face the consequences of not having done *his* homework when we meet. He would be pursuing me based on my pictures alone ... a big *No-No.* At times, I was pleasantly surprised at how many caught the discrepancy. They actually read my profile! I now am true to my age on all sections of my profiles.

By the way, I do look like my pictures, a match that helps ease any of my anxiety about the reality of my age. It makes the start of those *first dates* more relaxed. No lies to cover up. Make sure you look pretty much the same as you do in your photos, especially if you are going to fiddle with your age. Be as authentic as possible. You want someone to fall for the *real you* and not a figment of your imagination that you could never live up to long term.

As I did change my profile to reflect my real age, sadly but truly, I found doing so does affect the number of hits I receive. I am simply not in most members' search criteria range, the preferred age for the women they are seeking. The reality is that being in the latter years does limit the number of prospects you have ... both by SINS members' search parameters and their innermost wishes about the age of their ideal partner.

As more Matures join SINS, the field of daters will become denser. Perhaps lying about age will be less of an issue, as you will be part of the ever-growing dating pool for your true age range. More men will join who want to go out with 60+ year old women; more women will want to go out with 60+ year old men. If the gender numbers more or less balance each other, giving a truthful age will not be a set back.

All this having been said about the importance of your written profile, at times I wonder if some members even bother to read the text before they contact me when I see absolutely no areas of compatibility in our profiles. What were they thinking ... or not reading? Many SINS members respond to the visual appeal of pictures as they cast a large net. A big time-waster for everyone including you. Be realistic in your pursuits.

I see it as a good sign if someone cares about the details in my profile of who I am and how I live before he meets me ... and utilizes those details to imagine how he would fit into my life and I into his. You will find that you become a bit of a psychologist as you consider what motivates some of the SINS members with whom you interact and how they think their profiles mesh with your wish list for your desired future partner. You truly are entering a very exhilarating period as you extend yourself to find a new partner. The search is even more interesting now than in your youth because the *present* you is equipped with more life experiences and an accumulated wisdom that was not in play in those early days. Surprisingly, because of those experiences you have unknowingly fine-tuned some of your mating skills far beyond those you possessed in your 20's and 30's, even without dating all those years.

"Most of all, I like a man who can make me laugh."

The *About Me, About the One I Am Looking For,* and *About Our Relationship* sections are very important elements of your profile. Do not rush through them. Take your time and give a fair amount of thought to what you write. Revisit and rework; but don't agonize. These sections are your self-introduction to a potential mate, your *elevator pitch* so to speak. Put your best foot forward. In X number of words, you have to sell yourself ... that is why you are in SINS, are you not? You want to find that elusive special person and help your ideal one find you; so, put your utmost effort into writing these sections. Their contents and how they are received and perceived could change your life.

The focus of the first section *About Me* is the most challenging for people who are extremely uncomfortable talking about themselves. You can present yourself through any lens you want, in whatever manner you want to be perceived. Just do it well ... and ... make it realistic and truthful. Honest creative writing would be helpful here. It can make or break an average profile. Have a friend review it and perhaps give you a little constructive criticism.

Although it is certainly acceptable to be playful and flirtatious, no sexual innuendos in your writing, please. You could turn away the person you are searching for. Sexual conversation is not for the forums in traditional SINS sites. (The adult casual sex sites are for such pursuits.) Keep your descriptions classy, interesting, somewhat clever if possible ... *and* true. You will never regret doing so.

I highly recommend an excellent article: *How to Create the Perfect Online Dating Profile*, by Caitlin Roper in Wired.com.[38] The item gives incredibly detailed statistics based on the data crunchers from Match.com, OKCupid.com, etc.; stats of what SINS members are looking for when searching profiles to identify candidates. I have already covered the most important aspects of writing a profile. Caitlin Roper's article, with well-documented data research, will give you more very interesting specifics. They are thorough but far too detailed for me to cover here. Her data will give you a good idea as to what SINS members are looking at and looking for when they read your profile ... for both sexes. These items do differ! I strongly nudge you to google/search or click on this link for her very helpful article, http://www.wired.com/2014/02/how-to-create-good-online-dating-profile/#slide-id-410231

Many sites offer to write a profile for you (fee: under $50) that will present you in the best possible light using the information you provide them. That process will still take a bit of your time, though. You can also google/search for a *do-it-yourself profile*. You will find plenty of helpful websites whether for a *do-it-yourself* profile or for a *for-a-fee* website.

You may want to look over the many Internet dating concierge services available to you online. If you are a busy person and want to use your time productively to cut to the chase, consider their

---

[38] Caitlin Roper, 02.03.14, http://www.wired.com/2014/02/how-to-create-good-online-dating-profile/#slide-id-410231, accessed June 30, 2014.

services. These valuable timesavers provide written profiles, create your sites, scour profiles using the information you provided, filter and manage your communications and generally perform all tasks related to finding you interesting dates and potential partners. They even offer to arrange the dates, advise what to wear and where to meet. Their fees range from a one-time $49 to massage your already-written profile to $1,200+ per month to totally manage your online dating life. A few of them are listed below:

www.e-cyrano.com
www.lookbetteronline.com
www.virtualdatingassistants.com
www.profilewingman.com

First, try to write your own. Most of you will be fine; others might arrange to have someone who knows them check over what's been written. The whole process is also a good learning experience ... you are doing a little soul-searching as to who you are and what qualities you hope for in the person with whom you potentially want to partner.

As to the photos in your profile ... don't miss what is important about them and in them. They are the most critical element of your site for what they say and don't say. Mike Safka, the former CEO of Match.com, has stated that people who upload a photo receive 15 times more responses than those who do not. Most SINS members then read the profiles in great detail. The entire following chapter is devoted to photos because of their importance.

Chapter Eight

Photos

A picture is worth a thousand words
could not be truer than in online dating

Do not underestimate the importance of your photos! The majority of SINS members do not go beyond browsing over the numerous primary photos in their searches. They stop and read the written profiles of those members who catch their eye. Sorry, but the pool is so large ... there are so many of us! The good news is that you have the same privilege. And, you have the same option to browse their profiles *and* to make the first overture, as well. So, be assertive. Don't just wait to be chosen. It all starts with the pictures. Both males and females are encouraged to make the first move. No gender protocol here.

As the title of this book asserts: the SINS world is a version of Candyland ... offering all sorts of delicious treats. Eye-appeal in your profile photos is critical in order to tempt fellow searchers to stop at your pages to explore your profile further, to learn what you are about. If your photos are below the standard, your stop-and-read success rate will be low. Your primary photo is the first step to attract your prospective mate. Outstanding photos catch SINS members' eyes. If your photos are poor, you do not move beyond *Start*.

SINS members are looking for chemistry ... would your photo have them wondering what a kiss would be like? You may have a split second to tempt someone to pause on your profile. Read the following twice and say it out loud: *My primary photo is the single most important element of my profile!* That photo is your signboard on the Candyland highway. Your photo gallery can make or break your success in SINS. You absolutely must put time, thought and effort into your profile and your pictures ... and into your best appearance as well.

"I have a photographic memory, but I don't know how to transfer the pictures to my computer."

In a study by researcher Dr. C. Toma, photographs were identified as the single most deceptive element of the person's profile.[39] You want yours to be as authentic as possible, *but* you want it

[39] Kristi Dosh, www.womansday.com, http://www.womansday.com/sex-relationships/dating-marriage/online-dating-profile-lies, accessed June 30,

to highlight your best features and minimize your flaws. Do not conceal something that you know will be obvious when you meet on a first date. Don't waste your time or that of others. Doing so is both deceptive and very inconsiderate.

If you feel you are unattractive in some way, emphasize a positive element of your appearance. Present appealing aspects of your personality, your sports or other activities through your pictures. Let others see you in an interesting work environment or subtly allow them a glimpse of your lifestyle. Most of us cannot be of movie star quality and live a life of luxury. Yet, each of us has some combination of redeeming qualities other than just exceptional looks. Highlight yours. You will need to view potential mates' photos with that last statement in mind, as well, when you do your searches.

You should have current photos, taken within a year if possible, to show you as you now look ... and to reveal snippets of your life. Let these photos tell your story: what you love to do, where you love to go, etc. Let them demonstrate you *participating in life* ... your sports and other physical activities, with your pet, capturing your spirit and energy. You want your viewers to know you are interesting and interested in a life you enjoy. You should appear vibrant in your pictures and exude an energy and positive attitude about you. Could a potential match imagine being in one of your pictures? In a picture s/he is tempted to become part of?

EHarmony statistics presented in 2013 show members who offer photos are *nine times more likely* be sent communications than those without. Those who uploaded 4 or more photos received the most contacts from their matches. Women tend to post more pictures than men, averaging 6.4 photos for women vs. 4.2 photos

2014, citing University of Wisconsin-Madison and Cornell University researcher, Dr. CatalinaToma in a study commissioned by www.BeautifulPeople.com.

for men.[40] Some sites allow as many as 25 photo uploads. Have a tech savvy friend or grandchild help you if you don't have the skills to maneuver uploading them.

DO NOT BE LAZY ABOUT THIS! Photos will make the whole difference. They are absolutely necessary if you expect to maximize your chances for success in Candyland.

Perhaps too many photos may make you look a bit desperate to sell yourself ... or too pleased with yourself? Either can be unappealing. Hmmm ... I have 25 photos and their number has negatively affected neither my views nor my contacts. But, I have been in Candyland awhile. Because *you* are about to enter, I recommend you consider placing 6 to 10 photos on your profile and save the other great shots for later. Perhaps send them to your *interesting* first or second dates. A private viewing will be flattering, make them feel special. You can enlarge your photo gallery later on.

Men initiate communication 67 percent of the time.[41] But don't feel shy, gals. Men expect you to make contact in SINS if you are pleased with their profiles; they are usually quite complimented. Men are very comfortable with your contacts and are flattered by them. I have communicated with a number who are very proud of how often the first contact is made by a women; a reverse not common in the younger years of our generation but now very normal and increasingly acceptable.

An attractive upper-body shot that clearly shows your features is very important as your primary photo at the top of your page. This is the photo that will appear in a set of on-site search results. A full body shot or two among the supporting photos in your gallery

---

[40] John Cacioppo, the University of Chicago, Department of Psychology led the survey sponsored by eHarmony, 2013, accessed July 1, 2014.

[41] Ibid.

are always of interest. SINS members do want to see the overall you ... just as they could if they first met you in real life and not on a computer. One lone picture does not tell them enough about your appearance ... and you.

Your gallery of pictures should ideally contain landscape and portrait sizes; both receive the most interest, according to eHarmony's matching team. A medium-distance shot in your photo gallery is the best choice and offers the most action. A very wide, far away shot in which you are just an accessory is unpopular, as are those with you just one of a bunch of friends, and the very narrow portrait ... especially when that appears chopped because you have cut out a person, yet an arm or hand is visibly on you. Viewers naturally assume the severed anatomy belongs to an ex of some sort. They may subconsciously envision the missing person as still in your life. Not a good start!

Be sure to upload crisp shots. Ones that are blurry, too shadowed or too far away project a lack of motivation on your part. Shouldn't you want to make the best presentation possible? One that shows you are earnest, that you put time and energy into presenting yourself? Your photos relate a good deal about your personality; how much attention you pay to your photo details shows some of your character traits.

How to pose? Some studies imply that photos featuring the left side of the face are perceived by others as more attractive when compared with pictures featuring the right side of the face because people present more emotion on the left side of the face. Isn't that interesting? As with many things in life, there are exceptions, though ... as I was told by my sometimes photographer/SINS *special guy* ... the right side of my face is far more photogenic.

Another option for a gallery photo is the almost three-quarter angle portrait shot. The viewer sees you from an uncommon angle ... in not quite a semi-profile. This shot does not tell the whole story of your face, but can be quite flattering because it projects a sense of quiet reflection on your part. The angle also works well for a humorous or flirtatious shot when you are posing for fun. It is a unique addition to any sort of a photos panel.

As to whether or not to smile ... a smile is mandatory if you wish to win one in return when a SINS member views your picture. Just making the effort to exhibit these positive outward signs should make you actually aware of how good it feels to do so ... that you should be doing more of it. I personally feel you can never go wrong with a sincere smile. People always tend to smile in return, even emotionally, when reading a profile paired with a photo of its smiling author. Other members likely start reading your profile in a positive frame of mind.

Hint: One technique to smile in a genuine, non-forced way is to stand straight, take a deep breath with your mouth slightly open and then release that breath just before the click. Not only does the mouth generally make an automatic, relaxed mini-smile but the eyebrows go up just a notch ... which makes the eyes open wider just a bit, enough to make you seem more bright-eyed and engaged in life. Some photos can be so stilted. You want to project an easy affability.

And, make eye contact with the camera. Viewers want to look into your eyes. Let them sparkle along with your smile. A smile is a good motivator for both your viewer ... and you. ;-D A good initial contact, in my mind.

Interestingly, a study by Tracy & Beall in 2011 looked at the gender differences in ratings of attractiveness of different emotion expressions. The two determined men and women differed in what they found most attractive. Women were most attracted to men displaying pride and least attracted to those displaying happiness. Men were found to be most attracted to women displaying happiness and least attracted to women displaying pride. What's going on here? A woman's smile is often associated with low dominance on her part and agreeable femininity ... both indicating receptivity.[42] Hmmm ... a smile could be deceiving! The study also found men displaying pride appear more masculine to women. To emote pride tilt your head up, expand your chest, and raise your arms up over your head in tight fists.

Never post a sexually suggestive photo unless you are on one of the sites that promote sexual encounters. Inappropriate pictures always come back to haunt you ... many times as an embarrassment for you and your family. Please, do not take pictures in your bedroom. It is a personal part of your home few people enter in your daily life ... so why show this private space in a photo? Individuals who are confident and respectful in their sexuality do not have to advertise it. A future mate is looking at your overall personal profile ... an attractive entire package. If you reel in a SINS member because of your openly sexual beckoning, you may regret it down the line,

---

[42] Jessica Tracy & Alec Beall, May 26, 2011,University of British Columbia, Department of Psychology, http://www.sciencedaily.com/releases/2011/05/110524070310.htm, accessed June 30, 2014.

as that initial sexually-focused base for a relationship often fails to stand the test of time. Those members frequently move on to other prospects who have the same *come hither* look drawing them in ... at least for the short term. Attractive pictures of yourself are definitely important, but not suggestive ones, please.

Do not wear provocative clothing ... whether you are male or female. It can be a real turn-off for some SINS traditional site members. Most members are looking for a future partner, not a roll in the hay. You will send the wrong message if you are looking for a serious relationship. You will attract mainly those members who are just seeking a quick fling. Designated adult sites may suit you better if that is the direction you want to pursue.

What you wear in your photos should reflect your taste in clothing, your activities, perhaps your station in life, your work, etc., and show you to your best advantage. Again, be true to yourself. No surprises by you for the person you meet on your first date. You do not want to give a false impression to someone who is thinking you just might be a compatible future partner. Don't risk losing that person's trust at the very first moment of meeting ... a negative first impression can create a big uphill to overcome.

As you are no longer in the young prime of your life, a time you remember appearing beautiful or handsome, nicely appealing and charming in nearly every picture, quite a few shots ... dozens of shots even ... may be necessary to achieve a couple of excellent ones. The top models need to do it ... why can't you also enjoy the luxury of selecting perfect poses? Relax ... turn your present-day photo taking into a fun photo shoot ... take way too many shots, change your poses ... indoors and outdoors ... revel in the whole experience. Use the self-timer on your camera if you are shooting solo or ask a friend to help. You must shoot some close-ups for your primary picture ... SINS members very much want to see your facial features.

Even though the primary picture is the decision maker for someone to read a profile or not, it does not garner as much interest as full body shots in your photo gallery. These shots are sometimes tough for Matures to do, as they know they are not like the younger versions of themselves. A lump here ... a bump there. Placing photos of *the real you* as you *now appear* is necessary, though. No deceptive Photoshopping! Please. You will be fooling only yourself in the long run ... wasting your time and that of other SINS members.

You don't want to give your first date any surprises. It is best to be truthful in your photos if you are a bit overweight or show something you think might make another uncomfortable when you meet. A great guy wrote a wonderful profile of himself and sent me a beautiful email; he made a point to show his humpback in two of his photos. I admired him so much for his forthrightness and for his writing, I wrote him and enjoyably exchanged a couple of emails. The contact did not lead to anything in the long run. All emails do not lead to dates. Emailing is step two to come to know one another.

An aside here. Always remember the search process is an exercise in elimination ... similar to taking a series of job interviews. Doesn't sound glamorous, does it? Discovering a new mate can be, and most likely will be, very romantic. So, the underlying process is to find just one partner. Yes, along the way, some of us experience feelings of rejection when another continues the search ... leaving us behind ... or a touch of sadness when we reject someone as well. Always try to be kind. Remember, you appreciate courtesy and kindness, as well. I have been on both ends of the process ... which can be a hurtful one if not managed well by one side or the other. Cutting someone loose seldom feels good ...for either.

Back to your photos. Who is or isn't quite in each photo with you? Again: Please avoid any bits and pieces of an ex ... really a turn-off. Prospective mates do not want to subconsciously picture you with a partner's hand around your shoulder or on your thigh and the occasion you were sharing. You must have pictures without that negative distraction.

Your profile viewers do not want to see photos predominately of your golf and drinking buddies or social circle and sister club members, either. Or, your family tree. SINS members are initially looking to discover you ... not your whole entourage. Until things move further along, your family and friends are your personal life. Keep them that way until an appropriate time develops to share them with a new potential mate. Having others in most of your photos causes unnecessary bystander *noise* and confusion when SINS members are doing searches. Visitors to your profile look at it for only a split second unless something in it invites them to investigate further. Make yourself the center of that attention.

An extremely important concern for me is photos that include small children. Yes, you love them. Do you want their pictures lifted and used in disgusting ways on the Internet? I see lovely grandchildren so many times on men's profiles ... and I cringe. Please refrain from doing the same. Protect the children in your family ... and please, for those precious children, urge others to follow suit.

I have enjoyed viewing photos sent in emails from members who live a wide range of lifestyles that I can only imagine: from sea farmers to cattle ranchers, from metropolitan sophisticates to farmers in suspendered dungarees, from a yogi in his wrapped robe to an Indian chief in his headdress, and more. I will always remember the prisoner. I didn't see his surroundings, but the headshot in the orange jump suit was a big clue. He stated his profession as 'law enforcement'. I believe he lived in a gated community, just not the one that most would want to share with him. I can say he was creative. A large number of matching sites exist for both male and female prisoners. He picked the wrong site.

Now, let's step into your home. SINS members who read your profile and view your photos subconsciously think of how they would fit into your daily environment. This is one of the vital initial means of filtering a potential mate. Beware of the messages you are sending with the backgrounds of your shots. The important thing is to be authentic and not misleading, because your misrepresentation will eventually be found out.

What surrounds you is also very important. If you have pictures taken in your home, your surroundings reveal a good deal about you and your lifestyle. Not everyone can or wants to lead the lifestyle presented in your photos. That is part of the elimination process. Being in luxurious surroundings with shiny marble floors can be as much of a turn-off as a backwoods log cabin with rough-hewn cabinets to SINS members with different visions of how they want to live. Either possibility might also be just what other SINS members are looking for.

I cannot impress enough how important it is to have a neat and tidy home reflected in the backgrounds of your photos. Members go over these photos in great detail looking for clues about the person they are considering. They study your furniture, paintings on the wall, door moldings, kitchen cupboards, etc. Many members are not aware of how potential partners are influenced by the environments they see when they focus on a profile gallery shot. So often, a photo is posted without considering the details of what is before, beside and behind them. Clutter is a big turn-off in a photo of someone you are trying to envisage as a future mate.

It is natural to want to impress SINS members with your attractiveness, career success, sports agility, numerous accomplishments, exotic travels, home environment, etc., but try to avoid overdoing it. Near-perfection can appear obnoxious, even though the facts are true. If you live a privileged lifestyle and want someone who can support being a companion in such a life, show it subtly and tastefully. SINS members will read the signs when they note the details of your pictures. Sometimes your lifestyle is out of others' leagues. That is certainly OK. It is your reality, one of those filters by which others narrow their choices. Better they know before you both spend the time and effort on dates that most likely will not go anywhere. It is a bit tricky to show your fabulous home and/or all the toys, but that can be tastefully done with you the center of attraction in the picture and your possessions very much in the background

As long as your photos (and written profile) present *the authentic you*, you likely will not be rejected on a first date. A new interest will choose to meet you on the information and depictions provided. Next, chemistry and compatible personalities will be given a whirl. Example: some of your photos show you dressed for physical activity or sports in rural settings. Yet, in person you reveal yourself to be a city person, moviegoer, and TV aficionado. If your written information does not mention that you engage regularly in cultural and entertainment pursuits, you've created a disconnect.

Attempt to exhibit your personality in photos playing with your pet, laughing with a friend, cooking with a delicious smile, etc. And, try to show something unique about yourself ... are you a Karate black belt doing battle in your Dojo, a gourmet cook in a cooking school, etc.? Your gallery of pictures tells some of your life story. Exude confidence and indicate your life is a series of adventures large and small. Such an approach is very attractive to others seeking partners and mates. Do yourself a big favor: tell your real story through your photos. You will never be sorry for or have to apologize for the accuracy and authenticity of your photos.

The greatest easy-to-spot blunder is no photo in the primary photo space.

Never go incognito. Do not present a profile without a primary photo if you are seriously attempting to find a partner on SINS. You will be just a shadow in the SINS landscape. In addition to limiting access to interested potential mates because of their inability to see what you look like, you can be incorrectly judged as a possible Catfish ... a devious and/or sick person who does not want his or her identity known for unscrupulous reasons. [More on this intriguing topic later.] If you legitimately cannot show your picture, state why you cannot, such as your occupation or professional position does not allow you. Offer to send interested members a picture privately if you receive a request to do so.

A blank primary photo space severely limits your chances of receiving responses. Those that do respond to a blank photo space would most likely be suspicious, perhaps desperate ... or reckless. Do you want to meet someone like that? Your purpose of being in SINS is to find a stable partner. If you provide no photo, understand you are opening a window of interest to a marginalized fringe element. If you do not reach for the high bar, you are more likely to raise the possibility of being drawn in by a Catfish or someone who is playing a warped game.

Photos are the most easily accessible segment of your profile. However, if the profile does not present you effectively, the photos do not matter. Let's make a short return to the profile as a whole.

Have a member of the opposite sex read your profile; you may need to tone down your writing if it sounds intimidating. Many SINS members are very accomplished and successful; their CVs can be overwhelming. Early in my membership, I was told by a fellow SINS member that my first profile was just too much for many men to handle ... and, truthfully, it was boastful. I admit it. I was trying too hard to impress. I scared them away. I made the changes my new friend suggested. Sure enough, more of my *views* were converted into *winks, flirts, favorites,* and *messages* once I posted a profile that was truthful ... but more down-to-earth and not seen as bragging and intimidating. I had actually been accomplishing the opposite result of my intent. I had been chasing away credible prospects! Be careful of overselling yourself.

Between your photos and your profile writing, you can project a composite image of yourself that is problematic for some of your viewers. It's not that anything is blatantly wrong with you or your composite image. But, something is off. The lesson here? Scrutinize your total profile from several angles and ask trusted, thoughtful others to do the same. Remember the bit about being a work in progress. As I have shared, I have made most of the mistakes that can be made. Luckily, I seem to have learned from them. My mission now is to prevent you from making the same and other costly blunders.

I must mention that periodically you should change entirely or rotate your primary photo with others in your gallery. If I find my *views* are declining, it's an indication my photos have become stale to SINS members who have seen them before ... old news. I can look like a new user when I freshen up my page with new photos or rotate my old ones. Funny, when I do a rotation, many of the same men who viewed the initial primary photo return to the second but different primary photo to further view my profile. It appears they are attracted to the same type of gal, not noticing she is one and the same.

Last, if you are honest and consistent in your photos and manage frequent updates you should have no problem when you meet someone interested in you. Your effort in maintaining a crisp interesting profile will pay off. I see the difference when I become lazy ... contacts slow down. Like anything in life ... most of what you sow is what you reap. Great photos supported by an interesting profile should reward you with heart-warming contacts. Good luck!

Chapter Nine

How to Read a Profile ...

eyes wide open and between the lines
What they are telling you ...
and what they are not telling you

Save yourself time and money by learning how to read a profile. Read profiles with your eyes wide open, without colored glasses and with your heart held securely in your pocket. You should ask yourself what are you looking for before you begin. The homework you did in your personal essays ... *About Me, About the One I Am Looking For, About Our Relationship, etc.* ... has helped prepare you to now do a thorough Search with some knowledge of what to look for in others' profiles in order to find your potential mate.

You are trying to find an *energy* in the profiles you read. Although the photos are extremely important, you must feel a certain 'je ne sais quoi' once a particular photo stops you dead in your tracks and you read the related profile ... sometimes an attraction that can even be felt on your screen. That spark can be from members' descriptions of themselves, their activities or interests. That magical magnet can self-activate if they fit your conscious criteria, be sub-conscious or be a bit elusive when the SINS member is not what you had in mind at all *but* you find him or her very appealing anyway. Somehow, *it* is there ... enough to make you stop and take notice ... and perhaps contact that person.

THE PROFILES

Start with the obvious. Note how they were executed. If grammar and spelling are poor and the profile states they are highly educated, be wary. It is difficult to travel through higher education without being able to string a series of paragraphs together. If you see a number of blanks, follow up on filling those empty spaces in your emails. There may be a reason these were left empty. Or, these members were sloppy, lazy or even trying to hide something. Maybe those items were just not important to them or they did not care to fully honor the process. Too many blanks show little regard for viewers who hope to make a connection with a total person. Profile information spaces left blank do not offer a positive impression.

When you read profiles, do not eliminate yourself from the radar of members who interest you because you don't fit certain criteria they have stated, i.e., she wants a man with blond hair and you are bald; he wants a woman under 60 and you are 63. Take a chance. Most likely you have other traits more important to them. Many of us are unaware of what aspects of a person we are actually attracted to, studies have shown.

Profiles include photos. Yes, do examine them closely. Then, pull back from surface judgments. Most likely you do not look like a movie star. Nor are you as lovely or handsome as you once were. So cut the same slack when viewing others' photos. If even just the slightest hint of attraction is present on your part, take time to delve into the profile. Seeing the person in a different light will pleasantly surprise you. That average photo could be someone who might be accomplished, articulate, fun, funny, kind, gentle and have great values, etc. Appearance isn't everything. Emails and conversations can be very revealing ... and present some wonderful people, beyond those initial photos and profiles.

INITIAL CONTACT

Please put this early contact into perspective ... you are not asking someone to marry you. Do not place too much emphasis on its importance or become riddled with expectations. Your reach out is just an exploration to see if enough interest exists between you both to go to the next step ... exchange emails, speak on the phone or meet for a cup of coffee, etc. It's your call. Since you are in control at all times, relax and enjoy what comes next. Contact a few members who have the potential to become your friend, lover or lifetime partner.

© Randy Glasbergen
glasbergen.com

"I met a really cute woman online. I haven't seen her picture yet, but her font is gorgeous!"

Do not *attach* to your persons-of-interest or become excited too soon ... just look at the profiles, as if you would be interviewing them to see if you want to make contact with them. Very simple. Get this stage into perspective. You are still on the dock. You haven't left port yet, so no need for butterflies and love poems. I have had that happen ... men so anxious to find someone and wearing their hearts on their sleeves in their early contact with me. It actually is off-putting when someone appears needy. Save the poems and flowers for the romance stage of finding your potential partner; one who suits most if not all your criteria in Candyland. Candidates are out there ... be patient. You are still in the *Search* and *Contact* stages.

I always ask myself, "Could I kiss this person?" Perhaps it's silly, but it is part of the physical attraction filter, I guess. Please do not base your judgment of potential partners solely on photos ... although some can be quite tempting. In truth, most of us just display the everyday variety of looks. But, we possess quirks, qualities, interests, backgrounds, etc. that make each of us unique ... aspects to us that many members might find appealing. Be alert to interesting elements individual SINS members offer as well as celebrate them in your own profile.

Be prepared for some discrepancies when you meet for the first time. The previously mentioned UW/Cornell study measured participants in person and found more than 50 percent were untruthful about their heights in their online profiles, with guys fibbing "significantly more."[43] "People lie to embellish themselves, but not be liars," says Catalina Toma, PhD, an assistant professor of communication science who conducted the UW/Cornell study. "Weight fluctuates to some degree," which is why it's a popular characteristic to fib about. The UW/Cornell study found women and men subtract 8.5 and 1.5 pounds, respectively, on average.[44]

---

[43] Catalina Toma, PHD, Wisconsin-Madison and Cornell University researcher, in a study commissioned by www.BeautifulPeople.com.

[44] Ibid.

YOUR CRITERIA

Be careful with your ideal/search criteria. You can customize your ideal match when you register, but be aware that making your criteria too specific or unrealistic could eliminate good possibilities for successful relationships. We all have an ideal in our heads, but who ultimately spends the rest of his or her life with an exact version of a dream?

People's social values are often revealed by their activities. If you have no interest in volunteer work and would rather sit on a beach, then be truthful with yourself and those reading your profile. Do not present yourself as other than you are. Even if you develop a level of chemistry with someone, neither should hope to change the other to a new way of life. That intention very seldom works … for the long term. If you two do move through a stumbling point of incompatibility, better to think of your differences as enhancing each other's lives rather than changing the other.

With regard to differences, you may decide to become a bit deceptively proactive and mildly tweak your online persona to that of the person you are attracted to, or you may be content to remain happily authentic and continue to attract those you have attracted in the past. The choice is yours and one you will have to live with. It might be best to be realistic and content and not too much of a dreamer. However, sometimes life opens new windows for us to look through and engage in the world in ways we may have never imagined.

When you survey members' profiles it is up to you to keep in mind your own goals and desires in the pursuit of a potential mate … compare their written goals with yours. Look for a potential mesh, but exact *due diligence* to discover the potential personality flaws that could lurk behind their text. It is fair play for all involved if you can be as sincere as possible about your real objectives in regard to relationships and voice them in your own profile. You can only hope other SINS members whom you contact do the same.

THE LONG DISTANCE ISSUE

As far as I am concerned, distance as in geographical location is one of the main items you should consider. It is an important one. While many do not think distance (in my mind over a two-hour drive) is a problem, my experience has been that it is. With long distances your time to learn to know each other is severely limited; you are placed quickly in close intimacy decisions as to whether you stay with the other or one of you checks into a hotel. The overnight factor may induce you to go too far, too soon. (Of course, one option is separate lodging at a rendezvous point.) Long distance travel involves more effort and money, as well. And, safety issues. I drove through three significant snowstorms one winter in treacherous road conditions to spend time with a new relationship. I foolishly risked my life for something that only *might* have worked out ... and ultimately did not.

With distance Catfish and Scammers have more opportunity to manipulate you without any accountability. Please read the coming chapters on these characters before communicating with any member. You will learn what to look for in profiles and during interactions with these devious minds. When they have no photos and live at a long distance from you, you are at a higher risk of a possible fraud. So many wonderful members live near you ... proud to display their photos and share a bit about themselves and their lives in their profiles. Why would you go down a blind alley fraught with potential danger?

You may also discover too late that you should not have trusted and given your heart so soon. A long-distance special one may have more inclination to cheat on you once you have established an exclusive relationship, as well. I know this sensitive, potentially devastating situation is about trust that we want desperately to believe should be present and evident in a budding relationship. But unfortunately, many a time that trust has been broken when a long distance is involved. So many nights and days are spent alone when you are geographically apart … sad but true. Having cautioned you, if you are fortunate enough to have found a true partner for life, you should be able to survive those long separations. Remember, trust is earned over time, not bestowed without reason or with wishful thinking. Just be vigilant … please.

If your new involvement is a long distance one, be aware of RED FLAGS such as only being able to contact your interests on their cell phone, speaking at limited hours, speaking when they are mainly on-the-go in a car, etc. and not relaxing in their homes. Watch for calls they will not answer when they are with you. It is not always because they do not want to interrupt their great time with you, as you would like to believe. And, why are you receiving *unknown number* hang-ups? Where are they spending the big holidays? Are suspicious posts displayed on their Facebook page? Links that lead you to their photos on someone else's wall … links that show your special interests as more than *a 'friend'* to that someone? If you visit them in their environments do they never introduce you to friends and family, or take you to their clubs, events or hangout spots? These are all RED FLAGS. Your being curious about a potential partner's activities in a long distance relationship is not just about cheating and hurt feelings, but quite practically and most importantly about sexually transmitted diseases and your exposure to them if that someone is cheating on you. More about this important topic later.

Of course, checking cellphone call logs seems below your dignity; but seriously, doing so can uncover things you don't want to know are true but definitely should be made aware of. I can vouch first hand for that … having been unknowingly cast as *the other or another woman* a few times. I came to recognize the anxious voice of women on the telephone inquiring whether I knew a particular man. The women had found my name and number in their partners' call logs. I felt the pain in their voices. I, too, was a victim of these cheating men and hurting … but not seen as such by the women who loved them. We shall come to sites that will help you discover if your partner is cheating.

The wounded women were right … the men were cheating on them *with me* and I did not know it. I thought the men were free Singles looking for a relationship … like the majority of us in SINS. These occurrences were early in my SINS dating years. I did not have a clue as to how to weed them out … until I started to read the signs. Think of them as bad omens. Please remember these as you come to them … do not make the mistakes I made. Those mistakes can cause unnecessary pain and suffering … for you and for others. Better to err on the side of caution. Opportunities always come along in SINS. Thousands of new members arrive every day. Be alert … especially in long distance affairs.

RED FLAGS … Signs of cheating partners

- being able to contact with them on their cell phones only
- actually speaking with you at limited hours
- breaking contact for unexplained stretches of time
- unavailable for numerous and increasingly bizarre reasons
- touching and relating to you differently at times in intimate situations
- phoning when they are mainly on-the-go in a car, etc.
- not phoning while relaxing in their homes
- calls they will not answer when they are with you
- you receiving regular *unknown number* hang-ups

- consistently spending big holidays without you
- suspicious posts on their Facebook page
- links on Facebook displaying your love interest on someone else's wall that reveal him or her as more than a *'friend'* to that person
- when visiting them in their environments, they never introduce you to friends and family or take you to their clubs, events, or hangout spots

LEAVING LOVED ONES

From the very first glance at a profile, you must always consider what difficulties you might encounter if the involvement grows. If you love living near water, you probably do not want to spend your remaining years living on the plains ... or inland ... or in another country, etc. I have faced those choices and decided that living near my family was most important to me. You may decide otherwise. SINS have made these possibilities and similar options more common and possible than you realize.

My feeling is, by the Mature stage of life, most of us are settled in our communities and have our family love and social circles nearby. Some of us may not want or need those particular life enhancements. Personally, I would not be willing to give them up for a live-with situation more than a very few hours from my locale, whether married or not. And, I would not want the responsibility of having someone else make a possible sacrifice for me. Leaving behind a lifetime of family and friends is serious ... both for you and those near and dear to you.

So, I avoid that agonizing decision by never dating anyone long distance. I have had many tempting opportunities ... and have passed on them. I feel such involvements are not worth the possible problems. Long-distance involvements could become complicated, or dangerous and damaging, as previously mentioned. Even if they are successful, any might involve potential emotional pain ... for the people I love and for me. Long-distance dating is not for me, but may be for you. I will admit to the many success stories regarding both choices. Whether or not to consider members at a distance is an important item you must address when you are searching online and one you will likely need to act on. Expect to see many approaches from across the country ... and from other countries as well.

THE PROCESS

Some sites have tracked what profiles some members repeatedly visit. Many of those profiles are not within their stated criteria. Sometimes this factor is considered when the site *matchmakers* pair up members by applying algorithms.

Other sites do more than apply algorithms. Personality-matching sites such as <u>EHarmony</u> are in the top rankings for dating sites. They help you find a match based on mutual or complementary personality traits. These sites are quite successful and deserve high marks for their matchmaking skills and proven results. A personality-matching site may help you find partners better suited to you than you have been drawn to in the past. The sites may know you better than you know yourself.

As much as the customizing of an ideal partner in our searches is helpful and necessary, be careful; you could miss some wonderful people who could be great matches for you. The sites do not have a foolproof filter for chemistry, even though they have various tests that are fun and have some validity. Human chemistry is a big part of finding that elusive *special* someone.

You must remain mindful of what you want and alert to the persons with whom you are engaging. After all, you don't know anyone who is familiar with the backgrounds of those you are meeting online. You do not have check points, references from your community or social circles. SINS dating can become very personal and close. You must remain in control of the SINS process for your own safety and that of your heart, body, soul, and mind ... and your money. The elimination process basically narrows down your choices of which there should be many. Do not let it control you. You must maintain self-awareness and awareness of others' words and actions to allow SINS to work for your benefit, or you can be hurt ... well, perhaps at least a bit dented and confused. You are reading Candyland S.I.N.S., in part, to prevent all of that. I want your self-esteem to remain intact and your pride to glisten. And, your sense of fair play not to become jaded.

Do not narrow your searches too much if you want to harvest a broader spectrum of results. Open your horizons. You have many criteria options for different searches ... use them ... see where they lead you. You might find some unexpected contacts who fascinate you. I never thought I would go on a date with a country music singer/songwriter, a race car driver or a lawyer to the criminal underworld. But, never say "Never!" These men became friends and added much to my life. They certainly were not in my mind when I was setting my search criteria.

You can enjoy an early fruitful search if you view the profiles of new members or recently active members who seem keen to reach out. The date of their latest activity on the site is stated below their profile photos. Very recent activity indicates someone who is still looking and taking the time to check out their own site and perhaps that of others.

No one knows what you are doing when you are online on the dating sites; they just know when you were on the dating site last or if you are presently on the general site. Members *do* know that you open their profile pictures to read further. Your profile is logged onto their *Whose Viewed Me* page. You are listed anonymously only as a *view number* with no reference to your profile ... if you choose to hide your profile. No one will see that you viewed others' profiles when you are in the hidden mode. You can cruise the profiles on the site unnoticed.

If you see your *tempting* members remain online but appear to be in a long pause, they may not be so sure a current relationship, if they are in one, will stand the test of time. Or, they are just taking a break from online dating. Keep an eye on them if you think they have potential for you. Their status may change if their exclusive situation does not work out or they are back from their break. Adding them to your Favorites list accomplishes two things. Doing so makes finding them easier, and they are aware that you are interested in them because you are on a list of all those who have favorited them. Your favorited interest might just respond to that 'favorite' contact if s/he is ready to reach out.

The above situation brings up another RED FLAG I want to discuss. If you have entered into an exclusive relationship or believe you have done so and your partner refuses to deactivate his/her name on the site ... as I stated above s/he is continuing to indicate openness to new contacts ... a lack of commitment to carrying your relationship forward. Potential partners' continuing site presence is like their kissing you while their eyes wander around the room. If they refuse to take themselves off the enormous market on these sites, then you better follow suit and keep looking. They are not ready or may never be ready to further explore being exclusive with you. RED FLAG.

"You have a 30 year mortgage, a 5 year car lease, and a lifetime gym membership...but you're afraid of commitment?"

DECEPTIONS

Although you are likely to be forthcoming on the important points, most SINS members fudge something. I am not so hung up on *minor* infractions about height and age. However, the core values and the character traits members portray in their profiles are important to me, so I read them carefully more than once and carry them with me on our first dates.

A study conducted by researchers at the University of Wisconsin-Madison and Cornell University found about 80 percent of online daters lie about their height, weight or age.[45] Interestingly, the older you are, the less likely you are to fib about your age according to a study commissioned by www.BeautifulPeople.com.[46] This online dating site is one users can freely attempt to join, but they are only allowed to join when voted in by the members of the BeautifulPeople community.

---

[45] Catalina Toma, PHD, Wisconsin-Madison and Cornell University researcher, in a study commissioned by www.BeautifulPeople.com.

[46] BeautifulPeople.com; www.beautifulpeople.com.

Men are sensitive to their age and fudge it quite often. One SINS member who tried to go on a first date with me was 20 years older than his profile stated ... a totally unacceptable difference in my opinion. I tripped him up in the email conversation stage of pursuit when I asked him why he would be interested in a woman 10 years older than his stated age (RED FLAG) and shared I was not interested in a man that much younger than I. He said he was actually 10 years older than I. Oops, a 20-year discrepancy. Therefore, he argued, I should accept a date with him. I refused ... not because of his age, but because it was just too much of a fib for my liking.

A big RED FLAG! Watch when members say they want to date females older than their own age as stated in their criteria. Many men think they are cleverly disguising the fact they are older than their declared age. Women older than they are, *as a rule*, are not what men are looking for. They might fall in love with them, but are definitely not seeking them in the majority of searches. Hmmm, that's another interesting and controversial topic.

I dated a SINS member who had understated his age by 10 years in his profile ... a bit much. I discovered it on our first date ... SINS members usually do. It should have been a RED FLAG for me as to how much fibbing leeway he felt entitled to. I was new to the SINS dating world. I thought I would let it go. Big mistake. The fib proved to be the harbinger of a man who lied his way through our entire relationship of four years. I should have ended it on that first date before the saga really began, in order to save the self-esteem issues I eventually faced when dating and falling in love with a liar, as well as the inevitable inherent heartbreak that followed. Pay attention to RED FLAGS ... monitor them closely and hold your heart tightly to your chest until the flags are lifted.

As recent activity indicates which viewed members are still available, a very long pause since their last entry to their site usually indicates they have begun a sincere exploration of a potentially serious relationship. Most members truly looking for a committed relationship go off the dating sites for this important endeavor. It is tough on possible long-term partners when candidates are still lined up at the door of the other …an unsettling distraction.

Marital status should be closely looked at and watched as you move along establishing a relationship. It has been estimated that more than 13 percent of men on online dating sites are actually married. Although I could not find data to substantiate that item, I feel that it is accurate. I actually had an experience with someone who cleverly disguised his marital status from many women … a discovery not made until after his death. People with this M.O. are known as Catfish; they truly do exist in SINS. Be on the lookout! Note the RED FLAG. [One entire chapter on Catfish coming up soon.]

Many people fudge somewhat on a few things, such as their body-type, either attempting to be clever to attract more contacts or just practicing self-deception. When does *curvaceous* become *a few extra pounds*? Best to check the mesh of their photos and activities and interests to gain a good idea of a member's physical reality, so you don't have a big surprise when you two meet.

Another muddy area is income and occupation. "Men in our study thought it was more acceptable to lie about income or occupation than other profile elements," observes Dr. Toma. "They know it's important to women."[47] A survey by www.BeautifulPeople.com found that 42 percent of men falsified certain aspects of their jobs to enhance their image by overstating their position, or title or how many people they supervise. Some women demoted themselves and downplayed their intelligence.[48] I highly recommend you go

---

[47] Catalina Toma, PHD, Wisconsin-Madison and Cornell University researcher, in a study commissioned by www.BeautifulPeople.com.

[48] BeautifulPeople.com, www.BeautifulPeople.com.

to http://blog.okcupid.com/index.php/the-biggest-lies-in-online-dating/ for very detailed and fascinating statistics and charts in The Big Lies People Tell In Online Dating.[49]

Lying about lifestyle is a means to enhance the writer's image, so do not rely on all that you read as the gospel truth. Dr. Toma's study revealed that fibbers use fewer "I" statements; they are more likely to say, "Love to travel" than "I love to travel." In this way fibbers create a distance from their fibs. Dr. Toma states another sign is the use of shorter descriptions because "lying is cognitively taxing."[50]

Some deception may be unintentional. The formats of the Interests and Hobbies section of Match.com and a few other sites is a little ambiguous as to whether the member actually plays the sports checked off or just likes to watch them! I expect some honest mistakes are made there. Be aware of that possibility. For, it is highly unlikely that you will be going out with a 70 year-old rugby player. I have hesitated repeatedly over whether to check the boxes of a couple of sports I love to watch and would enjoy doing so with someone, but could never play in a million years of trying. For example, SeniorPeopleMeet.com provides the category *Pets*, but does not provide indicators as to whether the member owns dogs, fish, cats, horses, etc. or just likes them.

Another facet of deception in SINS is a bounce back to the subject of photos. So very important; so potentially misleading. Lighting can play a role in visual deception ... unintentionally the result of poor camera quality or intentionally the result of digital alteration to create a more flattering portrait style photo. Such fiddling is not the norm, but it can occur. Check the backup gallery of photos to see if they support the

---

[49] oktrends, Dating Research from OKCupid, http://blog.okcupid.com/index.php/the-biggest-lies-in-online-dating/, accessed July 1, 2014.

[50] Catalina Toma, PHD, Wisconsin-Madison and Cornell University researcher, in a study commissioned by www.BeautifulPeople.com.

image portrayed in the primary photo. You don't want any surprises. Dr. Toma concluded from self-reports, in which study participants admitted to their own lies: "Photographs were identified as the single most deceptive element of the person's profile."[51]

Here is another challenge you may encounter. You may spot some members who live with hefty emotional baggage. A profile loaded with negative statements is a good indication of someone who has a chip on one or both shoulders ... an axe to grind ... or is damaged ... sometimes not of his or her own doing. On-site emails that display mood swings and convey more than passing dissatisfaction with the scheme of things or make surprisingly strong judgmental statements likely indicate someone who is carrying around past emotional and psychological injuries that are tough to deal with at any stage of life. You may have enough of your own residual emotional weight to address without trying cope with or be kind/supportive/compassionate in a relationship with someone who is incapable of reasonably handling his or her own emotional residue. You want your remaining years to be as drama free as possible. No matter what your good intentions are, you do not want to be around people who might drag you down. I have been there and done that ... never a happy ending. Wish them well and move on.

You have written and submitted your profile. You have learned how to read the profiles of potential mates. You are now ready to launch into your searches ... to contact those SINS members who interest you ... and to respond to those interested in you. You will be busy, a happy and exciting busy.

But, not just yet! It's time for self-defense mode. Let's consider more of the warnings and necessary precautions of which you must be ever mindful.

---

[51] Ibid.

Chapter Ten

Scammers ...

one of our biggest fears on SINS

Trick or Treat

Let's wrench these lurkers out from behind
false profiles and discuss them and their ...

RED FLAGS

Scammers are essentially one very dangerous category of Catfish. You will learn about the latter and another damaging category in the next chapter. You are being introduced to Scammers first because these online criminals are the most dangerous. They want your money ... lots of it!

Scammers, like Catfish, present counterfeit identities and too-good-to-be-true profiles. Scammers' intentions, like those of Catfish, are deceptively evil. Scammers attempt to establish a relationship with you because they intend relieve you of any money they can get their hands on … either yours or that of your family. They attempt to literally capitalize on their targets' vulnerabilities. If they are successful, they leave their marks, their targets, devastated financially … and emotionally. Scammers have neither a moral code nor conscience.

Does the term *scam artist* ring a bell?

**"The identity I stole was a fake!
Boy, you just can't trust people these days!"**

Make no mistake! *If* you are unlucky enough to receive and naively respond to an approach or are too lax to detect the signs of a scam … *you will* become a business target. You will pay dearly. You will provide profit for their business. Although you will NEVER convert them to honorable and humane ways, they will attempt to tap the very genuinely humane traits within you. You must not fall for their heart-wrenching stories and deceptions. These masqueraders are incredibly creative with their clever well-documented profiles and convoluted lies. The personas you will encounter will be only figments of someone's imagination or of a group of imaginations … with one evil intent. To abscond with your money!!

Now is the time for three RED FLAGS. 1) Some Scammers quite often communicate in a distinctive grammatical style. 2) The structure of their sentences is not quite American English syntax and includes awkward uses of American slang. 3) Frequently their writing has a religious tone. Keep your distance. Better to lose one or two legitimate dating possibilities that innocently fit this description than to fall prey to heartless Scammers. Be forewarned: Once you engage with them, they are difficult to free yourself from ... especially if you start giving them your money. You are their financial lifeblood.

I cannot emphasize enough that the Scammers described above operate a business, a big business that has but one single goal: make money, no matter what devastation is left behind. The money they expect to come their way is yours; and, their way often leads across the world. They are usually nowhere nearby or to be found when you try to recoup your money which most often will have gone to distant lands. The majority of Scammers are part of documented international syndicates operating 'boiler rooms' filled with employees, each one pumping out hundreds of scripted emails per day. The complexities of the worldwide web provide such criminal enterprises total anonymity and you with no means to redeem your money and prosecute them. NEVER NEVER NEVER give money to anyone you meet online. Make that a mantra.

SINS offer fantastically rich hunting grounds for Scammers, as so many members are vulnerable after losses of partners in their lives and are now searching for friendship and/or love. Some are desperate for a special 'connection'. Scammers use their interpretation of your needs and desires to gain your trust and the closeness you seek. They will plink your heartstrings and appeal to your sense of charity. They mirror your interests, hopes and values. So, do not reveal much information about your emotional history and current state; your caring *friend* will take such information and run with it like a football team's running back heading for the goal line.

139

Online Scammers, as those we encounter in any walk of life, can be terribly charming and very believable. Or, they can be so outlandish and farfetched that you think they *must* be real characters. They have to be, right?!? Surely no one could make up lies on such a grand scale and expect you to believe them?!? Maybe they are actually who they say they are!! Someone has to be a CIA agent, a 5-Star general, or a diamond mining executive, etc. How exotic! Yes, I have met them all on SINS ... some of those stories later. And to top off their whole charade, they appear to offer the tender words and attention some of us have been desperately missing.

The slippery slope begins when you start to receive romantic emails, then quickly evolves to you both exchanging intimate details of your daily life, then progresses to them inevitably but 'reluctantly' sharing with you that they have been dealing with a big personal problem that needs some fixing ... with your kind help. With *your* money, of course. Millions of dollars have been lost to these Scammers ... not just on SINS but online in general. I think Scammers must have sociopathic traits to carry out such cruel crimes against the heart and its impulses for kindness, for compassion and generous acts by unsuspecting and/or vulnerable people.

I recommend an excellent book, *419* by Will Ferguson. He presents a detailed and riveting account of how many of the Scammers based in Africa operate and what their twisted motives are.[52] You might be surprised, but likely not shocked, at how some Scammers justify their unethical and criminal behavior as retribution for the devastation the West has levied upon their lands. One certainly can sympathize with the reality of their plight. You can surely understand their resentment and pain for their countrymen living in dire poverty while their land is stripped, economically raped

---

[52] Will Ferguson, 419 (Toronto, Ontario, Canada: Penguin Group (Canada), division of Pearson Canada, Inc., 2012).

and brutalized by big oil companies in order to put billions of dollars into others' hands ... those others being in the West. Some Scammers want *payback*; they justify they are entitled to have it. No matter how loving, sweet, good, kind, beautiful or handsome you are, you will not deter their aim. Know that from the get-go. I cannot emphasize this enough. This is one challenge you do not want to mess with. Delete them. Block them. Report them. Run from them. And, don't forget to cancel the personal email account you dedicated for off-site communications on which you communicated.

You will receive blatantly flattering emails from 'fantasy' younger men and women who are seeking an older partner, sharing tales of how they like the maturity of an older companion. Most are Catfish, out 'n'out Scammers or gold-diggers (the female version). Stay away from them unless you want to lose your pride, your peace of mind ... and your money. Your money is what they are after ... while you are alive or after you are dead ... or the money of your family. These deviants pervade the Internet in general and like to target the lonely. I have received many communications, mainly from supposedly younger men who are supposedly widowers with a supposed child who needs money for education, medical treatment, etc.

Scammers often say they travel frequently or work out of the country. Once they determine they have gained your trust they reveal they have a financial crisis that must be resolved immediately but, sadly, they do not have access to their funds. Could you please help? Could you wire a moderate amount of money to their bank? Then more amounts are required ... and more. The process is insidious and one that has destroyed not only individual lives but also whole families.

Once you realize you have a Scammer in your online life, do not try to dissuade or convert. You may be tempted to do so because your mutual emails have brought you to feel you actually know them well and have become close to them emotionally. That manipulated bond is their preparatory goal to set the stage for the big scam move. Your own goal should be to stay as distant from them as possible on all levels and disassociate yourself as fast as you can at your first suspicion. Hit your 'Delete message', 'Report a concern', and 'Block a contact' buttons immediately ... all are present on your site's screen to protect you from any further contact attempts by your *friend* and to alert the SINS site administrators that a predator has been discovered. The site will respond to your alert immediately. Administrators know how serious such an identity surfacing on their site can be.

You can then comfortably move on to spend time online responding to legitimate pursuers ... unless you gave the Scammer money and did not press the three magic buttons. S/he will not want to let you off the hook if you took the bait. You may have also connected with a persistent character who has several personae and email addresses and, therefore, could slip through site security and re-contact you via another address and under another identity. Another cycle launched. You now know how important it is to *not* become involved without personal meetings. To send someone *any* amount of money ... not one dollar. It is too dangerous. You have been warned ... heed that warning. Scamming is a paramount safety issue in SINS.

Do not be seduced by fantasy profiles: exceptional good-looks, a life of travels, a widower (or widow) quite often toting around the proverbial child, strong family values, possibly a dramatic life, possessing qualities most of us yearn for in a special contact ... and would like to think we possess. Most importantly, connection with such a person makes us think we are *special* ... lucky to have met them, even blessed. Yes, we are *special* to them ... because we possess money they are determined to take from us.

Real, solid individuals with many desirable qualities and lifestyle attributes are active on SINS ... maybe not quite all great qualities are found in one person ... I have met them and dated some. You just have to slowly and very cautiously allow these may be 'perfect' matches and potentially 'complete' partners into your world. Although they may be the real deal, do not share too much of your personal information or that of your family until you feel they truly are legitimate and trustworthy ... and such information as is appropriate for them to know at each stage of your involvement.

One key test is whether your still-new interests allow you into their world. Most Scammers have a conundrum ... how to achieve emotional closeness with you without physically meeting you, to become so close to you ... without an actual meeting ... that you would willingly give your life savings to them. A tough goal to bring about when they actually live in Africa, England, or the Philippines and you live in Wisconsin, New York, etc.

Online *couples* carry on for many years without actually meeting because one partner is likely a Catfish getting high on living a secret life or, perhaps, is a Scammer milking the other of his/her life savings. A Scammer does not want to meet you in person. A Scammer wants to meet only your money. A Scammer will never bring you into his (or her) personal life. RED FLAGS. Watch out!!!

I was very recently visited by a Scammer on one of the topnotch sites for Mature Singles. By unfortunate coincidence for him, I was working on this chapter. All his RED FLAGS were waving high, in vivid color before my eyes. His profile and email subliminally flickered 'too-good-to-be-true'.

I clicked my 'Report a Concern' button and filled out a very short form stating I believed this particular contact was a Scammer and why ... all done in a couple of minutes and, very importantly, a anonymously. The good sites are on guard for Scammers and take these reports very seriously. They have departments that specialize in such transgressions and dangers to their members. They make constant efforts to keep you safe.

The site quickly jumped onto my recent Scammer report to them, responded to me within hours with emails and with their 'live chat' function … which I electively asked for so site reps could give me immediate explanations and information. They promptly did their investigative follow-up work. My Scammer was off the site within the day. Not to bother another unsuspecting soul … how many women were saved from his scheming? Well, under that particular profile name, at least. That name and communication path are no longer available on the site for further contact with anyone. Another such contact can appear under a different name … you know the drill. Eliminate the new identity from your page and the site … as soon as possible.

Remember, the Scammer and his organization do operate a business. Discovery and reporting do not prevent the same person/ organization behind that name from setting up another profile with the same telltale RED FLAGS. That is why 'free' sites appear to have more Scammers and Catfish than the paid sites. It costs a scamming enterprise nothing but an employee's time and an Internet connection to do business. You must always be alert to Scammers' presence on the Internet in general and, in this case, within the world of online dating.

You should do your part to protect yourself … and other members. Look for the clues in emails and profiles as to who they really are. Stop them dead in their tracks. Vetting members' emails and profiles is a very important procedure to follow and not difficult to do. It is fascinating to read incoming emails and profiles with that in mind; and, it is personally very rewarding to actually uncover one of these predators.

Bear with me, please. This aspect of SINS is so important to me that I must offer one more compelling set of must-do's. To erase these schemers, remember to use the tools and procedures provided by the sites. Your power rests in those three buttons on your computer screen: 'Report a Concern', 'Block from Contact' and 'Delete Message'. Do not hesitate to use them to stamp out these parasites and piranhas. With a simple click on 'Delete Message' and another click on 'Block from Contact' at the bottom of every message profile, the associated name and email address are out of your communication pod forever. You can then click the 'Report a Concern' button next to them in order to give a report to the website. After your report is immediately investigated and found to be accurate, the identity will be eradicated. Your actions are and will be forever anonymous to the Scammer. Do not hesitate to use those tools ... keep yourself and others safe. You are part a community.

Unfortunately, although most sites make concerted efforts to keep you safe, it is impossible for them to know who is behind the profiles that constantly morph into whatever the Scammer or, more precisely, whatever you desire. As stated, Scammers *will* just keep popping up, being blocked and returning to the sites with another profile. Scammers sometimes Photoshop pictures with lips from one attractive image, hair from another, etc. to come up with their very good-looking versions of fictional 'member' pictures to lure you. Accompanying profile texts are constructed from bits and pieces of very well-written legitimate profiles. Truly, a deceptive business from start to finish.

Scammers follow protocols and a script in an attempt to quickly sweep you off your feet. They are on a clock ... so many days for each aspect of the ploy. Once you open the first email, within just a couple of days or just a very few exchanges s/he will tell you s/he is in love with you. You will read about 'destiny' and 'fate'. The rush will be on ... with you as the target *even though* you will likely never meet in person. Your Scammer will gently press and press and press because cash must continue to flow into accounts. For your Scammer, it is a living. For his/her employer ... it's a business. A dirty business.

One RED FLAG is the surprising speed with which the individual wants to rush you off the dating site platform and into a personal email account, one registered with a free server that is cleverly disguised within site-based communications with you ... because sharing of private email contact information is not allowed on most of the sites. Your Scammers often say they are leaving the site that day but would like to hear from you privately. They give a sense of great relationship potential and urgency to communicate. The rush on you is in order to redirect your mutual communication from the site before the Scammer can be blocked by its security administrators. Beware once more: You are on your own once you communicate off the dating site ... and on the Scammer's plate to be nibbled upon until all your money and, as so often happens, your heart are gone.

Sexy tomcat seeking cuddly feline
...that'll grab her
... and so will I !!

Many of the SINS sites offer articles giving you helpful tips on how to recognize a Scammer. Read them carefully. They carry my same warnings. To internalize them, read them again. You cannot be too aware. It is amazing how we can be duped ... even when we think we are savvy. As a result, many Scammer victims are too embarrassed and ashamed to report their experiences. Please do not hesitate to report them. It is an effective way to put a net around their tentacles, at least for the short term. Plus, you have taken positive action ... and control of an unfortunate situation

NEVER give out your personal contact information until you have developed some face-to-face contact and you feel a solid level of comfort and a building up of trust to share such mutual information with a new SINS acquaintance. I said 'mutual information' ... be sure the other is willing to share the same. If not, what do you see? RED FLAG!! Withhold any private contact details. Guard your safety as you do your money. You may unknowingly be doing both ... protecting your personal safety and the financial safety of your money, both yours and that of your family.

Scammers try to convince you to share personal information, which will ultimately lead to their desired goal and their disappearing with a chunk of your money. They will often ask for your private contact information under the guise of sending you flowers or gifts. In order to evoke your sympathy, they frequently say they are widowers or widows. They are anxious to pique your interest in them and for you to be flattered by their interest in you in order to lure you into an emotionally committed situation so they can ... yes, ask for money.

Now, enjoy my following true story. DO NOT DO WHAT I DID HERE. I have seen so many Scammers on my profile pages; I have to confess that I stepped *intentionally* into a trap one had set for me. I quite brazenly, though definitely unwisely, decided to bait one

Scammer to see how this type of despicable deception actually worked. Don't you do this! Sometime after my escapade, I read how dangerous 'scambaiting' can be. If you want to live vicariously in this regard, access one of the websites dedicated to surveillance of them. Google/search "scambaiters" and proceed from there to follow their reckless escapades.

To my tale. I decided if I were going to make an effort to understand this Scammer phenomenon, I would do it in a big way. How about finding yourself online-dating the Chief of Staff of the United States Army or a counterintelligence agent? I did! These frauds and every conceivable but eventually unbelievable scenario play their dishonorable games on SINS ... and in our everyday social frameworks.

Ah. My multi-star general. One email was all I needed to figure out where this 'Chief of Staff of the United States Army' was going with our communication. I decided to have fun ... not a good idea. Again: Do NOT do what I did. The idea might be an interesting way to learn how one version of a scam works, but it can be very dangerous. These inventive criminals are more clever and definitely more evil and dangerous than we are. As I read at a much later date, I had unknowingly become a 'scambaiter' in this instance. Don't you even think about doing the same. I would feel very guilty if you did and stumbled into a pot of trouble. With that being said, I hereby absolve myself from any responsibility.

I must admit I did have fun. I continued correspondence with this *fine* man for a month to the day; who knows what he really was? A woman, a very young adult, a prince, a pauper ... living in the U.S., in England or in Africa?

The Scammer sent his first email to me under the guise of an Army officer ... very believable. Eventually he wanted me to believe that he was the Chief of Staff of the US Army. Okay. He must have been chuckling as he wrote and embellished his life story. He wrote me love poems; I slyly reciprocated. Mine were original and outwardly heart-felt and, I thought, not too bad actually. ;-D When I googled/searched his achingly lovely poems, I found his were plagiarized. Oh, no. How could that be? For, he had proclaimed his own deeply emotional, immediate bond with me. Right. According to his plan, he *fell in love* with me immediately!

His stories became more bizarre as we continued our email conversations at all hours of the day and night. Remember, he was probably writing from thousands of miles away. So, time which seemed to separate us became a tool for 24/7 soft bombardment as well. My *Army Chief of Staff* confided to me that he had fathered a *love child* when stationed and living mainly alone in England while his wife had remained in the United States. Reluctantly, he had to leave this *love child* in England with its mother. He loved them both very much, but his position as a highly placed, married military officer would not allow him to publicly or privately acknowledge the child, now a handsome young man about to begin his university years. Next, I received emails from his *love child* saying he could understand how much his father loved me and he (junior) wanted to meet me some day. Hmmm. His sentence structure and spelling were suspiciously identical to his father's.

Then thirty days from our first email, the shoe dropped. I surmised the writer must have had a thirty-day window in which to close his deals. Poor fella. He was likely one of hundreds who sit in electronic scamming factories, part of big and frightening organizations, pumping out emails to lure in and nurture new victims. It is a worldwide business ... a lucrative, corrupt and dangerous business. Do not even think of doing what I did. Instead, immediately block a suspected Scammer from your site. Scammers and their operations are more wily than you and I could ever be.

After exactly thirty days, my fantasy Army Chief of Staff was stuck on a destroyer in the Pacific and could not access his funds without the government or his wife knowing about his financial transactions. His illegitimate son, who by then had developed his own *close* relationship with me, desperately needed money immediately to travel from England to the USA to begin his university studies. Could I loan him $2,000 and place it in a bank account for his beloved son? Of course! Of course, that would have been only the beginning.

I never answered that request email. The Scammer made one brief attempt to save the situation ... to which I replied in my best *school marm* scolding manner that he should be ashamed of himself, especially as he was always praising God and bestowing his blessings on me. I doubt he blinked; he likely swore, as he had wasted so much time wooing me.

Because some good-hearted people become caught up in well-choreographed games of emotional connection, nightmare stories abound about people losing hundreds of thousands of dollars ... with no avenue for the return of their funds. Multi-nationals for whom we have no legal recourses usually hold the money overseas.

Generally, we are not aware of the potential frauds that lurk around us daily; nor do we frequently come upon them because we are not conscious of how a scam plays out in our familiar communities. SINS are not only a concentrated environment of Singles in online communities but also one that is solely focused on romance and dating with members who are often vulnerable after losses in their lives. SINS are frequented by the same unsavory characters as in our immediate traditional communities, perhaps in varying degrees. Scammers and Catfish are in many online communities. These deceivers are clever and imaginative ... and have no conscience. Beware of them; they are very dangerous.

Because the purpose of SINS is so clearly defined, establishing connection with its members is generally easier for Scammers than is the case in our usual social environments. SINS members are exceedingly receptive to being approached. After all, close connections are our goal. SINS probably has more concentrated numbers of vulnerable members and more predators who feed on those vulnerabilities than do other social spheres in general, because of one fact. We are all trying to connect, to become close to others ... close enough to find that special someone with whom to spend the rest of our lives. And, the early communications are electronic and anonymous. Bearing this in mind surely can make reading the profile of a potential love match very interesting and very important. Pay attention!! Read profiles in detail, read between the lines and read what they are *not* telling you.

All that having been said and now having unsettled you with my warnings, I have done my duty as best I can. You must proceed with caution when communicating with any stranger who wants to become close to you soon after establishing contact. You are in control of your Internet-dating experience at all times. Be assured that you can remain anonymous until you feel ready to be known at whatever level of recognition you want to allow. I expect you will be fine if you follow the tips and guidelines here and within your chosen SINS sites. Add *common sense* and *gut feel* to the mix, as well. The importance of the latter two instinctive reactions cannot be underestimated.

The bottom line is you can NEVER give or loan strangers money. Carve that *no-no* in stone. When you consider we are open to fraudulent practices every day in many aspects of our lives, SINS is not much different. You have to be just as vigilant when playing the online dating game as you are about your other interactions with strangers, as you would be when engaging in car repair services, water heater removals, home renovations/repairs, motor vehicle purchases/sales, health & fitness clubs, collection agencies, home furnishing and appliance providers ... all top categories for financial crime complaints according to the Ontario Ministry of Consumer Services Top Complaints and Inquiries Report 2012.[53]

Yet, we continue to utilize all these goods and services. SINS is just another category to add to that list. You must take precautions with SINS, as you should with all your interactions and purchases of goods and services. SINS is just as much a part of our lives as the above financial complaint categories.

I wish the media would give greater attention to the plentiful *feel-good* success stories that occur because of SINS. From 2005 to 2012, 35 percent of all marriages conducted involved couples who had met on the Internet.[54] I know countless stories about Mature Singles who met online and married or are planning to. Their searches over, they have entered the *next hurrah* time of their lives. I am always thrilled to hear such stories ... happy accounts of good-hearted people who might have spent their later years unhappily alone. Instead they reached their journey's end holding the hand of a special *someone*.

---

[53] Ontario Ministry of Government and Consumer Services, last modified: March 24, 2014, http://www.sse.gov.on.ca/mcs/en/Pages/Top_Ten_Complaints.aspx, accessed June 30, 2014

[54] John Cacioppo, the University of Chicago, Department of Psychology led the survey sponsored by eHarmony, 2013, accessed July 1, 2014.

Chapter Eleven

Catfish & Players

You are now a member of SINS ...
how are you going to handle Catfish and Players?

Who are *they*? What do we look for in a profile to uncover them ...
better yet, what are *they* looking for in order to discover us ... the
unsuspecting and vulnerably hopeful members of SINS?

How about dating a sexy medical doctor or a drop-dead gorgeous,
powerful businesswoman? *They* are online and waiting for you.
Handsome, beautiful, wealthy and looking for love. Some of those
appealing characters are legitimate ... others, only if you *choose*
to believe them. CATFISH and PLAYERS!!! Beware ... *they* are
looking for you; with your broken heart, insurance policy payout,
inheritance, or divorce settlement. On SINS you must guard all
your assets, as you do in your daily life. Use your head and your
common sense in all aspects of your life to keep predators at bay.
Be disciplined in all your interactions to protect yourself.

CATFISH is an umbrella term, one fairly recently coined, which denotes a con artist who pretends to be someone s/he is not in order to satisfy less than honorable goals. A Catfish uses SINS or other social media to create false identities, particularly in pursuit of dishonest and deceptive online romances.

In the natural world, a catfish is a bottom-feeder. In the electronic world, a Catfish is a persona that swims up from the depths of human intention to operate in the sun-filled realm of Candyland. Of course, Catfish rise up figuratively in all areas of human activity. They may come online from anywhere in the world or operate much closer to home *and* in real life. Common Catfish and Players, just as financial specialist Scammers, are dishonorable, deceptive individuals who can endanger you on several levels ... emotionally, physically and financially. They, too, prey upon innocent people ... without conscience or regret ... upon SINS members they perceive as vulnerable, individuals they can 'work' to garner favor with.

Catfish, however, differ from Scammers because the latter cold-heartedly play others for financial gain. Catfish manipulate others for an invisible profit: enjoying the challenges and the thrills of carrying off a deception. Players deceive trusting hearts to serve their own impulses for egotistic satisfaction. Catfish and Players, along with Scammers, zero in on their victims' Achilles tendons and proceed to lure in their victims until they are ensnared. Catfish and Players curry their victims' favor so they can play their games for the emotional enjoyments they can create for themselves. While they derive warped pleasure as they snare, deceive, debilitate and often devastate their victims, they revel in games of deception for their own emotional and adrenaline-based high rides. Often their families are their victims, as well.

A CATFISH TALE

Early in my adventures in Candyland my biggest Catfish caught me. He presented a dramatic false identity. He told me that as he was a member of the NSA (the National Security Agency) he would not always be able to tell me his whereabouts. Guess what ... I met him ... and believed him!!! He would be late for dates because he was waiting for *top secret papers* to be flown in or he would have to postpone our dates until another day because of something dire. I was so new to SINS when I thought: *NSA agents exist ... why not him?* How gullible could I be? Well, that gullible! You see, I was naïvely engaged in SINS-based dating under a dangerous premise, one that automatically placed trust in my fellow members until they proved themselves otherwise unworthy of that trust. *You* must conduct your SINS dating with the opposite philosophy. Only bestow trust once trust has been earned. And, understand that the earning of your trust should take considerable time ... at the very least, a few private emails, a first meeting and a few dates.

I was the Pollyanna of SINS. I had entered Candyland believing all that was written and spoken to me was the truth. Since then, many years of dating have taught me lessons hard-earned. Reap the benefit of my mistakes. Although you will inevitably make your own, I want to eliminate as many of them for you as possible ... and give you a few laughs (or groans) at my expense while doing so.

You do not have to join SINS to find Catfish and Players. They are an unfortunate part of our society in general: human greed and evil in a disguise. Be very cautious ... they can be found in SINS because SINS provide them with continually renewed pools whirling and teeming with fish among which they can swim like sharks. *They will* find you. However, *you will* have coping tools to protect yourself ... the common sense, *gut feel* and precautionary general safety rules of conduct and the safety guidelines and tools of the sites themselves.

"As long as it's anonymous, put me down as 'dog seeking cats for discreet romance'."

SINS do their utmost to protect you and, even better, provide you with means to help you protect yourself. You're a truly mature adult now and should take total responsibility for your own safety because situations can develop beyond SINS' capabilities *and* purview. Be very aware that it is impossible for SINS to run background checks on the 100's of millions of members utilizing their services. You must exact your own 'due diligence'. [You have already come upon that term a few times ... and for good reason.] Do not jeopardize your safety by being desperately hopeful, trusting, lax or sloppy.

Catfish exist and flourish on many social media sites. If one finds you, s/he (likely) will groom you and prepare you to become his/her next victim ... most likely handling a good number of you simultaneously. This revelation does not mean that you should walk away from SINS or other social media sites. Just pay heed and proceed with cautions in place ... as you would if this arena were any other sphere of activity in your life.

I highly recommend you read Dr. Phil's book, *Life Code*,[55] to understand how common, even prevalent evil people are in our society, to spot them and to avoid being victimized by them ... both in your life in general and, by extension, in SINS. Apply the same protective measures on all fronts. Dr. Phil's sage advice on dealing with these predators and specific tips on how to handle these 'low-lifes' on SINS should safely bring you through Candyland's adventures.

Too, don't forget your common sense. You just have to be your own kind of sharp ... as sharp as they are ... and disciplined *and* vigilant. At all times! These perpetrators of deception operate not only throughout the entire Internet but in all levels of society: the rich and the poor, the beautiful and the ugly ... brutalizing victims in various ways from controlling others' lives emotionally to stealing money, kidnapping, to rape and even murder. Now that I have your attention ... it is still helpful to acknowledge Catfish and Players (and Scammers) are the exceptions to the norm in SINS. They are the odd story the media picks up. The vast majority of members are active in SINS for the same reason you are.

As hopeful, happy and golden as that ever-glowing goal might be, be mindful that Candyland is not LaLa Land ... an ethereal unrealistic zone where people float about aimlessly without rules of conduct or responsibility for one's actions. You would do best to possess both.

Pay close attention to the members you decide to meet and actually date; Catfish and Players are particularly charming, very disarming ... and very cunning. They apply time-proven strategies to manipulate your emotions and your ongoing assessments of them. Be aware of how a new acquaintance met online makes you feel. You may be *being played*. Yes, love on first contact or first date

---

[55] Dr. Phil McGraw, Life Code: (Los Angeles, California: Bird Street Books, Inc.), 2012.

does happen, but safeguard yourself, activate your pause mode. Maintain a sociable objectivity until your dates prove themselves worthy of the trust. Full trust is not earned in a couple of meetings. To flip the coin: If you appear to have earned another's trust too quickly, be on the lookout for a potentially desperate person or a naïve, inexperienced new member who could cause you grief. Remember, the bonding process generally takes time!!!

If, after kick-starting your *on alert* mode by seriously embracing my cautions, you still are ready and willing to proceed, read on and learn how to deal with potential traps and ruses so you may go on to enjoy what can be some incredible life-changing experiences. I have done so ... so can you. Begin to break through self-imagined boundaries and invalid or outdated obstacles.

SINS provide clear warnings ... easy and quick pre-emptive actions to take when you suspect you have met a predator. You will find excellent safety articles on their sites ... read them ... twice. Stay mindful of a site's security features, as well. With these tools you should always be in control of your safety and never close to true danger as you play by the rules in Candyland.

BLOCKING PREDATORS and others

A useful tool SINS offers you is 'blocking' unsavory characters from seeing your profile. Blocking is not only to be used exclusively for Catfish, Players and Scammers but also for any member you do not want contacting you for whatever reason you so choose ... an *ex*, an overenthusiastic suitor, a neighbor, a co-worker, a member of one of your physical–world community groups, etc. You can instantly respond with a click of your mouse or a brush of your fingertip on the Block Member and Delete Message buttons. No one is penalized, as potentially they are when you Report a Concern, but you have your peace of mind and privacy intact.

TELEPHONE NUMBERS

You must not give out the telephone numbers and addresses for your home and workplace until you are sure of your safety. While in SINS you can completely control a pursuer's contact with you. But, if you choose unwisely to trust too soon, once you release personal information, your security is out of SINS' control and likely out of yours unless you involve the police. You must realize that you are meeting complete strangers ... none of your or his acquaintances can give you a reference. Therefore, you must be on the look-out for RED FLAGS at all times. It is your responsibility. Never should you invite a complete stranger into your home or give out personal contact information to a person on the street ... nor should you do so on SINS. Also, because the electronic world conveniently enables searches in public records, too specific information early on allows anyone to dig for details on the life specifics mentioned.

Despite the difficulty protecting our identities in this age of easy access to such details, we should do all we can to maintain our security. SINS' warnings and safety suggestions, as well as my protocol SAFE (**S**afety, **A**ttitude, **F**un, **E**nthusiasm) exist to give you a *heads up* as to the potential approaches you may receive from some of these predators. Unfortunately, we might encounter unsavory characters anywhere in our daily lives. SINS are no exception. Up to this point in your collected years, you may have been fortunate to not yet experience the damages deceptive individuals can do to your life, your peace of mind ... and your heart. I have not been so fortunate ... and those incidences were even in a traditional social community before I entered SINS. You are about to enter a whole *new-to-you* world of cyber space where scheming individuals can hide under a cloak in complete anonymity and be protected from discovery of who they are, where they are and what they are.

I write here from experience. During my eight years traveling through SINS I have encountered and unknowingly dated a number of Catfish. In my early interactions with them, I believed and was fooled by so many ... a few for very short periods online, others for a meeting or two, and one for years. Some were so obvious I would never bother to answer their emails. A special one, I casually dated for years not knowing he led a parallel life very different from what I was led to believe. I am now more careful ... not as trusting. Experience is the best (and at times, the most painful) teacher. You have resources to avoid some if not all the pitfalls before you fall prey to a Catfish, a Scammer or a Player and experience the pain of lost expectations, lost money ... or lost love.

A PLAYER'S TALE

A most notable and rather recent shock I received four years after I had last dated a man who had been in my life intermittently for almost two years. He was highly regarded and extremely creditable in the very top tier of one of the most influential industries of the U.S. He made television appearances, he gave speeches and interviews, he was quoted in the media, etc. He had been known to be an established family man and community leader. I did not know he had fabricated a recent and ongoing *separation* from his wife. His post-mortem gift to me was shame and shock.

Who would have guessed this accomplished man needed the challenges and thrills of Catfishing, of being a Player, of leading a duplicate life in tandem with his ostensibly very happy and very much married life? Certainly not his family, including his very much still-married and in-the-dark, devastated widow, and their devoted sons ... one of whom contacted me after his sudden death. When the family was straightening out his affairs, they had discovered a *special* list of over 100 women with whom he had carried on Internet-based relationships over a number of years.

Some he dated were unaware, myself included, that he was still *very* married. As the secret unraveled, the grieving and now shocked family found that he had met me online as he had dozens of others. This Catfish/Player had been brilliantly charming and very believable. Enough of his story was true ... very public and verifiable. So, I did not question his honesty concerning his marital status. This crucial part of his story was always vague and not easily confirmable because we lived many states and even a country apart. He is one very real reason I will not date long distance.

One woman was never enough to satisfy this Catfish/Player's needs; each woman broken-hearted in the end. Right up until he died surrounded by his family, his supposedly ex-wife lovingly by his bedside. The perfect family for the *perfect* family man. His final moments were as much of a lie as his life. Each girlfriend had been excluded from his last months, never able to say goodbye ... some having spent years loving him passionately, selflessly, and fruitlessly, letting a completely-partnered life pass them by. Each kept in the dark as to his illness and even his passing. What a sad way for these women to end what they thought was a long-term romance. Don't allow this for you. Protect yourself from Catfish/Players.

"I don't want my husband to smell sexy. I want my husband to smell married!"

This is the time to give you grave warnings about long distance Internet dating. You have to extra cautiously vet an individual who does not live in your area. Do not worry about hurting feelings ... better to hurt that possibly innocent person's feelings than risk hurting your heart, losing your savings or costing you your life. The quote says it all.

"But if you're gonna dine with them cannibals
Sooner or later, darling, you're gonna get eaten ..."
- Nick Cave-

EXCLUSION

One of the biggest RED FLAGS a Catfish or Player can wave wildly in front of you is the one with the word *exclusion* stamped on it. Catfish never see you in their environment or include you in activities with their friends and family. You are never invited to company or business functions or gatherings of friends. Those 'nevers' create a most likely scenario. It is almost a virtual 'given' they have something to hide ... usually a spouse or a committed relationship.

When this warning flag flies, back away and end the contact as fast as you can. Not only might you be hurting an innocent family or partner if you continued you also would be leaving yourself open to STD's, i.e. sexually transmitted diseases. If you are an extracurricular activity for a Catfish, most likely s/he has others, as well. You have no idea of the breadth and depth of this person's previous and present experiences you are exposing yourself to. Do not be patient too long before asking for a date in the other's environment. In addition, I strongly suggest you pursue an *in-home-territory* date before you go to bed with anyone.

BED and STD's

Eighty percent of people between the ages of 50 to 90 identified themselves as sexually active in a report in the Student British Medical Journal, with accompanying implications for sexually transmitted disease (STD) rates, including HIV. Rates of sexually transmitted disease in the U.S. and Britain have doubled in 10 years, as fewer people are practicing safe sex.[56] Do not take the attitude

---

[56] Rachel von Simson, Ranjababu Kulasegaram, The Student British Medical Journal, 02 February 2012, **DOI**: 10.1136/sbmj.e688, Student BMJ 2012;20:e688, http://student.bmj.com/student/view-article.html?id=sbmj.e688, accessed July 1, 2014.

"It couldn't happen to me." You are at risk when a partner may have multiple partners. Catfish and Players are secretive, potential and quite probable carriers of hidden and dangerous diseases. Be on alert for their RED FLAGS.

GOING PUBLIC ... NOT

As a long-distance dating relationship begins to develop, set approximate time frames for a sequence of *home territory* get-togethers. If one does not develop or if you are given too many excuses, wave good-bye as you get out of Dodge. Once you realize what is not happening, make no exception. You have good indication your *friend* is a Catfish. Be firm; likely he (or she) will come up with the most incredible array of stories as to why that date with his/her friends or brother or sister can't happen or was cancelled: sudden deaths of friends or relatives, children needing them to emergency babysit, parents needing transportation to a vital doctor's appointment, etc. I have heard all of these fabrications. Believe them ... in that, those important and revealing introductions to their friends or family *will not* happen but not for the myriad of reasons they give you. Accept that your start to a fairytale has ended ... your coach has turned into a pumpkin. No prince; no princess. No happy ending with this person ... a Catfish or a Player. Face the likelihood sooner rather than later and move on immediately.

And, do not let them charm you, as is their *modus operandi*, to lie their way back into your life. They most likely will try to rekindle the relationship with you, not because they love you but because they love the challenge of bringing you back under their control.

After my first encounter with a Catfish, I grew to recognize their initial hang-ups then the sadness, insecurity, and anxiety in the telephone voices of a few women brave enough speak and inquire if I knew their man or his telephone number or his email address.

They had found my contact info among his personal items. These women were wives, daughters, fiancées; or, they were in committed relationships with these men. Of course, these found-out adrenalin-riding deceivers were immediately off my list of dates or even casual friends ... not to be trusted.

> *Oh, what a tangled web we weave*
> *When first we practice to deceive...*
> -Sir Walter Scott-

A SECOND PLAYER'S TALE

I did allow one particular thinly veiled Catfish, perhaps Player would be a more appropriate term, back into my life after discovering some of his lies. His identity was correct; he was no longer married. *But.* He cleverly continued to skirt the truth on countless occasions in order to keep me in his life while secretly pursuing and dating others. I wanted to believe him so much I shut my eyes to the obvious RED FLAGS. I never really knew what lives he led when I was not with him. I was in denial, as well. I had fallen deeply in love with this man and was lost in the maze of his lies, never knowing what was truth or fiction. No amount of well-intentioned advice from friends or even counseling set me totally free of his grasp, a dangerous emotional and mental place to be. Don't let this happen to you. Players can hurt you ... really do great damage to your self-esteem and happiness. Read the signs and exit the relationship immediately when you discover their lies or veiled truths before you get in too deep to pull away ... hanging on until the inevitable dispiriting end.

This Player who impaled me through my heart enjoyed a string of girlfriends, each unaware of the other. I surmise each believed that she was *the special one* in his life; each hoping that more commitment was sure to follow. I was one of them. He was so charming. I am sure he appeared to love each *so much* when with them ... at least he gave me that impression during the time he was together with me. He was a prime example of a man living in the moment. A typical Player, he loved the recurring thrills *his* women gave him ... knowing *he* controlled their hearts, their dreams, their thoughts and their bodies. Like a typical Player, just calling them gave him an adrenalin rush.

Players' intentions are not about pleasing you but about pleasing themselves ... about the emotional thrills they ride as they maneuver to bring someone's emotions under their control.

GLASBERGEN

"I'm not afraid of intimacy, as long as it's shallow, meaningless intimacy that doesn't reveal too much about me."

Gentlemen, you are also vulnerable. Certain aspects of a female Player's game will likely differ from those of a male Player. Her immediate motives might be the expensive things you can buy her and, likely, the exciting and exotic travel you can give her. As well as the longer term, lucrative divorce settlement. A female Player's *MOS ... mode of seduction ...* might be difficult to resist. If you deal with your suspicions early on, you will more quickly escape her determined grasp and recover from your emotional (and sexual) entrapment. Falling in love complicates recovery; nursing a broken heart takes an agonizingly long time. And generally after falling in love, attempts at decisive action and a quick dismissal only scar over deeper damage that might never be addressed.

ONE MORE TALE

Another Player I dated had me totally bamboozled. He was exciting and so full of fun ... when he wanted to be. I discovered after he ended our relationship that he had been communicating with other women the entire few months we were dating ... always looking for someone better while he appeared to be *exploring* a potentially serious relationship with me. I was stunned when I learned, on the Valentine's evening he spent with me at my home, he was messaging at least one other woman. I had bought filet mignon, prepared a beautiful dinner and executed the perfect Valentine's celebration. He was ecstatic and told me so. The evening was such a total success; he invited me on a trip to Italy in a few weeks. He also took time out during the evening to go on his phone a moment ... to text *her* and only he knows how many others.

What happens to the heart and the brain? You want to trust so much that you ignore the RED FLAGS. I have long said if you don't know why a partner is acting strangely and the relationship is falling apart for some unknown reason, usually another outside love interest is behind the scenes or an attempt to find or snare one is underway. I have experienced the scenario enough times to know my theory holds water.

Many Players appear needy. You, in turn, unknowingly feel you are the perfect nurturer. Right?! I thought I was, as well. Don't do it. Neediness usually translates into *their* need to enjoy yet another thrill ride topped off by constant affirmation of their desirability ... from more than one *innocent* ... while each is told she is the perfect *one*. Then comes the big *discard/disappearance* out of nowhere. They are gone ... until they return and want your affirmation once again.

Don't let a Player happen to you. You are now too informed to let their lies pass over your head. Fool you once ... maybe a misjudgment on your part. Fool you twice ... an uneasy feeling. Fool you three times ... cut off contact before they gain such control over you that you succumb again ... and destroy your peace of mind. Believe me, a broken heart really hurts. If you've been there, you know. It hurts as much at 40 and 50, or 60 and 70 as it did when you were in your teens, 20's and 30's. Perhaps more so, because you don't have decades and decades ahead to regroup and charge on. You are anxious to start to live your final chapters with a loving partner. Falling in love with a Player can be devastating; s/he will give you great heartache. Enough said ... heed my warning.

What deeply drives and motivates Players and Catfish is the subject of other books. Suffice to know, interaction with them is about *their issues*, deep and tightly secured motivators. A victim will never break through the bondage of those *issues* unless these perpetrators, these damaged human beings commit to serious counseling over a long period ... probably years. Don't go there. You can't really help. Too much baggage for you to sort through. They themselves must face those deep causes ... if they are even curable. Some Catfish and Players have little, if any hope, of being able to change. Others do not want to change. In any case, they are prisoners of their own device.

The latter stance was what I faced and refused to acknowledge until the passing of the one man I had loved so much. I learned that lesson too late. Step away and stay away. Tend to your own life issues, with professional help if necessary, for however long that recovery takes. Take time to explore new-to-you theories about how to enjoy a truly fulfilling life. For a while, *you* will be enough to handle. In time, you will be ready to full-heartedly enter Candyland once more.

I sometimes wonder if the other jolted saddened women finally cut their ties and left the men we unknowingly shared; if these Catfish and Players I knew so well (I thought) ever straightened themselves out, or if they went on to inflict more pain upon their wives, fiancées, girlfriends, and future unsuspecting conquests. Most likely the latter; for without serious, long-term counseling, these damaged individuals cannot rise out of patterns of self-serving and manipulative behaviors. Catfish and most Players have deep problems that need to be resolved, not just an *I'm sorry. I promise I won't do it again.* Come to recognize them and act accordingly.

BETRAYAL

I was sure a fiancée of one of these Catfish was legitimately going insane because of his betrayals. Catfish behaviors can do that to you: their charm, their declaration of love and their promises to change ... with the inevitable back-sliding. The sad and broken fiancée contacted me, one of his unsuspecting victims. She tried to stay in touch with me for a sympathetic ear and a shoulder to cry on while I was doing my own crying. I initially thought of myself as the victim, but swiftly grew to understand how much these Catfish hurt, maim and damage their ongoing relationship partners. I could do little for this particular wounded fiancée, as I could see she was an active participant in a dysfunctional relationship driven by his infidelities. Too much for me to handle; I was not the woman for the job. They both needed serious therapy. I remain mildly curious as to whether or not they received the professional guidance and counsel they needed to survive and move healthily beyond his Catfish compulsions.

BIG RED FLAGS: All Catfish (and Scammers) usually have a glowing profile, almost too good to be true, they quickly ask to communicate privately with you and they want to prematurely exchange their personal email addresses. Don't do it. Big trouble! Stay protected under the SINS umbrella until you meet and feel confident about your interesting someone.

Your encountering one or even a number of these evil individuals on SINS, is a matter of bad but not uncommon luck. You must develop a radar for them. They trawl on SINS for victims, as bottom feeders do for food ... only theirs is a dark business (Scammers) or a compulsion (Catfish and Players) that can't be denied. They fill their pockets and/or feed their illnesses and egos. True feelings for you never enter the equation.

You can fairly easily avert any harmful contact with Catfish as I now do, since I became aware of their presence on SINS. *Now that you know about them,* exercise your good sense to make a preemptive escape when you see the RED FLAGS. Be consistent and disciplined. Follow solid safety procedures to avoid suspected perpetrators altogether. Prepare yourself emotionally and logically for Scammers, Catfish and Players before you enter Candyland. Even though its shops offer all sorts goodies, a few baddies will appear. Apply your new awareness and all safety measures. They could be lifesavers.

"Nothing of me is original.
I am the combined effort of everyone I've ever known."
-Chuck Palahniuk-
--Invisible Monsters--

Chapter Twelve

Safety is paramount ....

Luck runs out, but safety is good for life.
Author Unknown[57]

Assurance of informational and personal safety is one of the most frequent concerns of potential SINS members ... and the most important task of all SINS sites and members. Stories abound about physical assaults and worse, murders, financial scams, etc. I cannot deny that such crimes exist; I know they do, but not to the extent that the public's taste for sensationalism demands to hear. Remember, SINS is a microcosm of the society we live in. That larger society itself seems heavily darkened by behaviors ranging from criminally stupid to heinously horrible. Prowlers, scammers, con men, players and cheaters were not created by the Internet. They have always existed and will continue to do so outside the cyber world. These predatorial types have just expanded their

---

[57] http://www.quotegarden.com/safety.html, last accessed August 12, 2014.

territory. You must be alert and cautious, be your own detective and enable your own precautionary diligence. Be a pre-emptive self-guardian. Aspects of your life may depend upon the cautionary actions you take.

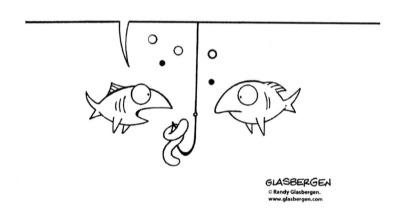

One important key to your safety is to maintain a discipline in all matters of your well-being … without becoming paranoid. Doing so will never hurt you and will ensure your SINS experiences will be safe and relaxed, while allowing for healthy communication and mutually satisfying interaction with the right people, similar security-minded and thoughtful members.

If you miss one or two dates because your caution has dampened the interplay, feel confident you will discover many rewarding opportunities awaiting you just around a sunny corner in Candyland. I encourage you to practice **SAFE**. Once more: This self-coined acronym neatly sums up your sure and simple approach to Singles Internet-dating: **S**afety, **A**ttitude, **F**un, **E**nthusiasm. If you enter SINS with **SAFE** in mind, you will have a secure and happy journey through Candyland. **S**afety procedures are paramount. **A**ttitude is *the game-changer;* without a forward-looking *attitude* you could have a very disappointing experience. **Fun** is in the enjoyment of your journey, one that should bring you the joy of a new partner as you exit. And, **Enthusiasm** is the fuel that propels you through.

The overriding element of your adventures in Candyland is your safety. Truly. Its importance cannot be underestimated; it must be your ever-active, over-arching priority. You have heard stories of unsavory characters prowling for connections on the Internet. These types do exist, but are not as prevalently as we are led to believe by publicized real and tragic incidents. Still, one unfortunate safety mishap and you could be quite unsettled or so traumatized that you do not allow yourself to further enjoy the flirtatious fun interactions that are genuine and innocent and so plentiful on the sites of SINS.

The vast majority of SINS members are just like you ... very credible sincere singles looking for a compatible companion and/or a romantic partner. The villainous ones are the odd exceptions. As I shared earlier, SINS is a reflection of society that focuses mainly on supporting single people looking for a partner or mate. It is a particular community of people heavily populated with similar single status and goals. No legally unavailable members should be on the traditional dating sites ... no 'Committeds' or 'Marrieds' with intentions to cheat, no members only online for sex or personal gain. In nearly every grouping of human beings the odd one will slip in. For those seeking other than companionship, affection, love and lasting commitment, other types of interactive dating sites do exist. [Some were mentioned in the earlier chapter on picking your sites.]

Despite all the security efforts of SINS sites no foolproof methods monitor SINS members' credentials even though these sites take their members' safety and security very seriously. Many SINS entities use fraud detection algorithms and employ living, breathing people who review every dating profile at the time of registration.

You can browse, connect, flirt and email with confidence. *Unless* you foolishly break some of the safety precautions recommended both in *Candyland S.I.N.S.* and on individual sites, your privacy and security are pretty much secured.

You must do your own preventative police work and you must do it well because these predators do spring up on mainstream sites ... your life or at minimum your financial, physical and mental health could be at stake if you do not closely monitor how your 'relationships' proceed. You can become a victim very quickly if you run into the wrong potential someone and are not perceptive and alert.

> *When you gamble with safety, you bet your life.*
> -Author Unknown-[58]

You would take extra special care where to invest your money, would you not? So it follows, your heart and your emotional wellbeing should be even more of a priority. You vet people proposing to invest your money and earn your trust ... do the same with your heart. Start from a position of responsible guardian of your affections. You must allow individuals wanting those affections to earn your trust because you will not blindly bestow it without reason. Doing so will likely prevent much heartbreak ... emotionally, physically and financially. Believe me.

Once again: The most important rule for your safety is: Withhold your trust and allow potential partners to earn it, at a rate with which *you* feel comfortable. Do not discard this very important rule! I have done so and still have regrets. I learned the hard way; I want to save you the same conceivable consequences.

---

[58] http://www.quotesdonkey.com/333-safety-quotes/15862-when-you-gamble-with-safety/, last accessed August 12, 2014.

To prevent most possible, if not all, problems when you navigate the meandering pathways of Candyland follow the excellent guidelines from respected sources set out below. Use their information as a trip planner for a safe and pleasant journey. To stick to a safety protocol requires a discipline that is sometimes very difficult to adhere to in matters of the heart, as I know. Always be aware you have no community or social acquaintance references for your new interest. You must be your own security guard.

Do not forget that SINS is populated with vulnerable members recovering from deaths, divorces and breakups and abandonments ... individuals who are perfect targets for predators ... whether for control, sex or money. Deceptive people know SINS offer perfect hunting grounds, so be more vigilant than you normally would be in your traditional communities. I cannot stress enough that you must be very cautious and not let your guard down until your new romantic interest progressively earns your trust.

Early in my SINS membership years I started dating from a position of trusting potential mates until they proved themselves otherwise. HUGE MISTAKE. I paid for it; I don't want you to have the same opportunity. Never give your heart away until you are confident your new romantic interest would not abuse your trust. Easy for me to say but, as I know, it is tough to do. I still have a problem following my own advice in that regard. So, I understand if you would as well.

The safest risk is the one you didn't take.
-Author Unknown-[59]

---

[59] http://www.quotesdonkey.com/333-safety-quotes/15928-the-safest-risk-is-the/, accessed August 12, 2014.

The following rules for financial safety have been gathered from very credible and broadly scoped sources. Pay attention and plan to follow their advice.

The Ontario Ministry of Consumer Services warns consumers to be diligent and cautious when engaging in financial transactions not in person. Some of the below tips may be helpful in preventing this type of fraud:

"Never use verification information provided by the other party engaged in the financial transaction. The address provided by the other party may be false and the phone number may be registered to a fictitious name. Many scammers use toll free phone numbers to add to the appearance of legitimacy. They use mailbox addresses that appear to be suites in well-known financial districts.

Conduct independent research prior to engaging in the transaction. Have you searched the names and addresses on the Internet for reports or complaints made against the company or person?

If you are using a bank, money transfer service or e-commerce service for payment contact them directly. Never use email links provided by the other party engaged in the transaction."[60]

The Ontario Ministry of Consumer Services also provides a series of very helpful lists presenting safety procedures to follow with regard to potential Scammers, both online and offline. The lists that address the top ten complaint sites are footnoted and linked herein. Do make checking them a priority. Become aware of all that

---

[60] Ontario Ministry of Government and Consumer Services, many warning lists and safety procedures to help you both online and offline, http://www.sse.gov. on.ca/mcs/en/Pages/Scams_romance_scams.aspx/, http://www.sse.gov.on.ca/mcs/en/Pages/Top_Ten_Complaints.aspx, accessed July 1, 2014.

you can do to become alert to signs of Scammers and, at the first signs, stay clear of them.

Also, most SINS sites post safety guidelines as part of a strong effort to protect their members from fraudulent activity. Be sure to read them and then read them again. You must endeavor to protect yourself. The following material is based on the excellent guidelines on OurTime.com, other online dating safety advice and my experience. The content is crucial for you to follow; make sure to adhere to these guidelines at all times when meeting new people online:

"NEVER send money to anyone online, especially by wire transfer. Wiring money is the same as cash in the mail: the sender has no routes of recourse against loss. Those who insist that people wire money to them, especially overseas, do so because reversing a transaction or tracing the money is nearly impossible. No matter how dire the financial emergency presented to you, do not send money in any form to strangers met online! In fact, be very sure to crosscheck the identity of someone supposedly known to you who asks you online to wire money, write a check, purchase a money order, give out your credit card number or your bank info.

Do the same when someone wants your SSN. Just say NO [61]. (Your telephone numbers and address may be available via public information records ... something you can do nothing about.)

---

[61] www.ourtime.com, http://www.ourtime.com/v3/datingtips, accessed July 1, 2014.

*"How could somebody steal my identity when
I still haven't figured out who I am?"*

More tips for dating online and offline are drawn from <u>www.
ourtime.com</u>. It is a leading site for the over-50 online dating
community. The material below is gleaned from their sage advice
and my experience:

*Guard your identity until you have created a proven level of trust.
Do not share while messaging or chatting online your life-specific
information ... your full name, phone numbers, place of employment,
any addresses, any identifying information. Be sociable, but be wary.*

*Remember, a false profile can be posted by anyone who wants to
appear as someone else, never mind commit identity theft. NEVER
post personal information in your profile or username that could be
used to trace you in either or both your every day and cyber worlds.*

*As to your online access information: Be cautious when employing
Wi-Fi or accessing your account from a public or shared computer.
And, be aware of others' line-of-sight when you are onscreen or
using a public access keypad. You do not want anyone to be able
to view or record any details of your personal information. If you*

share a computer you should disable the auto sign-in feature if you have initiated automatic log-in functions for your accounts.

Take advantage of the onsite email features that protect your identity until YOU choose to reveal it. Until you feel some measure of ease about your security and others' identity, maintain your real-world identity.

Use an indirect electronic route to you via a third-party, anonymous email address ... especially for dating purposes. Doing so adds another layer of safety. Instead of to your personal email address, have your SINS emails sent to a third-party address such as Yahoo. com, Gmail.com, Hotmail.com, etc.

Respect your instincts. If you feel unsafe or threatened, immediately drop contact and report behaviors that give you cause for concern. Should a contact pledge deep and abiding love after a few online chats or after the first meeting ... if you don't step away totally, proceed with caution.

Develop some non-manipulated mutuality online before you meet the other person offline. Use the tools available through dating sites such as www.ourtime.com that will protect your anonymity as you learn to know someone before you meet her or him in person. Keep a notebook or folder on your computer. Record details about this-new-to-you person that you can gather by using sources ... such as Internet searches, government resources and various databases. Consider a background check ... at your cost. However, because background checks may have glitches you can't rely fully on their results. ... They are not foolproof. All the dating sites do not perform background checks on their members for this and other reasons.

Discontinue contact with people whose answers are not clear-cut. If someone seems uneasy when you ask about various things and/or frequently talks in circles, cease contact. Watch for indications that may signal your contact is not single or is hiding something ... speaking in hushed tones, 'got to go now' and a hang up, vagueness rather than openness, meeting only at odd hours and not replying to direct questions.

Deflect potential future abuse. Block abusive users. Block members who express forms of abuse toward others, treat you in an abusive way or refer to others in an abusive way. Promptly report the behavior to your site administrator. Cut off communication immediately with anyone who pressures you ... for personal data of any kind that involves your identity, full name, and relevant numbers or financial information. Any profile page or message board offers quick action features to block and then report violations of terms of use as well as your concerns.

Terms of use violations include:

- *Use of the service by married people or minors*
- *Transmission of offensive or harassing emails/IMs*
- *Inappropriate behaviors after meeting in person*
- *Use of the site by criminals or other questionable characters*
- *Member registration or profiles that are fraudulent*
- *Solicitation**
- *Spam*
- *Infringement of Copyright*
- *Requests, Invitations, Pleas, Pressure for money or donations*

*Immediately notify them if another member sends you links to a pay-to-view site or includes instructions about how to call a 1-900 number. Also, immediately report any invitations to join other singles

sites, emails about modeling opportunities or attempts to sell any merchandise or service.[62]

I highly advise the following safety measures:

- NEVER GIVE MONEY TO ANYONE YOU MEET ONLINE.[63] The above wording is quite simple and succinct. This one sentence from www.SeniorPeopleMeet.com, another leading site for the mature daters, is the best advice to always keep in mind when communicating with strangers or new online contacts.
- Arrange your own mode of transportation to and from your first and early dates and never get into a vehicle alone with the new acquaintance.
- Do not let a new acquaintance know where you live or work. Suffice with telling them the general area you live in and what type of work you do.
- Speak in general terms concerning this information and that of your family.
- Try to avoid consuming alcohol on the first few dates. Imbibing does heighten reactions, lessen your inhibitions and lead to poor judgment calls.
- Always keep your drink within your sight.
- If you leave your drink alone, do not finish it.
- And do not leave your personal belongings unattended. Take them to the washroom with you.
- Keep your cellphone switched on at all times.
- Leave full contact information with trusted others for where you will be and with whom, along with the contact info of the person you are meeting.

---

[62] www.ourtime.com, http://www.ourtime.com/v3/datingtips, accessed July 1, 2014.

[63] http://www.SeniorPeopleMeet.com, http://www.seniorpeoplemeet.com/v3/datingtips, accessed July 1, 2014.

- If you two are about to transfer to another location, text or call someone to inform that person where you will be.
- You might even have your back-up person call you about an hour into the date to see how you are. A call can also give you a reason to cut the date short if it is a no-go.

Long-distance dates which require an overnight demand an additional layer of precautions. Never stay with a new potential partner ... no matter how practical and wonderful that person may seem. Just accepting such an arrangement can be wrongly interpreted and may put you in a difficult situation from which you might not easily extract yourself. (If I felt such anticipatory unease, I probably would not be traveling to this person, at least not early in our acquaintance. Everyone is different. You have to find your comfort levels.)

- Some advisors suggest you keep your hotel location confidential and place your valuables in the hotel safe.
- If you cannot afford your own room in a hotel, do not go until you can save your money to easily do so. Perhaps the other interested member is more financially comfortable and can prepay for your hotel stay or travel to your locale and be the one to take a room. Do not be afraid of giving offense. Your wellbeing is the overriding factor.

I follow the last policy above; my visiting suitors stay in a beautiful (but haunted!) bed and breakfast century home in my historical shipping Great Lakes town. One visitor in particular was a very fine man ... handsome, cultured, worldly, charming, and intelligent. A real gentleman. He would have preferred to stay at my place I am sure, but graciously accepted my rules. We had a wonderful three days' visit. Although we were not to become a romantic match, two years later we are very good friends who email and phone chat regularly. We had done our homework before we met; we knew we could become friends. So we have. You can develop relationships such as this, loose bonds which broaden and enhance your life. Rather than a life partnership, you and someone you meet will share and enjoy a lifelong friendship.

Back to budding online friendships. Most sites have wonderful messaging systems. They keep you completely anonymous. You can use their emails, chats, and audio; some offer visual interaction, as well. You need not switch to personal calls or meeting each other until you are ready ... or not. You are always in control *if* you consistently follow safety guidelines. You can cut off communication at any time with someone you feel bothered by. You can block that person and even report her or him to your site administration teams with one click to prevent that identity from harassing anyone else.

PLEASE do not become overly anxious due to the intensity of my cautions and warnings. I have been involved in SINS for many years and know online dating requires members to use common sense based on the safety guidelines presented here and elsewhere. As we conclude this very serious chapter, you are not only intensely forewarned but also fore-armed because you now know what to expect and what to do.

If you are careful in certain venues and situations in your daily life, you do not fear danger lurking in the shadows. I have spoken with many women who have that negative image, in regard to online involvements paralyzing them. It is such a shame to see them be prisoners of their fears. Enter Candyland armed with safety guidelines, a positive attitude and common sense based in what you are learning in *Candyland S.I.N.S*. Because you now know what to watch out for and what to do, you will be AOK. You will trust your instincts. You will not underestimate your gut feelings, which have likely served you well at some time in the past. Do not allow desperation or wishful thinking to compromise your sense of the best thing to do.

Safety doesn't happen by accident.
-Author Unknown-[64]

As a counterpoint to practicing continuous safety, always remember so many wonderful members are waiting in SINS to meet you. If you must pass one by, others wait ahead around the next curve in Candyland... for *you* to come along ... with warm smiles and open manners. Be assured you will meet some wonderful people. The great majority of SINS members are just like you ... looking for a special person to be part of their lives. Maintain the right *attitude* and enjoy the adventures that should come your way. You will most likely emerge with a wonderful new friend or two and a close companion or the *love of your life* strolling beside you.

---

[64] http://www.quotegarden.com/safety.html, accessed August 12, 2014.

Chapter Thirteen

Online Dating Etiquette

"I used to feel so alone in the city. All those gazillions of people and then me, on the outside. Because how do you meet a new person? I was very stunned by this for many years. And then I realized, you just say, "Hi." They may ignore you. Or you may marry them. And that possibility is worth that one word."
-Augusten Burroughs-

How you handle the subtleties of online dating can make or break you and totally affect outcomes at the different stages. Internet dating is about having many choices, a deep field of potential life partners. It is also about the process of eliminating the great majority of them to narrow down your selections. During that process, you are trying to save and savor the prime candidates and let the others move on. Those prime candidates are doing the same. Therefore, how you conduct yourself and whatever gives you the inside edge are important for you to make it to the finish line arm in arm with *the one*. Online dating etiquette savvy is important for you to have right from the starting line. We'll begin with a recap

What follows is a quite inclusive review of the previous chapters for those who are truly new to the SINS experience.

SINS make your journey through their sites quite simple. Their directions are clear and their many helpful articles enable you to not only technically navigate their sites but also help you deal with some of the inevitable bumps in Internet dating or any dating for that matter. For, much of the advice is similar to that one should follow in dating in one's own traditional communities.

The process begins by taking a free trial membership or joining one of a multitude of sites. You essentially set up your profile, read the matches the sites regularly send you, do your own searches, decide which members you find interesting and contact your choices through a myriad of clicks such as winks, flirts, favorites, virtual gifts and emails, etc. At the same time you will be receiving similar approaches. You will be kept busy!

If you do not have a photo in your profile you will be far less busy! Remember this. As you now know by this point, many members do not respond to contacts without photos. People simply do not want to spend the time to find out if a potential connection awaits behind the blank photo space. I never answer advances from someone without a profile photo. A blank space is not in the spirit of the game when other members have taken the time, energy and care to place photos on their profiles. They are sincere and deserve courtesy.

Do not become too hung up and uptight on every approach you receive or give, but give each one the attention it is due. I have noticed many members agonize over any perceived slight or criticism. Doing so destroys the intent and spirit of the advance. So often, something can be taken in more than one way. Prickly is not a warm character trait. Compliment the other member with a thank-you and by telling him or her you have interest in something in his or her profile. Most missteps or offenses are unintended, given by people who haven't dated in many, many years. They are a little rusty in the art of romantic pursuit. Give them leeway here. But, be sure you pay very close attention to their profiles ... what they say and what they don't say. Profiles are so very important; slowly read each one you select and then read it again for the implications of what is said and what is not said.

Be polite to the senders of each approach, say *thank you.* In other words, play nice. Honor their own search by mentioning or even complimenting something in their profiles. If you do not wish to engage in further contact, at least wish them well and good fortune in their ongoing search.

Dating online takes a good deal of thought, time and effort. Since most of you are seriously looking for a long-term relationship, it is important to give the search the attention it deserves ... and requires. Do so with respect, particularly because you are interacting with real people with feelings, most of whom are sincere very nice people. Please, never lose sight of that in your journey through Candyland. You must show other members the courtesy and kindness you expect to receive from them.

"When I agreed to have dinner with you, I accidentally hit 'reply to all' on the e-mail. Long story short, I'm now dating 112 people."

The SINS sites generally give you the option to set up custom search bundles for yourself using whatever criteria you choose ... gender, age, locale parameters, appearance, interests, background/ values, lifestyle, keywords, with or without pictures, etc. You have a multitude of options with which to begin your search for a special person in your life. However, the more restrictions you place on your wish list, the less likely many members will come close to meeting your criteria for an ideal partner. You decide how to fine-tune your parameters. Always remember your chances of success increase if you follow basic protocols. You are always in control, unless you break safety rules.

Internet dating protocols ... may seem like a boring term, but what it encompasses is important for you to know and follow for successful results. Your online dating set of protocols and how you conduct yourself and interact with other members really constitutes your philosophy of online dating. You should think about it before you begin. I have observed two basic approaches to online dating, initially casting your net wide and deep or casting a single line ... with a fishing pole ... under perfect conditions. Of course, variations lie within these two extremes.

Since dating choices are so wide and varied in SINS, some members like to sample a variety of members to test the solidity of their initial criteria for a new partner. You may want to open yourself to new people and experiences, as well. Perhaps you were too narrow-minded or conservative in your initial wish list? Within SINS you have the opportunity to test and expand that list and broaden your possibilities.

Other SINS members choose to date as few contacts as possible to find *the one*. They attempt to do their vetting via emails and phone. Then comes the initial interview meeting to learn if what they expect in their choice is a very close approximation of the person they hope will be *the one*. That mode works well for very busy people who do not have or want to spend the amount of time required for a round of coffee dates. But, this approach unfortunately eliminates some very good potential partners from their lists of choices.

Ladies, please feel comfortable contacting the males you see as possible mates. SINS is not a men's domain. In fact, men enjoy the attention and the opportunity to share the responsibility of finding a mate in this Candyland of possibilities. POF claims 36.7 percent of all long-term relationships on their site are the result of a female contacting a male.[65] So gals, get busy and pursue your dream match. Now!

Is the initial meeting an interview or an actual date? My style is somewhat a combination of both: to make the meeting a conscious interview with someone I have determined as a very strong possibility to mesh with me ... and a *real* date that allows for easy conversation.

---

[65] www.pof.com member entry page accessed June30, 2014.

But, members develop their own approaches and comfort zones. You will find yours after a couple of dates with each new *possible one*.

I have a friend who met a gem of a life partner through a coffee date. Her strategy was to meet with candidate after candidate who fulfilled her basic criteria. She considered these meetings as interviews for the possibility of planning actual dates with potential mates. The format made perfect sense to her, as it does to many other members. You never know what special person you might be eliminating too soon who does not strongly appeal to you in print or photos but shines in person. She went to over 100 coffee dates before she met the man who perfectly suited her.

Remember, in SINS you skip the more normal introductions made through social activities, work and friends. You lose the natural in-person filtering process which transpires before you actually go on a date. The coffee dates fulfilled some of that role for my friend. With carefully thought-through questions and honest responses to her dates' queries, she was able to determine whether potential existed for further exploration. It worked incredibly well for her ... it may work as well for you.

You are not really playing a game with Internet dating. But, the process is based in a procedural structure, as games are. Since real people engage themselves, you all play by the protocols ... do unto them as you would want for you. Do not intentionally hurt, disappoint or waste other members' time. Show them the authentic you in your profile; be considerate and trustworthy in all your interactions. A relationship built on lies will never work. Be truthful with your intentions; expect they be truthful with theirs.

Be sure to establish a separate email address for all your online dating correspondence. You can always close it and create another if you have poor judgment and give your private email out too soon, before you really know the person with whom you are becoming acquainted. Be careful giving information out too soon. I usually wait until I meet my choices and am comfortable with their expressed character. This stage may take another meeting or two. They typically say they understand, because I explain it is a general safety policy I follow, nothing personal. If they don't understand, they are not good long-term relationship material in my mind.

You don't need to respond to all the advances you receive, especially the generic greetings prepared by the sites. You will not have the time. The senders just click on ones they feel suit their interest and most likely are doing it for dozens, if not hundreds, of profiles. They do not expect you to answer if you are not interested. Respond to only those you want to give a closer look. Senders of generics understand if they do not hear from you, you are not interested. Also comes the question of whether they would prefer to be outright rejected by a response from you or just quietly left to pursue more receptive matches. I am sure most prefer silence for a response to their unsuccessful advances. Other appealing members are always waiting for them to approach.

If you are genuinely interested in the sender of a generic greeting, answer it. Such greetings are a mild-mannered way to initiate a connection with you, one the senders hope will develop into something. They may be shy … give them the benefit of a doubt if you like something about them and see a potential. But, I do think it is very respectful and almost morally mandatory to answer contact attempts personally written to you, if at all possible, even when you want no further involvement beyond that. Their personal reach out shows they are interested and hopeful enough to make the effort to really connect with you. Respond in a timely manner, as they are most likely waiting for your answer. Do not play games waiting a few days to answer personally written advances. Most likely these initial contacts will have moved on to other more enthusiastic members by then … the senders with whom you really do want to pursue contact could be gone. So, do not delay responding when possible.

Do not be shy to answer advances. That is why you are a member of SINS … to be a participator, not a spectator! If you reject some contact attempts, you have many gracious ways to do so, even if you must kindly fib a bit to save face for them. You may say that you are starting to explore a new relationship and you only date one person at a time. Or, the timing might be bad because of other obligations filling your calendar at the moment. Or, you are just taking a break from dating for a while. All have frankly been the case in the past for me … and can be true for anyone, including the ones you approach. The process is not all about you.

It is tough to tell senders they are not a match without hurting them. Some sites have a button that responds with "Thanks, but no thanks." I prefer a short note maybe using one of the reasons above but no detailed explanations why we are not a match. I then wish them good luck in their search. I usually add something like, "So many great gals are on the site. I hope you and a special someone find each other."

Do put your better self in play … don't be hurtful as you move on. And, do not hurt yourself. Never must you feel guilty about rejecting seemingly nice persons; know that they most probably will meet someone special if they have realistic expectations.

You can see which members have viewed your profile right up to the minute. They took the time to stop and consider you. Be proactive. If a few interest you, email them. You can say something along the lines of *"I see that you have visited my page; I find your profile of interest, as well, and would enjoy more conversation with you. If you are interested, I look forward to hearing from you."* Short and simple. I bet you receive a good number of responses … not from all your follow-ups but from many of them. They liked you enough to have taken a close look once and perhaps even have read your profile. They may not have followed up with a contact if they decided you were out of their league, were in a temporary search or dating burnout when stopping by your site, felt overwhelmed by so many choices or life became complicated, etc. Help them along if you are interested … make contact!

Since you are not on an adult niche site, never mention anything sexual or ask members for pictures that show their bodies. They should include body shots in their profiles. If they do not, ask to exchange more photos and you may receive a body shot in the group to help you determine whether these contacts are close to your ideal body type. Never say anything in an email that you would not say to their faces. Also, never bombard them with emails when they have not responded in a reasonable time and continue not to respond. Read their likely silent message … they are not interested. Numerous repeated emails is *email stalking*. Most members will find such continuing contact attempts aggravating; some will find it frightening. You will achieve the opposite of your intent. Members could block you from accessing their site altogether *or* even report you to the site administrators. I have done so a few times for this very reason.

Always be aware that online dating is an elimination process and usually narrows down to just two people sincerely exploring the possibility of a serious relationship. Be prepared for some rejection. It is inevitable. In return, do not give an angry or nasty response. Exit gracefully. You cannot suit every person you contact, just as every person who approaches you will not suit you, as well. Plus, members may have other reasons to not pursue anything with you. The dropped connection is not all about you. Again, all sorts of reasons may lurk in the background. The drop could be due to overwhelming family obligations, a returning spouse, overriding work commitments, settling on an interest, too long a distance, etc. I have experienced them all ... on both the giving and receiving ends of these reasons. Believe them and move on. So many more wonderful SINS members are waiting to meet you.

It is best to keep your early/pre-coffee date emails brief, polite, interesting and usually under 100 words. Make the reader curious to hear more and get back to you. Compliments are always nice, as is a reference to a hobby or sport the reader had mentioned. Doing so shows you really read the profile and you may possibly have something in common.

Many new members make the mistake of telling their life stories in the initial emails. No matter how glowing your life was and/or is, the too-early life story can be a turnoff and even reek of desperation to be accepted. Once again, never give personal contact information to your new romantic interest, such as your last name, your phone numbers, address, where you work, etc. The time will come for exchanging personal data when you know each other better and sharing that would be appropriate. If I am asked directly for such information, I reply my policy is to wait until I know my dates better. My non-disclosure is not directed strictly to them.

Always check your emails before you send them. They are an important first impression of you. You do not want to be rejected because of poor grammar, punctuation, spelling or nonsensical sentences. Sorry, but it does happen frequently. I've done it! Remember, this is an elimination process. Write a friendly greeting and sign-off. I begin with the Username (or true name if we are further along) in the greeting and usually signoff with "Joan on a beautiful day on the bay". The descriptive is friendly and sets a picture of me in their minds. You might try a similar sign-off pertaining to something about you, such as " Sally in the city" or "Jim on the road again" ... better to use just your first name if you cannot make up an appropriate sign-off. Try to send a few each day. You cannot rely on one big catch! The members with whom you choose to communicate are likely sending and receiving other emails, as well. Engage in this online dating process the way the successful daters do. Play the field, carefully narrowing it down to *the special one* for you. You have so many possibilities awaiting you.

After you have reached out but do not receive responses within a week from recipients of your new or follow-up emails, give them the benefit of the doubt. Once again, one or more of the aforementioned reasons ... and others ... could be in play. Or, silence could just indicate no interest. After two or so weeks, if the members are still on your mind, make one more try. Send a brief email stating you wanted to touch base and still would enjoy hearing from them. If this approach yields no reply, move on.

Timing *is* sometimes everything. It is very important when meeting someone. I have a friend who had enjoyed early promising SINS-based email conversations with her potential romantic interest; he suddenly dropped off the face of the earth. A year later she saw him back on the same SINS site. She did a friendly follow-up email. It is now seven years later; they have been happily living together the last five of them! Timing is everything. Do not be afraid to initiate contact or to follow up.

Some SINS members go quickly from emails to instant messaging or to face-to-face dates. I highly recommend at least one live, telephone conversation before you make a first date. You can tell so much more and connect better in a live conversation than you can in multiple emails or live chats. I suggest three to five email exchanges are enough to move to the next level of communication. The practice of having at least one voice conversation before meeting has saved me from a few disasters ... and much time. Suitors can say they are anyone with any background in an email. When they speak with you, you can develop a better grasp of whether they are who they say they are. And, whether or not they might be a little crazy. Keep your antennae up for RED FLAGS. This is the most important stage in which to weed out the Catfish & Players.

With one prospective date, I engaged in a telephone conversation during which he asked me to take some pills from Canada into the U.S. for him, as he had a small natural vitamins company over the border in a near-by state. He felt I would have an easy time, since I am a dual citizen of Canada and the U.S. He said, "I can really use you." He sure could *use me!* I couldn't hang up fast enough.

He was a prime example of being okay looking, having an impressive profile and writing well; I needed to hear him tell some of his story before I realized he was not the kind of person I wanted to know. He followed up my polite *rejection* email to him with the only poisonous email I have ever received in all my years in online dating. I blocked him ... as you can do if you find someone with whom you don't want to communicate further. This man would have been someone with hidden agendas and a dangerous temper. You must be careful. Always keep your antennae up looking for RED FLAGS.

When you go from emails to phone conversations, the normal protocol is for the man to ask the woman to call him. He quite often initiates this stage by asking in an email if she would like his phone number in order to call him. She can agree or decline. If he receives a positive reply, he then shares his number with her so she can move to the next stage ...telephone contact. She does just that, and for the first few calls she engages in a security conscious way by first blocking her phone number before she keys in his number. After she picks up/activates her phone, she keys in *67 followed by his phone number. The call will ring through to the contact with Caller Unknown displayed on his phone instead of her name and/ or number. She is thereby protected from any harassing return calls. In order to protect herself, she should keep contact in this way until they meet and she feels comfortable enough to give her phone number ... likely after a couple of real dates.

Both parties may also ask each other for private email addresses. If they wish to share these before they meet, they should only give the email addresses they have established for online dating. Each always acts in a way that will not to compromise their individual privacy and safety.

When you make that first date, arrange for a public place with plenty of people around. Always give a friend or relative your detailed plans, including whom you are meeting and where, along with the date's contact information. Drive to and from your meeting separately. Some women park their cars at a distance or around a corner where the dates cannot see their license plates. NEVER get into a car with a man until you have met with him enough to feel comfortable about placing yourself in what could be a vulnerable situation. He should understand and accept your caution. If he does not, I say again, move on. He is not relationship material.

A short meeting of about an hour is usually recommended, but I must say ... if you have done your homework well ... you may want to stay on and chat longer if the feeling is mutual. A magical moment happens when you two have clicked ... when you both are fascinated by everything the other has to say and when the chemistry is right. It can happen. That *click* has happened to me a few times and it is special ... something to strive for. And, to always remember.

Other times, that first meeting may not be stellar. The immediate chemistry might not be tangible, but many things are right about the other person ... enough mutuality to build on. Allow for the fact that most SINS members are nervous on the first meeting and may not shine as they might when they are relaxed. You can help yourself with this common anxiety by being genuine and honest in your profile and communications. It's the best way to enjoy your SINS experience ... both for you and your dates.

If you feel some potential could blossom, suggest to your date another meeting. Do so either on the spot or by email. I prefer email unless encouraging sparks are flying and it is obvious you both would like to see each other again. If the other person does not wish to do so, try not to be offended. You two are in the very earliest stage of face-to-face. Be gracious about the decision. Any pains of rejection should not last long because you have others you are communicating with or dating or you will be moving on to new searches and new contacting.

> *"Rejection, though—*
> *it could make the loss of someone*
> *you weren't even that crazy about*
> *feel gut wrenching and world ending."*
> -Deb Caletti-
> --*The Secret Life of Prince Charming*--

Sometimes the person asks on the spot for another date, so just in case be prepared with a refusal response. It can be awkward if you do not want to try for a second date. Although unfortunate, it is just an uncomfortable moment ... you both will survive it. I usually say something like: *"Thank you for making the effort to meet me. Although perhaps neither one of us truly feels a strong need to continue, I always think of how it makes us a bit wiser in what we are looking for. It has been a pleasure meeting you. We must realize Internet dating is not as simple as one initially thinks. It is as diverse and complex as the people on the sites. You are a great person who will meet someone special soon; there are so many wonderful members. I wish you all the best."* You may have a better way to ease yourself out of this awkward situation. Do it and move on.

"I prefer online dating. Deleting someone with one click is less exhausting than a long and painful breakup!"

I usually follow up a successful first meeting with a short email the next day telling them it was a pleasure to meet them and thanking them for traveling out of their way, as I live a couple of hours north of the city and not near too many of my suitors. If I would like to see them again and it had not been discussed, I open up the possibility by stating so. Simply, that it would be fun to meet again if we both feel the same and can arrange it. If you are phoning to follow up, wait just a couple of days so you do not appear desperate. Sometimes both parties are too nervous on the first date to broach the subject of a second date, so attempt it by email or phone if you are interested.

If you are not interested, you may still want to email a thank you to the other person for taking the opportunity to meet and to wish him or her luck in further searching. An amicable parting allows each of you to keep the other in mind if you have friends ... or meet others through the Candyland process ... who might be more suitable for such a match. Because finding the right partner online can be a complicated process do not worry if you strike out a few times ... or more. The search for the love of your life generally takes time, effort, and more than the appearance on a silver platter. If you realize the futility of continuing to pursue anything further early in an acquaintance, best speak frankly but gently about it.

For you both, all is certainly not lost. Your good news is many more potential partners await you on the sites. When I go onto POF (Plenty of Fish) I notice consistently close to 500,000 members are online looking at any one time. And, that is just one site ... all age groups. Surely you could find someone among them who is compatible with you! Your chances are certainly greater there than walking down your Main Street or standing in your bank line or having dinner at your favorite restaurant, etc. And, if you did meet intriguing individuals in such places, do you think they would fit the criteria that you have now given so much thought to and filtered in your searches? Do you get the drift? Don't be discouraged if you must move on. Continue your search in SINS. You just haven't met the right one yet. Relax and enjoy the process ... so much fun can be had on some of those *interview* dates.

Most members initially date a few people simultaneously online and offline, narrowing their selected pool down slowly until ready to commit to an exclusive exploratory relationship. Even though you are a one-partner person, pursuing one individual at a time can come back to hurt you, if the early relationship stage you are exploring with only one person does not work out. You must then start all over again interacting with other members; going through the steps ... contacts, emails, phone calls, first meetings, etc. The smartest procedure is to date a few members for a while until one stands out as the most mutually compatible with you. Then, focus on each other. Another situation to face at this stage is when to become intimate and have sex. [More on *this* subject soon.]

When you find your perfect mate a time will come when you both mutually agree to remove yourselves from the SINS websites and from dating others to focus on furthering your long-term partnering potential. The logic is so simple. It's tough, if not impossible, to grow a relationship when other dating partners are in the background, a lineup sitting on the bench. It is difficult to play a sincere committed role in someone's life when others are auditioning for your part. You may feel diminished. Even if not, prepare to move on.

"The women in your dreams kept me awake all night, chasing the men in my dreams!"

If one potential partner balks at removing his or her profile it is a clear message the readiness to commit is not at hand and/or a huge ego enjoys affirmation from many sources. The very same happened to me while writing *Candyland S.I.N.S.* How could I not see what was to follow? Me, a now-Seasoned Mature online dater ... it must have been wishful thinking and trying to be patient with this three-month rollercoaster relationship. I did not see the big RED FLAG as his profile remained live on the site where we met ... as he happily flew away, traveling around the world for a few months without a thought of us as a couple. I had helped him to prepare for the trip until the day before he left ... I was by his side with his packing, book selections and travel presents ... all at his request. Like a loving wife. He liked my company and my help, but he obviously wasn't where I was in our relationship.

> *"I really wish I was less of a thinking man*
> *and more of a fool not afraid of rejection."*
> -Billy Joel-

A profile that remains on one or more SINS sites sends signals out to those dating communities that someone is still available. This is not a good thing for a partner who is ready, expecting to move on to the next stage of the relationship. It is the *big talk* time. Good luck. It is a difficult one to handle correctly. The real challenge is not merely about your profiles being removed from the SINS sites; it is really about where you both are in your relationship and what commitment issues each has. It is a major juncture. Be prepared ... you may have to move on.

© Randy Glasbergen
glasbergen.com

"Are you my knight and in shining armor or just another guy with intimacy issues?"

Committing to exclusivity is very complex and must be addressed delicately; or you can lose ground or even the whole connection. Relationship coach advice may needed ... or, perhaps, my next book. As you cannot wait for that, I recommend a few of the following online relationship coaches who I have found very helpful throughout my dating and relationship experiences. They offer dating programs for males and females at various levels and costs, also excellent email newsletters gratis from which you can learn so much for free.

MiMi Tanner: www.mimitanner.com
Michael Fiore: www.digitalromanceinc.com
Nick Bastion: www.nickbastion.com
Christian Carter: www.catchhimandkeephim.com
Bob Grant: www.relationshipheadquarters.com
Emily McKay: www.clickwithhim.com/
Scot McKay: www.deservewhatyouwant.com/
Mirabelle Summers: www.meetyoursweet.com/

Or, google/search *relationship coach online* on your search engines to find others.

> *Sex relieves tension—love causes it.*
> -Woody Allen-

If you decide to break off at this stage, after a period of some level of intimacy, try to be brave and do so face-to-face. It can be difficult, but do it cleanly and kindly ... if possible. Your partner and you deserve that respect. If you two have shared just a few dates that were not leading anywhere, an email goodbye is fine. Your relationship began with an email, did not go much beyond that, and can end with a gentle goodbye and good wishes for the other's future. Word it carefully and consider his or her feelings at all times. Also, you might offer that person two options for true closure. Ask if he or she feels a need to clarify things. If so, would a conversation by phone or one in person be better ... if you both can handle such a discussion. Many would prefer to deal with a break-up privately at an early stage rather than deal with rejection in front of you.

In the happy event that you both decide to take your profiles off SINS, away from its unnecessary interference in order to pursue deepening your commitment, you can move forward in your exclusive relationship in order to further your close and special connection, to perhaps move into *love.* You are well on your way to achieving the goal with which you set out when entering *Candyland S.I.N.S.*

Congratulations ... to you both.

Chapter Fourteen

First Date ... and beyond

Will the last pieces of the puzzle fit?
Fit to be **Tied**?!

Seventy percent of success is showing up.
-Woody Allen- [66]

While this quote applies to such matters as being in the right place at the right time, etc., far more is involved in being successful in the dating world than just showing up ... especially on those important first dates. You want your *first date* and every following initial date to become your *last first date.* A successful first date requires preparation, not a dash in and out, greet and meet for five minutes at the local coffee shop for a quick cup of coffee and a speedy once-over. True coffee dates are acceptable and financially more

---

[66] Woody Allen, www.brainyquote.com, http://www.brainyquote.com/quotes/ authors/w/woody_allen.html#IktcCr5fDawHI4sY.99, accessed July 1, 2014.

practical if you are arranging several new partner possibilities within a short span of time; but, respect the occasion and each person. If a only a sip or two of coffee and a quick dash off does happen to you, is that person likely the one with whom you want to start an extended online and offline relationship? Be happy to offer a so long and farewell. Any friendship or relationship should begin with and end with respect.

My very first SINS date was memorable ... he ran away when he saw me. I saw him dash from the coffee shop and jump into his car as I approached. Eight years later he is still searching for a partner on SINS. Hmmm ... but then, so am I! Another *first date* made a second *first date* with me two years apart. He seemed to have a poor memory. For both dates, he cancelled a few hours before we were to meet because he had a last minute call from his mother to take his father to an almost forgotten appointment ... the same excuse both times. You have just encountered two examples of cold feet from grown men running well-established businesses. You cannot imagine how anxious some members become on those first dates. Be prepared and be forgiving ... of them and yourself. Those early first dates with potential romance in mind can be quite intimidating ... as some of you enter the dating scene after a substantial number of years.

You should be appreciative of someone who has taken the time to plan and commit to a *first date* that is convenient and safe for you both. Anticipate the meeting with sincere light-heartedness although the meeting has serious implications. Arrive on time dressed to impress in a low-key way. You have done your homework and possibly will want this to go farther. Ideally, you will pay each other respect and not pre-judge by a first glance or the first few minutes. Arrive with an open mind and an open heart; allow your dates time to show you who they really are. Expect they will respond with the same courtesy.

With me it's always about first impressions ...
-Billy Zane- [67]

Where to go on that *first date*? Most advice recommends just a coffee, a glass of wine or a light beverage, so you may relatively quickly end what could be an agonizing, seemingly endless couple of hours with someone you determined early on you never want to see again. So, plan something casual that you can conclude at any time you feel has been enough yet is respectful.

It seems to be a universal that the place and activity do not really matter. These details never make-or-break the success of your mini-date. It really is about people meeting. Here is one of the best ideas I have seen. The source is an article on Match.com about unusual first dates.[68] The unique first-date activity? Going to a planetarium. Replace that destination with any activity for which you wait in line and, so, have a chance to talk, get to know each other and experience some physical closeness. How romantic ... looking at stars. Along that line, my second date with someone who became very special was going to a themed photography exhibit at an art gallery. That venue proved to be the just right for us because it allowed us to share some of our tastes in art and to meander chatting lightly about our lives while experiencing physical closeness.

Be authentic, but be on your best behavior. Do not act too nonchalantly and disregard your manners. Gentlemen, tend to the doors and pull the chair back for the ladies. Ladies, say *Thank you.* etc. Although it may have been a while since you dated, good

---

[67] Billy Zane, www.brainyquote.com, http://www.brainyquote.com/quotes/keywords/first_impressions.html - 5va2UQUsvQZ3i0ck.99, accessed July 1, 2014.

[68] Laura Schaefer, www.match.com, http://www.match.com/magazine/article/12828/First-Dates-Men-Expected-To-Hate-But-Loved/, accessed July 1, 2014.

manners have not gone out of style; they are noted and appreciated. One no-no: Never flirt with anyone else while you are together. Such interaction is very rude and disrespectful. And, hide your electronic devices. You could be setting up a roadblock to romance right there on the table. Keep your gizmos out of sight but easily accessible for safety reasons. Very few of us are so important that we have to be available every hour of each day. Try to make those *first dates* distraction free. Focus on your date ... your person of interest will probably return the favor.

I had another notable *first date* with a new man who was aware I was going out for the first time after surgery requiring many stitches. The first thing this 6'2" husky man did when we met was lean on me to walk because he had hurt his foot that day playing golf ... RED FLAG!

Let's consider wardrobe and appearance. Ladies: Do not dress too sexily. Doing so sends the wrong message. I think everyone agrees that most men have vivid enough imaginations when it comes to sex, so allow them to work them. What they imagine most likely is better than any provocative clothing you may wear. Most women have their own style. For the *first date* make it casual and classy within your normal taste ... and appear how you presented yourself in your photographs. Wear something striking but not showy. Feel comfortable in what you have chosen ... do not wear a favorite outfit now too tight and gaping when you sit. I've done it ... not a good feeling when you are trying to impress. If you didn't have make-up on in your photos don't go heavy with it on your first date ... if at all. He liked what he saw on your profile. Stick with it. Your best accessory is your smile ... you don't need much jewelry when you flash your smile.

Men: You have not been forgotten. Some of you may live alone and not regularly keep up your appearance ... just not high on your priority list. Well, it should be when you go out on those important first dates. First impressions do count. Be neat, clean and current in your style. Though you may dress traditionally, do not wear something that has been kicking around in your closet for 10 years. Even in the dark, luster fades away.

Some of you present yourselves in fine casual and dressy casual fashion ... I am happy for you and for those in your lives. Others of you may need a nudge or two ... especially if you have been sitting on a shelf with the elf for a while. If you've lived alone for a bit, you may usually dress down ... spiff and polish not part of your daily routine. They should be when go to your *first dates and first meets,* especially. First and early impressions do count.

Let's take it from the top. In addition to a pleasant, easy smile and genial manner you want to present a you that is clean and crisp (as in streamlined). Present a self that looks maintained. Invest regularly in hair and mustache trims. A first date one week does not benefit from a hair trim the week after. (Check the ear and nose hairs, too.) If you enjoy after-shave, just go lightly with it to start. Later on, this item might become more-or-less negotiable. Regular use of a mouthwash that lightens the teeth is a pretty solid small investment. Nails, anyone? The cleaner and more smoothly-edged the better. Do you need to aim for male model twin of the year? Of course not.

Now, on to clothes. Don't dress too sexily! Spruced–up casual is fine. For most guys, a dress shirt, patterned or plain, with an open neck collar is all-round best. If the weather is warmish, roll up the sleeves. For now you can diss the tie. Fresh dress jeans or slacks? If the weather is coolish consider a sports jacket (as opposed to a suit jacket). The right kind of sports jacket can look as terrific with a pair of nice jeans as it would with dress slacks. If you don't have an up-to-date one in your closet, now may be the time to bring one into your life. Clothing stashed away can look lifeless. As to the feet: Perhaps dressier sneakers, casual oxfords, boaters? This complete look is called 'dress casual'... you can go just about anywhere with it if you add (gasp) a tie.

The unadorned usual you and high-soled motorcycle boots or trail clompers can work fine ... later.

For now, make the effort! First meets and dates are special occasions ... every time. Special occasions call for something extra. You might be happy with the guy you see in the mirror! Even *authentic* needs a dust- off and a polish-up every now and then. What better reason than in anticipation of first dates?

Also: As a relationship progresses, be alert. Sort of touch base before some doings. Sometimes a guy's version of agreed-upon casual is 180 degrees of separation out from a gal's. You did not know that!?!

WHETHER GAL OR GUY

Make sure you have your facts straight. I usually save a profile in a folder on my computer when we start to communicate, then print it off and take notes on it when we reach the phone call stage. I read my notes over before we meet. How awkward and even insulting when a date confuses you with another s/he has lined up. Definitely not a first-date enhancer. And, try to mention a couple of things that you found interesting in his or her profile. S/he will be impressed that you really read it through and did not just look at the photos.

Relax and feel as confident as you possibly can. After all, you both have done your vetting and should be looking forward with much anticipation to that important first meeting with each other. A positive frame of mind ... is a great start, the best start! Will the last piece of the puzzle fit ... the one you could not test through emails and phone calls? Will that all-important chemistry bubble up inside of each of you that so many speak of in their profiles and yearn for in life?

Suspend judgment as long as you can in the meeting. Doing so will give you more opportunity for a successful outcome. Some people are shy and need time to shine. Some are humble and slow to reveal inner qualities and share some of their interesting talents. Look and listen with an open mind and hope they will do the same.

This is serious business. Each person could be *the one* you have been searching for. Give this get-together, one you both have planned for, your full attention. You each have work to do, asking the right questions and listening to answers. What they tell you and what they don't, are equally important. Listen carefully to these people, to their answers and to their blanks. Remember those blanks and try to fill them in as you move along.

211

And above all, maintain a sense of humor. A ready appreciation of the humor in things is one of the main traits I see requested in the wish lists for a prospective partner. Yes, a sense of humor ... and a climate of all-around respect. They should be right up front and present on your first dates. Along with that positive *attitude* ... and a readiness to smile.

> *When someone **shows** you who they are,*
> *believe them the first time.*[69]
> -Maya Angelou-

I cannot stress enough that from the get-go you always must be your authentic self ... bearing in mind you know you are not perfect and are making ongoing efforts to improve aspects of yourself and your life. Otherwise, if you present a false picture of who you are and plan to continue to be, you are setting the framework for big disappointments time and again for you and your dates. A potential mate will eventually discover who you really are and vice versa; the true you could reveal itself too late for one or both of you to redeem the situation. One of you will sadly find that you have given your heart to a stranger, someone who cannot live within another persona for all his or her life. One of you will walk away or, even worse, will stay! One of you will remain with someone, a stranger whom you had never bargained for when you committed to your relationship. Not what you wanted for your next hurrah, is it? Be truthful and authentic and encourage any potential mate to be the same. You want the final relationship in your lives to be the best it can be. A great *next act*.

Arrive at your date locale expecting a successful outcome to all your preparation. The Law of Attraction states you will attract what you project. Extend a positive attitude and expect you will receive the same in response. Smile ... a sincere smile. The same

---

[69] Maya Angelou, www.brainyquote.com,
http://www.brainyquote.com/quotes/authors/m/maya_angelou.html - mUVObx2dZXARW6HB.99, accessed July 1, 2014.

should come to you. Many people find it tough to be unhappy and displeased with someone who is smiling. Repeat this process for every date. You will find many potential partners lose their self-consciousness and tenseness as they bounce your positive vibes right back at you.

As your series of first meets and greets proceeds you may be pleasantly surprised that eventually you must fine-tune your criteria to keep whittling down so many prospects ... picky, picky, picky. ;-D Next up: the elimination rounds ... just as in many competitions. Sometimes you do the eliminating and sometimes *they* do it. Be prepared for feelings of rejection. Remember the goal is to arrive at the final match with one loving partner. Only two of you can play on the court in that final ... one from each side of the dating equation who has met his/her match. Game over!! Winners declared as *tied.* Hopefully forever and however they both so choose to lead the rest of their lives together.

What you've just read is the ideal scenario and the most ideal conclusion to a search. Can the same happen for you? Of course. But, you must operate within a frame of mind that will accept new partners into your life, as well. Many of us have mental or emotional blocks that we may be not aware of. Possibly we are still residually in love with an ex or we cannot imagine anyone filling our deceased partner's place ... even though we want and are eagerly trying to make that very thing happen.

Or, deep down we do not feel worthy enough to enjoy a totally loving and fulfilling relationship. Perhaps we are our own saboteurs of the good prospective matches we find in SINS. We could be the real problem, not the caliber of the people we are meeting. Here may be one reason we are alone at this time in our lives, even though we are told we are excellent relationship material ... good-enough looking, loving, caring, smart, talented, fun to be with, good values, etc.

If you are struggling with why *it just isn't happening for you*, objective self-examination, some appropriate topical reading and/or a good therapist may help free you of hidden chains. And remember, if you struggle with one of *your* mental *saboteurs* on your dates, your feelings of rejection could be very unfounded ... your dates may have eliminated you because of *their own* issues, not your self-perceived inadequacies.

Some painful dates are inevitable; they can only be endured ... politely. As the old saying goes, "You have to kiss a lot of frogs before you meet your prince." In practice, you do not have to kiss them. But, you might have to sit through some boring conversations and grin and bear them, knowing that the first-meet date will not go anywhere. Sometimes our vetting in emails and on the phone is not enough to catch the flaws. Or, everything about your date is as you expected but you sense no chemistry. This failure to launch has happened to me a few times. Always remember that your dates deserve respect; give them an appropriate amount of time to try to connect. You are not out to destroy anyone's self-esteem just because you are not interested in him or her. Your basic human values should prevail.

You will meet some opportunists looking for a free ride or, at the very least, seeking the 'security' that has evaded them or been lost along life's way. Who are we to judge why? But, we do have the right to offer, accept or deny sharing our comfortable life situation and security with another. You must be sure very early on that your potential partners are pursuing a relationship with you for love, not just money or security. That assurance is a big and important topic you should explore with further reading or conversations with friends and financial advisors.

You are in a vulnerable position having been left alone in a society that does not necessarily welcome you with open arms. You could be quite lonely or give the impression of being so. Predators ... Catfish, Players, and Scammers are drawn to such people and rely upon their vulnerability. You must thoroughly vet possible partners.

One example of not thoroughly vetting a potential partner before you engage your heart was an experience of a wonderful man, a widower whom I dated. He discovered a woman he had met online who worked at a financial institution had used her position to check into his accounts and financial status. Luckily, he had an alert and trusted account manager who delicately asked him if he was considering changing institutions, as a competitor was quietly making inquiries about my friend's accounts. After some cross-checking my friend was smart and strong enough to cut the relationship immediately, even though he was entirely smitten with the woman. Again, guard your heart as you guard your money ... they may become hopelessly and painfully entwined.

Another instance of poor vetting was my first date with Jim. He was attractive, active and a personality full of life, but I soon realized in our conversation that the farm with all the acreage he said he was living on was in fact owned by a woman for whom he did odd jobs. He actually lived in the barn. He appeared anxious to find another similar situation where he could hang his hat. That certainly wasn't going to be my place. I couldn't end that *first date* fast enough. I stayed and listened politely, but I knew a second date would never happen. He did not meet some of my basic criteria of established stability and ability to maintain himself ... you may have very different criteria.

Criteria-matching reinforces what make SINS such an important tool when you are looking for a partner. Its large membership pool vastly increases the chances to meet candidates for your *wish list* and to find that one match right for you. The SINS collective memberships form a pool unrivaled by your circle of friends and your various communities. Almost 50 percent of Singles have tried online dating (of 107 million Singles in the U.S.).[70] If you can't find your mate in Candyland, you are most likely not going to find him or her anywhere ... unless fate and a version of 'some enchanted evening' appear.

My previous example of a disastrous first date with the country gentleman proves the wisdom of planning a short but focused first meeting over coffee, etc. If interest is mutual and the sparks of magic begin, you can extend the length of the date and/or make plans for a second date soon to follow. I went out with a man who shared with me his experience on a first date when he was new to online dating. He had naively planned a golf game for his first get-to-know-each other meet. He and she both were avid golfers; their phone calls showed such promise. Those 18 holes of golf? The longest in his life. As soon as he met her he knew he had no interest ... he had to endure 4.5 more hours of being pleasant while

---

[70] www.Match.com, http://match.mediaroom.com/index.php?s=30440, Match Fact Sheet 2014, accessed June 30, 2014.

avoiding any behavior that would encourage her. She was obviously keen on him. Save the lengthy golf game and/or similar outing for a later date, after you both know that you enjoy each other's company and want to explore more time together sharing a mutual interest.

Another man whom I met for a first date had posted a great profile. He stated he spent his summers on his sailboat in the northern lakes of Ontario and wintered in Arizona. He owned a couple of properties in Arizona. The "properties" turned out to be one small rental home ... a home I saw in reviews online in which a renter stated when the family arrived they found the property filthy *and* a dead rat floating in the pool. As I learned from my date at lunch, his boat was his single real residence ... for summers only. In winter he lived with his daughter and her nine cats in a rented house in Arizona.

I believe he lived, as well, in his truck. When he took me to see his artwork ... made of tumbleweed painted in gaudy colors ... I also saw his truck loaded like a hoarder's home. This person was someone I had vetted by phone and for whom I thought a full lunch date was warranted. He was warm and funny, well-spoken, good-looking, and had created a profile that indicated a financially comfortable, stable man. I broke my first date rule of just coffee or *one* glass of wine on a first date *and* I had to pay for it, both in time and money. For, I always insist on paying my way on the first date. I may relent on that rule if I think a second date will happen and he insists to pay. Be prepared ... a good talker can fool you, especially a very attractive one. We sometimes do not want to see the RED FLAGS. We sometimes do not read the *blanks* in their profiles and conversations ....

Enough recollections. Please, do not attempt to be affectionate and *touchy feely* on the first date. Doing so most often will backfire and push the potential partner in the other direction. The first date is all about getting to know a bit more about each other and not testing physical boundaries. If you have a good first meeting, plenty of time will develop later for handholding, hugs, kisses ... and more. Some men can be skittish about forward actions made toward them, having been accustomed to taking the lead. Others may not be the touchy feely kind of guy, as well, especially with a woman they've just met. And Mature women in general do not expect men to make any moves on a first date. Doing so could ruin any possibility of further dates. So. Relax, stay in the moment and gather information that will help you both feel comfortable with each other so you can each decide whether pursuing another date together would be a good idea. If good vibes are mutually felt, a friendly 'peck on the cheek' goodnight is very acceptable.

Women tend to be more conservative about physically touching early in an acquaintance. Experts say a primal instinct in women goes back the historical necessity to decide if a particular male would be stable and able enough to care for her and her children before she allowed him to come close. Remember, as well, that many SINS members have come out of painful situations and are cautious. On the up side, withholding any physical contact on the first date can heighten anticipation and add to your appeal! I vividly remember a man who did not attempt to kiss me goodnight or hold my hand on our first date. That relationship became one of the most passionate of my life ... after time was allowed for it to evolve. I like to explore and develop the friendship part of a new relationship first. This personal protocol has worked for me. For that reason, many of my first dates are still my friends.

It is wise not to give your heart away too soon, no matter how enthusiastic you are about a new person in your life. You are able to make a wiser assessment about how much potential a relationship might have with such a person if your emotions are not running rampant. Lust and passion are wonderful highs but if they are shared with someone who is totally inappropriate or likely to break your heart you can be easily devastated.

First, go slowly and diligently to see if he or she might be a person you want to spend considerable time with ... perhaps, even the rest of your life. Are your values and ethics in line? Is your potential partner truly free? Can you live with his or her baggage? Be fair; maybe the other person can do the same. We all have some baggage by this age, especially if we have lived interesting lives and/or pushed boundaries. Reverse the focus and ask: Does s/he appear comfortable dealing with *your* complexities and idiosyncrasies?

"You seem like a nice gentleman, but I'm not sure I could ever get serious about a man who has a laxative jingle for his ring tone."

While I am querying you, I want to offer you a few questions you might ask on those first dates. Some are meant to relax you both and others to give you a fuller picture of the person you are considering as a potential mate. Questions to help you find out who they are; to see if you truly do have common ground as a good start to explore a relationship. Such questions give you an easy narrative and chronology of their lives as well as basic bits of information. Exact, open-ended questions (no 'yes' or 'no' replies) call for your interest to share hopes, dreams, expectations and his or her values as well as, perhaps, some of his or her failures. [71]

I have assembled some open-ended questions from various sources including my own experiences. The most comprehensive list of such questions can be found in an excellent book on online dating I highly recommend ... *Awesome Secrets for Men* by Denversky5280. [72]

- "How has your life differed from what you had anticipated?" How do you feel about the variance from your expectations?
- What are some of your favorite foods and drink? Any particular reasons why?
- What are you looking for in your future ... a friendship, a casual dating situation with no strings attached, a committed companionship seeing each other regularly, a travel companion, an exclusive committed relationship spending lots of time together, a long term live-in situation, a marriage, etc. (Every couple has to find a mutual ground on this one or they are traveling down different paths with painful endings.)
- Are you a type A or type B personality; what type do you co-exist well with?
- If you believe in inter-personal chemistry, how long does it take you to feel it?
- Are you a homebody or do you like to go out frequently? If so, how often and to what sorts of venues?
- If you could change your chosen career what would you choose? Could you see yourself doing something associated with such a career now in your later years?

---

[71] Nick Baily, Charming, www.Quora.com.

[72] Denversky5280, Awesome Secrets for Men (Denver, Colorado: Amazon.com) 2010. P. 324. Similar and further excellent questions can be found in this detailed and fun online dating book I regard highly.

- How do you like to show your affection for the one you love? Why is it important for you to do so? To both give and to receive?
- What are some of the simpler pleasures of life you engage in? What are others you would like to add to your 'to do' list?
- What types of holidays/vacations do you like to take? Are you able to fit some of those into your life?
- How many times were you married or in long-term committed relationships? For how long? Reasons they failed?
- What do you usually have in your refrigerator and food cupboard?
- What are some accomplishments you are most proud of ... even the smallest but meaningful to you?
- What one thing in your life would you change if given an opportunity to do so?
- What do you believe is the first impression people have of you?
- How do you approach meeting someone new?
- List 5 to 10 words or phrases that you feel characterize you.
- What are your 3 to 5 best features that you feel would be welcome by a potential mate?
- List 5 to 10 words or phrases that characterize the mate you are seeking.
- What are the 3 to 5 best features your potential mate can offer you?
- How much *alone time* and how much *together time* do you require?
- How do you deal with conflicts?
- What are your least attractive character traits, if you are willing to share them?
- What do you believe most people do not know about the *authentic* you?

- What are your 3 biggest *deal breakers* in seeking a new relationship?
- What are your 3 biggest *deal makers* in finding a new relationship?
- Who are your best friend/s and what makes them so important in your life?
- Other than your visual appearance, what do you think some people notice about you when they meet you?
- What one thing in your life would you want to do more often?
- What one thing in your life would you like to lessen or do away with?
- Besides the basics in life, what are some of the things that you would not want to live without?
- What would you like to add to your life? Hopes, dreams ....
- What type of relationship are you seeking?[73]

A myriad of other questions may come up that are important for you to know the answers to. To receive the best answers try to construct your questions so they do not have simple *yes* and *no* answers. You need to learn the details and reasons surrounding the answers to help you know whether to go forward with this person. Add your important *get-to-know-you* questions to this list and copy it. Look it over thoroughly before you meet. Try to cover as many as possible without making it sound like an interrogation. (Avoid early-on controversial topics such as politics.) Many of the queries are important and are your *need-to-knows,* if you want to proceed to a satisfying second date and beyond.

Do give their answer your full attention ... listen and responsively interject with expressions such as *I understand, I see, Ahh* and the like. These small comments show you are with your date in

---

[73] Ibid.

the conversation, your mind is not wandering. Maintain good eye contact. Appealing connection through the eyes can be the beginning of the chemistry you seek.

"I thought this was a date, not an interrogation!"

Be very careful how many questions you ask. If you ask none, or just too few, they will know you are not really interested … or, perhaps you are extremely shy and private. If you ask too many, you may give the meeting all the charm of a job interview. Rather, enjoy the date … give it a chance to flow at a natural pace. Because flow is sometimes tricky to maintain, be sensitive to your dates' eye movements and body language. If eyes and body are shifting about, you know you have lost the connection between you two … for some reason that may not necessarily involve you. Slow down and relax. Be your confident, entertaining and interesting self. Lift them off the *hot seat* and attempt once more. Not every beginning is a good one. But, some can be turned in the right direction.

As for your responses, be sure to answer questions in a lively tone. Remain upbeat and positive. Don't talk about your previous partner … that history will come up at a later more appropriate time. Do not relate too many details of your private life. Reason one: Doing so could come back to bite you. Reason two: These could be dangerous to reveal to the wrong person. Reason three: They could be just too uneventfully boring for a still-new acquaintance.

With regard to conversational expression, unsavory words may be part of your vocabulary when you are with *the guys* or close friends or in certain environments. Avoid particular words. They will show a lack of regard for your new acquaintance. Even simple negative words such "hate" or 'worst', "disgusting" or 'gross', etc. set a negative tone for your conversations. Referring to your past partner as your "ex" is also not recommended ... it implies disdain. You cared for that person once. Say *my ex-wife* or *ex-husband* or *my previous relationship*, etc. Avoid being overly dramatic or excited. Be more reflective than damning. Do not create your own RED FLAG. It is best not to have more than one strong drink. Loose lips ....

Please remember many Mature Singles may not have dated for a very long time and are attempting a crash course in 21st-century dating skills. Allow your dates some slack if you are more recently experienced. Some have literally not had a date in 40 to 50 years! Just trying to brush up on rusty dating skills is stressful ... never mind the important reason for you meeting: to explore the possibility of furthering your initial optimism in each other as possible mates.

One widower I went on a first date with had wed his high school sweetheart. The marriage lasted 47 years. As a successful businessman, he assumed he would chose a Mature Single lady in the community and she would gratefully and immediately be his, just as he had experienced 47 years previously. Wait a minute. Mature women in this day and age are more independent than young brides of decades ago. Likely, more than a little wooing and some money will be needed to budge women from their liberated state, comfortable homes and freedom to set their own schedules with no one to answer to, etc.

Copyright 2004 by Randy Glasbergen.
www.glasbergen.com

"I started a new relationship. At the end of our
first date, I was ready to slip into something
more comfortable—my old relationship!"

Finding a mutually satisfying arrangement with someone you desire in your life may take some SINS searching, negotiating, and compromise. That three-part process was almost unheard of in our youth ... a time when life was more one dimensional and simple. Many mature women I know are interested in an exclusive dating relationship, including one that involves physical intimacy, but are not interested in a live-in situation and definitely not marriage. Men: be prepared. You will be facing a different sort of women than the ones you dated in your youth.

Congratulations. You both enjoyed a terrific first date and feel a second look is in order. You can suddenly see yourself headed for a committed relationship ... halt!! It is important not to have too many expectations or become too excited and enthusiastic on your first date. You are still in the interview phase, just in the rudimentary question and answer stage. Do not put unnecessary pressure on your date or yourself to meet unrealistic premature expectations. Just be your authentic selves, go with the flow and see how you get along. Determine what you find interesting about each other and allow the relationship to develop depth. Is there something worth pursuing further each time you meet?

"Do you want me to tell you something really subversive?
Love is everything it's cracked up to be.
That's why people are so cynical about it.
It really is worth fighting for, being brave for, risking everything for.
And the trouble is, if you don't risk anything, you risk even more."
-Erica Jong-
--*Fear of Flying*--

Always remember: It's just a *first date*. Even though it is roaring success, go easy. I have had it happen ... that initial flare to soar up and fall quickly down to earth, its flame extinguished. You just cannot know enough about someone from a couple hours together. Even when the chemistry is off the charts, a relationship is built on more than an initial rush. Besides, good old-fashioned courting is still romantic. A little bit of *cat and mouse* is far more fun than the almost inevitable rollercoaster ride of two people too anxious to dive into a deeper relationship prematurely and possibly too damaged to stay in it.

"We met, fell madly in love, got engaged, had a lovely wedding and honeymoon. Then things turned sour, we grew bitter, separated and divorced. It was quite a busy weekend!"

You should have an active or inter-active second date, an activity as the center of shared conversations. Plan something where you can have fun together and start to bond, enjoy a common interest like an art gallery, a bike ride, a picnic, a sporting event or a cooking class. I created a cooking school for *Seasoned Singles* when I was left *suddenly single* in order to do just that ... have fun and bond.

My final bits of advice for your *first date*? Remember *attitude* is the game-changer and have realistic expectations. Amen.

You are looking for perfection, but are you offering it?
-Unknown-[74]

Did someone mention *sex*?

---

[74] I believe this phrase was coined by me, as a former important man in my life reminded me ... he thinks of my biting words each morning he looks in the mirror! I do not believe it was a subliminal reference to something I had read. I could find no such phrase in my research. It was just appropriate for so many of us ... unrealistic expectations of a relationship considering what we have to offer it.

Chapter Fifteen

SEX ... intimate engagements

Almost forgotten, illusive,
highly-prized and sought-after

SEX in your Mature years ... such a big subject needs more attention than I am able to give in this book. I hope my overview, along with suggested reading and information sources will help guide you through what is a very important part of Mature dating. You cannot ignore that it will be at minimum a focus of your thoughts and, likely, of discussions with potential partners as you continue to see each other. If you are both agreeable and sexually compatible you can enjoy some of the best sexual sharing of your lives ... into your 60's, 70's and beyond. Your experiences will depend somewhat upon how you rate your earlier sex life or your memories of it. Many of you have had at least a few dry years, as well. Companionship, love, and perhaps ... an intimate sexual relationship or two ... can develop when you join SINS.

When you were young, sex outside of marriage was taboo for most of you. Now its existence is not just acceptable, but also sought after and quite prevalent ... even for traditional grandfathers and grandmothers on the Seasoned Mature dating scene. What a shock this can be for children and grandchildren! They may look askance at you now ... not so pure and perfect. They are right!

Another situation to face at this stage of dating is when to become intimate and have sex with your possible *special one.* I have heard general expectations for the third to fifth date. The matter is one of mutual desire and comfort levels. To take this next step certain issues must be considered and discussed first. If you become sexually involved and your partner is not sexually exclusive to you, you have to factor in serious health-related issues, such as sexually transmitted diseases (STD's). This particular issue is tricky to address and resolve. Especially in the heat of that first moment. Let level heads prevail.

> *For the first time in history,*
> *sex is more dangerous than the cigarette afterward.*
> -Jay Leno-

Trying to exchange clean bills of health with potential intimate partners is difficult enough, but how do you monitor their other sex partners if your candidate insists s/he does not want to be exclusive? I am still trying to cope with the difficulty of resolving this situation of sexual exclusivity. It is a battleground littered with broken hearts ... generally the men wanting their freedom to enjoy many partners and the women wanting the security and health safety of one exclusive partner. The obvious way is to resist any sexual contact until you are both ready to commit to exclusivity or to break off dating that person altogether. Both decisions can be very challenging but definitely doable and wise. STD's are growing in the Mature dating crowd; they should be a serious consideration and discussion if you are dating a person sexually active with other partners.

I find men very reticent to agree to STD tests. I must tell you that STD tests are the best way to protect yourself when intimate outside a committed relationship ... start with a clean bill of health. Otherwise, it is a crapshoot. Believe me, I have heard horror stories. You cannot take someone's word for it, or just hope for good luck and a fussy potential mate who would not expose him or herself to these diseases with a questionable partner. Even when dating a seemingly fastidious partner, you never can really know what lurks in the sexual health charts of sex partners once or twice removed from you ... or them. STD's are not stamped on sex partners' faces or bodies. And, of course, as an added safeguard use condoms. The post-menopausal segment of Mature women no longer need to prevent pregnancy but do need to prevent becoming the recipient of an unrevealed or undetected STD.

The big difference between sex for money
and sex for free
is that sex for money usually costs less.
-Brendan Francis-
--Playboy, 1985 --

Some Seasoned Matures married very young, knowing very little of the world of sex. Sex was probably never discussed as they were growing up; it continued to be spoken about in hushed tones or joked about in their adulthood. Well, times have changed and so has their exposure to good healthy sex. It is no longer a dirty word or activity ... never mentioned as though it didn't exist.

Perhaps this is the age in which you can finally shed those ligatures and cobwebs to glory in sex. It is still available to most of you if you make an effort to adapt to your ages with the aid of modern science and medicine. Mounds of information are available to you on the Internet and in bookstores. Reach out, gather information, talk to your doctor and to friends who are willing to discuss their views and experiences. A whole new learning experience could be waiting for you ... and possibly for your new partner. In fact, s/he may have some helpful hints to make the sexual intimacy more pleasurable for you both.

> *Love is the answer,*
> *but while you are waiting for the answer,*
> *sex raises some pretty good questions.*
> -Woody Allen-

What comes next when approaching and considering committing to exclusivity? Do what comes naturally. His *moves* and her *moans* ... your SINS dating progression. When is the *big event*? I believe for the first time to be a positive experience for both partners, perhaps even memorable and bonding, it should come about when you both feel comfortable enough with each other to passionately share some of your perhaps rusty moves and moans. They may be awkward or jerky, or creaky and croaky ... or come off just as you remember from your younger days of glorious sex. I would say, no matter how the sex or you unfold, enter into it with gusto believing it will be a stellar event for you both ... most likely it will be. Go into your first sexual encounter with your new partner without trepidation and with guns blazing ... perhaps not fit for the big screen but as fulfilling as you might remember. Give your most sincere effort to express your feelings toward your new partner. You have nothing to lose and much to gain by pleasing each other.

Some people cannot imagine older bodies engaged in sexual pleasures. The ecstasy of exquisite lovemaking is not wasted on bodies in their advanced years. Perhaps tender lovemaking is even more heightened as we know how fortunate we are to still delight in sexual pursuits. Many of our friends cannot ... be grateful for your pleasure and the pleasure you give your partner. Enjoy every moment to the fullest.

Our minds and our emotions can respond to the same stimulations of our youth. Granted, we may need a little help from modern science for our bodies. Use it ... it can help us reclaim and extend our sexually active years. Our supporting structures are not quite the beautiful taut bodies some of us once possessed. But damn it, our emotional responsiveness is still very much intact and can be more in tune with our bodies than they once were when we were so distracted by life's demands of work and family. We probably are now more appreciative of tender loving touches because we know they can be fleeting ... and can perhaps never return.

Romance without sex is like cake without the icing. Most of us just love that icing! I remember how as a kid I always lined up for the corner pieces of my friends' birthday cakes because corners had the most icing. As adults, you and I don't do that anymore, mainly because of the calories. Guess what ... sex is the icing on your romance. Sex does not add calories but actually consumes them. Surely, a win-win situation.

Since so many Mature Singles are in the population these days, you are not alone ... not the odd man or woman out. In fact, you are very in! The U.S. has the highest divorce rate in the world sitting at 45 percent in 2010.[75] The divorce rate among adults ages 50 and older doubled between 1990 and 2010. Roughly 1 in 4 divorces in 2010 occurred to persons ages 50 and older. The rate of divorce was 2.5 times higher for those in remarriages versus first marriages, while the divorce rate declined as overall marital duration rose.[76] As our

---

[75] Susan L. Brown and I-Fen Lin, Department of Sociology, Bowling Green State University, August 30, 2012, The Gray Divorce Revolution: Rising Divorce Among Middle-Aged and Older Adults. 1990-2010, p.1. citing Amato, 2010; Cherlin, 2010, National Center for Family & Marriage Research, Bowling Green State University, http://www.ncbi.nlm.nih.gov/pmc/articles/PMC3478728/, accessed July 1, 2014.

[76] Ibid. p.1.Susan L. Brown and I-Fen Lin http://www.ncbi.nlm.nih.gov/pmc/articles/PMC3478728/, p.1, accessed July 1, 2014.

life expectancies increase, the likelihood of more of these divorces among Matures in later years increases.

More recently, Wu and Schimmele (2007) suggested that broad cultural shifts in the meanings of marriage and divorce influence all generations, including older adults. Specifically, the weakening norm of marriage as a lifelong institution coupled with a heightened emphasis on individual fulfillment and satisfaction through marriage may contribute to an increase in divorce among older adults, including those in long-term first marriages. Marriages change and evolve over the life course and thus may no longer meet one's needs at later life stages. Qualitative research indicates that many older couples that divorce simply have grown apart (Bair, 2007). Life-long marriages are increasingly difficult to sustain in an era of individualism and lengthening life expectancies; older adults are more reluctant now to remain in empty shell marriages (Wu & Schimmele, 2007).[77]

"Our underwear spent 30 minutes tumbling in the laundry. Our underwear has a better sex life than we do!"

---

[77] Ibid. p.3. Susan L. Brown and I-Fen Lin, Department of Sociology, Bowling Green State University, August 30, 2012, The Gray Divorce Revolution: Rising Divorce Among Middle-Aged and Older Adults. 1990-2010, citing Z Wu and CM Schimmele, Uncoupling in late life Generations 31, 41-46, accessed July 1, 2014.

You are single but not alone, as you read in the excerpt above ... and you are free. You no longer have to depend upon well-meaning family and friends for introductions. You can craft your social life and your love life through your participation in SINS. Your privacy will be intact. It can be an unexpected rebirth for you. Wake up and smell the roses. Do not lament your single state in life. You are luckier than most, if you have your health and your freedom. Enjoy this journey through Candyland.

You will definitely face some *issues* as a Seasoned Mature dater that you did not have to cope with in your youth. The dating routine is essentially the same. But, you are entering it with a lifetime of experience and baggage ... and some sensitive scars. I suggested to you earlier to address these.

And, your life may no longer be clothed in the fit and active bodies of which you were so proud, or at least accepting. Now some might want to hide under the bed instead of lie on it when it comes to sex. Through the work I discussed in earlier chapters I have come to feel better about my inner and outer self than I have since my twenties. I did so with discipline and taking actions to better myself ... and with help from my friends. Many of them are thanked in my Acknowledgments. You can improve upon your well-being on all levels, as well. Romance and sex are best when experienced in a body in good physical shape and a beautiful mind honed through life's experiences. Both are doable for most of you with a little *work*.

—GLASBERGEN

"Sex is healthy, natural activity between consenting adults who aren't afraid of going to Hell."

Some of your biggest hurdles to overcome when confronted with new sex partners may be those created in your past. Many of you were raised in traditional families where your parents showed no affection and certainly never discussed sex with their children. You may have been given very little sexual guidance and made to feel shame or guilt to harbor those feelings, which you had to keep hidden. Sex education for many of you was learned in the biology lab or from stolen moments reading *National Geographic*. Sex was a dirty word; anything to do with it was taboo.

Sex is emotion in motion.
-Mae West-

Some religions taught you that sex was for procreation only. Sex and pleasure were never equated. In fact, for some of you sex was emotionally painful because you had been sexually violated, most likely by someone you trusted. Molestation was a crime seldom reported or talked about within the families where it occurred. It was understood you brought it on yourself as your body matured.

235

Due to lack of sex education and information and sexual abuse, some young girls became pregnant and were sent away in shame to return without their babies. They were disgraced ... some even ostracized. A sick, dark society placed these young innocents in situations with raging hormones, no information and no protection. A society which could not deal with the consequences.

Don't knock masturbation—it's sex with someone I love.
-Woody Allen-

Masturbation was the usual way out for the guys. It was accessible, easy and obvious as to how to please themselves. Girls were left to muddle about, thinking they were sinning if they ever touched themselves in those pleasurable places. Most of you had your first sex with the person you married and relied on each other's help to fumble through what pleased the other. If you were in a long-term relationship with your partner before your current single state, you may have some relearning ahead.

The good news is what you will learn is pleasurable ... very pleasurable. That is why I say you may have the best sex of your life during these Mature dating years. Do not be surprised when you do. Remember my words and smile while you explore sexual pleasures with your new partner, each learning how beautiful it feels to please the other, giving and receiving with the newfound abandon you may have been denied for so many years.

Many of you have been through a period of grief due to the loss of someone you loved through death, divorce or a breakup. Sexual arousal may still be the last thing on your minds. However, you might want to be able to enjoy sex with a partner in the future. The adage 'use it or lose it' readily applies to sexual intimacy. You should keep your juices flowing for many reasons. For example: Repeated contraction of a female's PC (*pubococcygeus*) muscle increases blood flow to the vaginal tissues ...action which helps her feel more sensation, more pleasure and stronger orgasms. Such contraction helps lubricate and prevent thinning of the vaginal walls ... two of the prime causes of painful intercourse for many Mature women.[78]

> *To succeed with the opposite sex, tell her you're impotent.*
> *She can't wait to disprove it.*
> -Cary Grant-

A painful sexual problem for mature men is more emotional ... coping with erectile dysfunction. Approximately 20 percent of American men, almost thirty million, are affected by erectile dysfunction, sometimes accompanied by loss of libido.

© Randy Glasbergen.
www.glasbergen.com

"I would climb the highest mountain and swim the deepest ocean for you. But don't be upset if I'm too tired for romance afterwards!"

---

[78] Candida Royalle, porn film star and founder of Femme Productions, Staying Juicy and Fit During Celibacy, in Joan Price, Naked at Our Age (Berkeley, California: Seal Press, 2011), p.141.

If you do not have a partner both men and women not only can but should nurture arousal and orgasm through self-pleasuring. Regular activity keeps your sexual responses vital and healthy ... not a tough prescription to take. Such personal engagement is indeed very pleasurable and will keep you healthy and ready for your next sexual experience. In the meantime, you should be having an orgasm at least once a week with a partner or alone. Orgasms exercise the muscles that keep your internal organs in place, which ultimately prevent urinary and bowel incontinence or a prolapsed uterus in females. [79] You can reduce your risk of mild to moderate depression by 30 percent if you enjoy one to three orgasms per week. Such a regimen reduces your incidences of colds and other viruses, as well! One study found that at least one orgasm per week reduced the risk of heart attack by 36 percent.[80]

> *Having sex is like playing bridge.*
> *If you don't have a good partner,*
> *you'd better have a good hand.*
> *-Woody Allen-*

Sometimes celibacy is cast upon us or at times is self-imposed. Either way, you might make a concerted attempt to maintain your sexual and bodily health through self-pleasuring if a partner is just not in your cards at the moment. The hormones and endorphins released into your system will put a smile on your face and pink in your cheeks.

Consider going to one of the tasteful sex shops that are in most densely populated areas and, for starters, pick up a vibrator and a lubricant ... all to the better for both female and male enjoyment. You

---

[79] Ellen Bernard, MSSW, Reasons to Keep your Sexual Self Alive and Functioning, in Joan Price, Naked at Our Age (Berkeley, California: Seal Press, 2011), p.139.

[80] Ibid. Ellen Bernard, MSSW, 139, 140.

can use these alone or with your partner. While you are browsing, explore the intimate play (sex) toys available. They are usually very pleasingly packaged and delightful to discover. I promise you a fun outing whether alone or with a partner or friend.

All this is preparation to feel comfortable with your body and to be cognizant of what pleases you sexually. Otherwise, both you and your new partner will be literally groping in the dark. A new partner wants to know what pleases you. Help him or her by doing a little reconnaissance work before the 'big event'. You will both feel more relaxed and ready for the best sex of your life!

"Do not go gentle into that good night."
-Dylan Thomas-

Studies and Statistics
Additional materials for Chapter 15 -- SEX

Note: Related to Brown & Lin material citing Manning & Brown:

In a 1980 and 2008 comparison of adults age 65 and older, the segment who reported their marital status as divorced *doubled among men*, rising from 5 percent to 10 percent.

During this time, the same descriptive *tripled for women*, going from 4 percent to 12 percent.[81]

---

[81] Susan L. Brown and I-Fen Lin, Department of Sociology, Bowling Green State University, August 30, 2012, The Gray Divorce Revolution: Rising Divorce Among Middle-Aged and Older Adults, p.2. 1990-2010, citing Manning & Brown (2011) the Demography of Unions Among Older Americans, 1980-Present: a Family Change Approach, p.193-210, accessed July 1, 2014.

Chapter Sixteen

Going Solo Again ... with SINS by your side

This chapter could make you laugh or make you cry.
If you decide to ...
Go solo again ... is it rare?
Go solo again ... is it despair?
Go solo again ... is it narcissism?
Go solo again ... is it just 'settling'?
Go solo again ... is it bliss?

Solos expanding boundaries and creating options ...

You entered SINS in an attempt to find some level of connection with a special someone or perhaps plural 'someones' for friendship and/or love. You have winked flirted, 'favorited' and dated dozens or more qualified members. So, why are you still Single and Solo?

Truthfully, some of us have experienced unrealistic expectations or have held onto unfulfilled dreams. Some have been spoiled by such great previous but *to-be-no-more* relationships; tough acts to follow. Others have deep personal issues holding them back from fulfilling their wishes for a lifelong partner. I think I qualify for all four.

In my seven decades I have wended my way through a few relationships I will neither forget ... nor regret. But, they did not satisfy my search for my intended life partner. I discovered a part of me kept emerging that wanted to remain Solo, a very unexpected turn in my thinking. The shift was not one of despair or 'settling'. Rather, it was based in discovering how much I enjoy myself and my time alone. I feel complete.

"I need you, darling. You complete me."

Here is what I came to realize: Another person is not necessary to make me feel fulfilled and whole. I have evolved and grown in this direction throughout my SINS experience. In my search for my special *someone* I found me! Such a totally unexpected revelation could happen to you, as well. Believe me. I was told by many Singletons that I could quite possibly morph into that mode of thinking and feeling; I truly never believed them. I was wrong. Despite meeting wonderful partner material, for whatever my reasons I have found peace and contentment living Solo ... although I have been *tempted.* I continue to utilize SINS for companionship and travel. I feel I have found the best balance for me. Who knows? That balance could fluctuate again.

Review all your lifestyle options periodically; I have been doing so. You may be surprised how your favorites seem to move up and down the scale. If someone were to come along who would totally captivate me and add even more dimension to my world, I might be tempted to change my Solo status. But in the meantime, I have the best of all worlds and am very content. You can sculpt such a life fulfilling your criteria, a life which would quite likely be different from mine.

To remain Solo does not eliminate my use of SINS. Quite to the contrary, it gives me opportunities to enjoy all the benefits of going Solo without giving up the social aspects of dating and romance. I think going Solo would not be so appealing to me without the social options provided by SINS. Many of us do not want to share a home again. We prize our freedom and independence, and seek companionship in small doses. More about the pros and cons coming up

Most people assume you are looking for a life partner when you are engaged in online dating. Such an assumption is not necessarily true for all members. You should clarify your feelings on this important subject when you first 'connect' with a member. The goal of partnering is dependent upon each member's definition of partnering and her or his genuine desire to achieve such an arrangement. When we were growing up our standard relationship anticipation was pretty clear ... you were supposed to be either 'single and dating' while in the process of finding a mate or be 'married'. Once the latter was achieved, you met society's expectations of being tied to someone for the rest of your life in order to complete you. Times have surely changed.

The 'connected' state in which you exit SINS is reliant upon how capable you are of being realistic as to who would be interested in you and as to how willing you are to adjust unrealistic expectations. The once-Marrieds among you may have been very fortunate the first time around with your marriage partner and are now starting to realize that lightning may not strike twice in the same place.

Most likely you will not be reconnecting with your previous partner ... and most likely would not do so even if you had the chance. Maybe a new connection will lead to the love of your life *or* to the opposite extreme ... you might ultimately choose to remain Solo. What you *will* do is make wiser and more educated decisions for your 'next act' knowing that you have covered the broad spectrum of what the Singles dating scene can offer you as you seek your desired lifestyle.

How you expand your boundaries and morph your expectations while meeting members from many walks of life depends upon you ... and a bit on fate. I suspect most of us, if we met the absolutely right one who *knocked our socks off*, would settle into partnered life. I know I have been tempted once or twice. But in this era, the alternative lifestyle of self-determined Singleton living (living Solo) is not at all a negative one and certainly better than so many Marrieds tied down and drowning in unhappy relationships. The Solo living option may be one you want to explore as an alternative to full-time partnering. Here is yet another lifestyle choice.

Perhaps the stars were not aligned for me to find Mr. Right in eight years of being single and active in Internet-dating. I certainly have enjoyed many exhilarating close hits and near misses, but never a direct bull's eye. I have come to the very comfortable conclusion that another very appealing option exists for me. I am most likely a *Suddenly Single* who will be remaining Solo during my final years ... years blessed with family, wonderful friendships and, perhaps, romances. Such choices are possible in SINS. You might consider variations of Solo options, as well as partnering. You will have opportunities to explore such thoughts with SINS members also seeking to sculpt fulfilling lives.

SINS certainly make the choice to live alone not one of despair but one that is viable, appealing, even exciting and fun. You need not be totally alone and celibate; you can enjoy dating when it suits you ... to whatever emotional depth suits you. You can visit the appropriate sites to find like-minded Singletons who enjoy the friendship, companionship or casual dating aspects of SINS as well as those who pursue the more prevalent, loving long-term relationship path while still residing apart. You are single and you are free ... you can do what you like. That privilege is precious. Utilize it to your advantage during these later years.

'Going Solo Again' as a choice is not so uncommon or so skeptically judged in today's more tolerant if not enlightened society. Many independent spirits have long selected to remain Single. Many have discovered this alternative lifestyle, also, through necessity or fate ... never having found the *right one* or living in the aftermath of a divorce or passing of a partner. Many have accepted Singleton living after unsuccessful attempts to bond with someone new, etc. Some of us were reluctantly cast back into the Solo state. Perhaps, we thrashed wildly looking for a partner or we paddled passively along. Some of us perceived our Single living as just bad luck while others enthusiastically embraced Solo living right from the start.

GLASBERGEN

"I need someone who would always love and adore me, always find me fascinating, someone to spoil me rotten and never leave. So I married myself!"

I highly recommend a game-changing book, *Going Solo,* by Eric Klinenberg. It reframed my whole perception of Single living. His book nurtured in me a real comfort level, one I would not have believed I could develop: I am not an oddball, defective, or a castoff. In fact, I am one of a growing majority! My new understanding of how common being a Single really is now allows me to make very positive, non-desperate and non-self-conscious choices in my life. I have become more deliberate. The combination of *Going Solo* with its affirmation of Singletons and *Candyland S.I.N.S.* with its open discussion of a rainbow of Singles lifestyles could do the very same for you.

Eric's statistics are not only fascinating, comforting, and thought-provoking but also revealing and relevant for both Singles and the Partnered:

"In 1950, only 22 percent of American adults were single. Today more than 50 percent of American adults are single, and 31 million, roughly one out of every seven adults, live alone." Single adults are more common than any other domestic unit including the nuclear family. They constitute the biggest demographic shift since the baby boom. [82]

According to Eric Klinenberg, we Singletons are not alone but in the middle of that massive demographic shift ... we are far from being alone!! He defines, validates and explains the development of the Solo circumstance that so many of us live in during our final years. Eric's book lets us know that it is OK to live alone and, most importantly, that *we* are OK. We are not losers. We are increasing in numbers ... many Solo by choice, not forced situations. In so many respects, we are to be envied.

The now certifiable Solo concept and its prevalence offer us more control of our lives ... intellectually, emotionally and physically. We are a recognized demographic force. At one time, being Single was a state between other Partnered states ... time frames in life that dictated we live alone due to loss of a partner through death or divorce (in some cases a *shedding*) or to long-distance work assignments, etc. 'Single' was assumed to be just temporary until we would be able to attain once again a 'normal' Partnered state. Eric's figures belie that present-day myth of us being outside the crowd and not within the norm. Singles are becoming the majority demographic; Solo living is gaining predominance, desirability and acceptability.

We are no longer misfits but people who forge our own directions, meet its challenges and seize its opportunities ... one of which is Mature dating (almost publicly non-existent in small communities of our parents' generation).

---

[82] Klinenberg, Going Solo, front flap.

To now know that we are not really alone but among many who share our desire to remain Singletons gives us permission to make intelligent and healthy choices about whether we want to live alone sharing just portions of our lives with others or want to share our lives totally with another ... to not let society's outdated opinions and judgments guide us. This knowledge allowed me to feel empowered; so should all of you feel that power. We've got a lot living left to do!

Mature Singles need not be isolated; they can live very interesting and fulfilling lives. They no longer 'lurk' about in clubs, volunteer organizations, at dances and dinner parties, etc., perhaps considered with sympathy, or falsely suspected of wanting to steal someone's husband or wife. Singletons are learning that we no longer live in a society of married vs. unmarried but one composed of many shades of each. Online dating plays a role in those variations.

We should be proud. We Singletons are actually the secret envy of so many Marrieds tied down by too many years of too many problems, hurts, scars, etc. I have come to the conclusion that Singles, if we live within some degree of *financially comfortable*, are often the lucky Matures. Not at all to be pitied. Now that we Mature Singles have the resources of SINS, our perhaps unsolicited freedom is a blessing and our alternatives greater than even just a few years ago. Our freedom to self-determine our lifestyle, along with society's growing acceptance and recognition of the *validity* of Singleness have changed for the positive in our communities.

Living alone has been so often rhapsodized in movies; in truth, it can be very romantic. I know ... I live it. Thanks to SINS you and I can date as much as we want, but I must admit I have found some my most beautiful and cherished evenings are spent alone at home cuddled up with a book and a glass of wine by my fireplace. That happens frequently, as often as I want it. You see ... I am the only one with whom to plan the evening. Those gentle, get-away, candle-lit evenings can happen for you if you have romance in your heart and intentionally set the scene ... for you.

The thought of such a scenario possibly being so much better if I were sharing the experience used to plague me, but it now seldom enters my mind. Truly, my situation is *as good as it gets*. Many of you can find that same peace hiking or kayaking solo or floating alone in a pool ... feeling no void spaces, no need to better those moments with a partner.

Narcissistic, perhaps? I must admit that we Singletons possibly become a bit self-oriented with all that time and attention we are able place on ourselves. We are bound only by what we choose to be bound by ... family and social bonds and a range of commitments notwithstanding. We enjoy the relaxing feeling of no one else's wishes to be fulfilled or demands to be met. Our time clock to be set only to our schedule. An easy and self-indulgent life perhaps.

But, going Solo again is a double-edged sword. Counter to the benefits are the disadvantages of living Solo. No one ever-present to take out the rubbish, carry in the groceries, run to the store for a forgotten ingredient when preparing a meal for guests, drive when you are exhausted, take you to doctors' appointments, pay the bills, share expenses, cook your favorite meals, make the house smell fresh and look great, to do the gardening, to change the light bulbs, hold the ladder, give you a hug when you are feeling down, give you a hand when you are overwhelmed, remember everyone's birthday, shut out the lights, etc. Also missing are spontaneous physical touches and yearned-for versions of intimacy. The list of what Solo living is *not* is just about endless and sometimes nudges me to reconsider whether I should partner again ... or not.

I must admit the times I miss having a partner most are when I carry the groceries from the car and when I travel alone. My travels have been frequent and widespread for extended periods. Loneliness can set in during those long journeys. I have noted the wish for travel companions in so many SINS profiles, probably the majority of them, the large number of members who would like a travel partner to share the beauty and the adventurous fun they are fortunate enough to make happen during these remaining years. Those are my sentiments, as well. You may want to contact SINS members who express the same preference. You could find stimulating and compatible companions for your travels.

Yes, many Singles in all age groups have chosen the Solo lifestyle. Some of us were drawn by the 'pull' of the Singleton lifestyle as well as the 'push' of circumstances. The 'push' to become a Singleton is frequently involuntary due to having been left alone ... formerly considered a temporary situation. The 'push' to be coupled is more dominant, more naturally gravitated toward. Sometimes social circles are more welcoming to a married member, as Singles are not always comfortably invited into mixed social situations. Perhaps some career/work-related events are more couple friendly as well. Or, you simply are lonely and want the companionship and intimacy that a life partner offers. The idea of finding a life partner can be quite appealing. Many feel full partnership is nature's first choice for humans. The latest studies reveal that individuals in a committed relationship, especially marriage, do live longer than others not living that lifestyle.[83]

The 'pull' of Solo living comes from all the benefits it offers us: we are allowed the simple daily pampering luxuries of living alone like the selection of special soaps, foods, TV programs, music, bed times, room temperature, eating schedules, etc. We luxuriate in

---

[83] www.huffintgtonpost.com, http://www.huffingtonpost.com/2013/01/10/marriage-research_n_2450639.html, accessed July 1, 2014.

the pursuit of singular interests, joining with others as we please, to play and to work with only one schedule to consider ... to feel no need to share anything. Stretch out on the sofa, clutter the counter, leave our coat draped on a chair, socks on the floor, toothpaste cap off, bed unmade ... all at our will. No one to tell us that we should or must tidy up after ourselves. We are free of another's set of family, work, and friend obligations which can weigh heavily on a partner ... as well as be very time consuming.

We have no need to justify how we spend our time and money, no need to twist ourselves into knots trying to please someone who has different priorities or inclinations that strongly conflict with how we want to spend our time. For some of us, our treasure box of interests overflows ... we don't have enough time to devote to them even as a Single with reduced distractions. Imagine trying to accommodate another's needs while engaging in this lifestyle some judge as narcissistic and others see as personally *free-to-be*.

Matures pursue second careers or focus on hobbies and dreams left unfulfilled when they were obligated with the responsibilities of a spouse and possibly a family, home and mortgage. Hallelujah, they have reached the Promised Land! Do they want to return to that same racetrack again? Even to walk, not run this time on the raceway that consumes energy, emotions and, maybe, too much of their financial resources?

Do you really want to give up your peaceable lifestyle to move into a committed relationship? You may. Many Solos do. SINS exist to help you whether you pursue a long-term committed relationship or casual dating. You need not be lonely within a Solo lifestyle ... enjoy a travel partner, an exclusive non-live-in companion or commit formally to a marriage or many other variations of these. SINS give you the means to find like-minded people.

Society's definition of success has slowly incorporated values such as pursuit of an individual's personal happiness and fulfillment in areas other than in work and careers. A survey done in 1957 found the majority of Americans believed that unmarried people were "sick", "immoral" or "neurotic" [84] as well as "narcissistic". We still suffer somewhat but, thankfully, to a lesser degree from that same stigma of being Single and living alone by choice ...once considered by some as 'going against the laws of nature'.

You are part of the largest demographic shift since the baby boom. More than five million Americans have places of their own ... and live alone.[85] Going Solo has become a very acceptable lifestyle and increasingly a very livable one. SINS have played a part in the contemporary affirmation of the Singleton approach to life.

Hmmm. Perhaps that now waning stigma of being a Singleton is morphing into *envy* by those who do not have your freedom of choice?! You have gone through the pain of loss for a reason ... could the peace of living Single be your reward? Could you turn the curse of that loss into something positive, something you'd not dreamed of a year or two or more ago? You are free ... to utilize Candyland as a way to meet your new life partner or to enhance a lifestyle that leaves you uncommitted and free.

Living alone has been romanticized in many movies as in *Something's Gotta Give* starring Jack Nicholson and Diane Keaton. Their characters led lives many of us dream of ... successful, wealthy, attractive and dynamic members of their communities. Such lifestyles raise the ante on 'romance', take it to a level that includes creating settings around us that visually and sensually (as in related to our seven senses) enhance our well-being. Although

---

[84] Klinenberg, Going Solo, p.12.

[85] Ibid. p. 48.

most of us do not have the ability to lead life to movie-style extremes, we can still create a more realistic but still romantic lifestyle. We just have to focus on that goal and sculpt a life within our means. Lives of Singletons are now more fulfilling and diverse than many traditional nuclear family marriage situations.

Take this time alone to better yourself, and pamper yourself and the people in your life. You may find you enjoy the spontaneity now possible and want to make it a way of life. Enliven your at-home life by bringing company into it occasionally. Cooking a gourmet meal for yourself can be fun, but eating it alone is generally not. Why not invite one of your new SINS friends and/or other long-known ones to join you for both the prep and the meal in a food-based adventure? If they are Singletons, male or female, I can almost guarantee they will be at your door in minutes ... a bottle of wine or 'somesuch' in hand and a smile on the face.

Yes, you could surprise yourself and be caught in the 'push' and 'pull' of Singleton living. Perhaps you may spend time living alone, content to know that within SINS probably awaits a partner with whom you might someday be ready to renew your life. Until that day, you can utilize the time to revitalize yourself in your now romanticized personal space ... engaged with all 'things' about you and your recovery and further growth. That includes dating interesting SINS members, some of whom you hope will become your friends because you all would have done your homework ... meeting each other's criteria for values, ethics, lifestyles, and interests. The icing on that beautiful social cake would be if one of those SINS members became your committed life partner. Many hundreds of thousands have found their perfect icing. Why not you?

"You keep me on a chain, you make me eat on the floor, you never let me go out in public alone. We need counseling!"

On a personal note, I believe my philosophy is changing concerning dating at this age. Because of my research for the writing *Candyland S.I.N.S.* and the sum of my experiences, I have become more relaxed about my dating. I am no longer in such a hurry to meet Mr. Right. Maybe I have given up finding him or I have just become comfortable in my own life. I am not sure. I love the company of a special man in my life and all that entails, but I can't imagine spending the rest of my life 'surrounded' by one person.

I have long chipped away at my personal *big block of marble.* Time and experience have taught me what is important. I now have the full life as a Singleton … a life even better than I aspired to because my vision of life morphed and expanded as I moved through the years. I continue to grow, to think more deeply about how my remaining years should be spent. For these moments I am happy Solo but if *someone truly special* were to appear, my life might morph once again. I have always led a life open to new people and experiences and will continue my journey in my style. Doing the same is what I hope for you.

My world has been significantly enriched by the various special members I have met on SINS. Some I could call any time day or night; they would respond. I have done so. Our mutual bonds have given me a community I can relate to and rely upon while I remain Single and, likely, beyond. They have made that Solo state I so hated initially into a warm, welcoming community. You may decide to experience the same. Expand your world and create a real sense of community around you ... with Candyland S.I.N.S.

"Some girls need men to take them places.
Others just click their heels, spread their own wings, and fly."
— Coco J. Ginger-

"Every couple needs a song. Ours should
be 'You'll Never Walk Alone'."

Exit

Candyland S.I.N.S.

Take time to reflect ....

- Have you stopped to pause and give serious thought to your 'next act'?
- Are you anxious to make positive, proactive changes in your life?
- Are you ready to launch into action ... to take control of the remaining years of your life in a world much larger than you have ever before experienced?
- Are you anticipating the joy of shedding your cocoon and revealing the beauty of the butterfly that has been hidden within?
- Are you willing to come out of the hibernation in the fall or early winter of your life ... to happily flap your wings and fly with the multitudes of SINS members into full sunshine?

- Have you found the possible key to renewed excitement for life, contentment, fun, and perhaps even years of love and happiness? Partnered or Solo?
- Are *you now ready* to begin your journey through Candyland SINS?

I hope *Candyland S.I.N.S.* has given you incentive to consider these thoughts, as you face the remaining years of your life and how you want to lead them, rather than be lulled into a mediocre, boring existence. *Candyland S.I.N.S.* has been written to shake you out of your pause in life, your stupor or your paralysis. It has been written to help you understand the 'mysteries' and the misconceptions of Internet-dating and to give you a realistic view of what transpires for many of us ... Mature Single members with good attitudes and safe practices. I wanted to help you enter Candyland S.I.N.S. fully prepared and armed with the tools and emotional support that lie within these chapters; to guide you through the SINS' process and, most importantly, to keep you safe as you explore the Candyland we call SINS.

An expert is a man who has made all the mistakes
which can be made,
in a narrow field.
-Niels Bohr-[86]

This wise and so *applicable-to-me* statement, along with my experiences handling over 22,000 views and the ensuing contacts and events in SINS, has qualified me to write Candyland S.I.N.S. with faith that you will benefit from my trials and my errors ... and my triumphs.

---

[86] Niels Bohr, www.brainyquote.com, http://www.brainyquote.com/quotes/quotes/n/nielsbohr385596.html#IUdmT7tcbvKuZGJx.99, accessed July 1, 2014.

I have approached this stage of my life with a positive, practical, yet romantic attitude. How you shape your *here and now* and find the happiness and contentment you seek is your choice. I have found both (Well, most of the time!) through gratitude, maintaining strong family and core values and taking control of my personal social life with SINS. You can do the same. I am proof it can be done.

My little boat these last eight years could have been stalled in years as *dull as ditchwater;* instead, they have been anchored by SINS in a glorious, azure blue sea ... at times with waves rising high and crashing on the shore and other times as calm and peaceful as a mirror's surface. I wish the same for you, my friends, my fellow and sister Mature Singles as we move toward our last years. Let us live them with all the gusto we can muster.

Before you picked up Candyland S.I.N.S. you may have been drifting in your pity pot ... feeling somewhat OK. But, history tends to repeat itself. Frozen acceptance of the status quo easily becomes a way of life; eventually such a life rides a slow current composed of boredom, loneliness, regrets and sadness How almost unbearable. Nearly unbearable not just for you, but also for those surrounding you.

If you find yourself, as many have, in a personalized version of a pity pot, begin your transformation ... follow its outlet to the main stream even if you envision yourself struggling against the current and facing unconquerable rapids. Believe me ... I have paused at the mouth of such a stream. I know moving yourself into action takes strength. You have that within you whether you sense it or not. Commit to the clear intention to change your life for the better. Strengthen your body, your mind, your will and your heart to accomplish more than you ever dreamed you could. The difficulties you might anticipate should fall away and your journey be enjoyable and heart-warming. May you find yourself moving easily with the current, navigating your way ... on the ride of your life.

Because you have read through *Candyland S.I.N.S.* I hope you now firmly believe life can be sweet once again. That realization is possible ... light and laughter have returned to me and so many millions of SINS members. For as much as you might have been skeptical when you opened these pages, variations of light and laughter and sunshine can be yours.

You are now ready to successfully follow the guidance and advice herein. Probably the best advice that will save you much heartache and, possibly, physical danger are those tips gleaned from the missteps of those who have gone before you. You want to travel through Candyland enjoying the good and, perhaps at worst, chuckling about most of the others.

What I don't want for you is you blithely bouncing through, tripping and falling, emerging bruised and dented. Believe it ... good experiences can happen in SINS, if you properly prepare yourself, heed experienced members and avoid all the RED FLAGS of which you are now aware. Conduct yourself honestly and maintain that all-important good *attitude*.

This book has been written for SINS members, for those who are curious about what lies behind the gates of SINS and for those who are cynics of SINS. My hope is the curious, and the cynics as well, thoroughly read *Candyland S.I.N.S.* to enhance their understanding of what transpires in this magical realm ... this mystical world they have not experienced. We members welcome you to Candyland S.I.N.S.

Explore. You may like this Candyland ... even revel in it. Should you exit SINS without meeting, for whatever reasons, a special *someone*, you will at the very least emerge knowing yourself better. If you stay and play in SINS you will become an ever better version of yourself ... one on the way to becoming *the best you*!!!

GLASBERGEN

"Are we in Heaven?
Or, are we still in Candyland S.I.N.S.?"

Enjoy your journey.

Candyland S.I.N.S. may be nearly as much fun as the destination!

And, the destination the most rewarding one of your life.

Wishing you the best in life ... and love,

Joan

"Because if you take a risk,
you just might find what you're looking for."
-Susane Colasanti-
--Take Me There--

Acknowledgments

Most grateful thanks to Dianne Pierce, my tireless arrived-on-the-scene editor, who flew in from abroad on her magic carpet, for a stopover visit before her return to Tennessee. I had just begun the first revision of this book. She tuned in immediately to the overwhelming task ahead and shared that, by the way, she taught writing and she edits books!!! Before she left, she began to sprinkle my words with her editing sophistication and sparkle. How could such a special someone I had seen once or twice in 50 years, a childhood friend, appear on my doorstep to visit me on precisely the days I had begun revising my manuscript for submission? What are the chances of such a double coincidence? She was sent to me ... we both knew it. There is *no* coincidence. We fondly reminisced about the dedicated and capable teachers in the small-town Webster/Dudley schools who taught us so much. How they would have loved to see, several decades later, two former students discussing the fine points and twists of the English language. Dianne worked with boundless energy to help me meet my ever-shifting deadlines.

Thank you, Dianne, for being a compassionate support during those professionally demanding and personally emotional days together that turned into long-distance weeks ... months. (I know she thinks just one more read-through would do it.) Your expertise and sharp eye have given Candyland S.I.N.S. the 'spit and polish' it sorely needed. Gotcha!!! I could not resist one more catch phrase ... needed to have the last words!!! ;-D

Thanks to my friend Jack Whyne who was always willing to take a few moments from his exercises at the YMCA to hear a recount of my latest escapade, advise me to be patient about blending with a new potential partner and at times nudge me to be not so patient and walk away from a likely unhealthy developing relationship. Jack's advice was so *spot-on* even my therapist wanted to meet him. On the days before I met with her Jack would offer observations and advice similar, at a basic level, to what she would present. Double-teaming in the best of ways. And, so well worth it ... the cost of a month at the YMCA in the company of my dear friend Jack was a fraction of the cost of an hour with my professional!!! ;-D

And, truly, deep gratitude to my therapist Judith Smith, MSW RSW, whose wise and professional advice expanded Jack's kind counsel. Judith opened my eyes to my past and how it underpinned so much of who I am and how I act and react today. She made me a believer in the benefits of therapy.

To Nonnie Griffin who has spent (I am sure) hundreds of hours being a true girlfriend as she allowed me, after I became Suddenly Single, to share with her the emotionally exhausting aftermath of such an unforeseen experience. Her kind love and patience will never be forgotten. We all need a Nonnie in our lives. If you are lucky enough to have one when you see very little sunlight ahead, you will travel along your rocky roads and steep hills with greater ease and borrowed strength when you believe you have none left of your own ... emerging with some remnants of self-esteem still intact. She is a bottomless well of support ... where does she always find the right approach to a girlfriend's struggles? I thank my Nonnie and the other Nonnies of the world who are present for those friends who seek their wisdom and experience.

To my incredibly patient and wonderful brother Paul (with his common sense and sage advice ... "Why don't you just call him and talk?" ... offered as I writhed in variously imagined scenarios *tearing* my 'relationships' apart.). Paul and I are living proof that no matter how differently lives evolve, family roots and love can bind and ground us all.

To Philip Dyke who helped me navigate through some of the most difficult waters of my life. Philip's expertise and sage and practical advice kept me calm in those stormy seas. I shall forever be grateful.

To Donna, a friend who has weathered much turbulence in her life yet gives so much of herself to others. While I pursued this book she kept me and my surroundings in order. I am grateful to her for all she did to make my life and my home comfortable during seemingly endless challenges ....

To Liliana and Odi Fass for sharing with me their knowledge of the latest laser anti-aging treatments. Their laser clinics beam clients into a world where bodies melt into desired shapes. Their most precious beam sets their clinics apart from others ... the beam from their hearts. They understand not only desires of clients who want to improve upon that which genetics and the natural passages of time have given them. They also discern what underlies their clients' resolve to be the best they can be. Liliana and Odi's thoughtful and helpful insights into all aspects of their patients' care are part of the package at Liliana Laser Clinics.

To Dr. Deniz Akyurekli, of The Best You enhancement clinics, whose enlightened and humane approach to cosmetic surgery, laser procedures and their psychological benefits inspired me to write more extensively and very positively on what can be done for ever-maturing bodies and spirits. Dr. D is a wonderful ambassador for the science and art of cosmetic surgery. His The Best You clinics and staff *beautifully* reflect his philosophy.

To Dr. Alex Graham who took precious time to enlarge my background knowledge of what goes on in men's minds and bodies as they age and what products are available to them. Besides being a wonderful doctor, he is one great guy and respected player on the tennis court.

To Elaine Saunders, makeup artist extraordinaire, who has encouraged my forays into the worlds of entertainment and media ... her worlds, the same she enthusiastically shared with me. She encouraged me to push through my self-imagined boundaries. This book is only one result of her support. My deepest thanks and love to a wonderful friend.

To dearest H, most special SINS friend, an accomplished man who emerged from a childhood that dealt him less than nothing ... who against all odds achieved so much. A man who shared generously with those whom he later saw experiencing the same dismal shadows. H, who through his search for what he never had or knew, taught me much about the complexities of deep struggle and compassion for others. I thank him for his help as he counterbalanced my lack of aptitude for most things electronic. I am especially grateful for his photography on my behalf, creating as he did, something beautiful out of what I gave him to work with ... much as he did rising and soaring above the early years of his life.

To Pat Irwin and Sally Bradley, a marvelous couple who met on SINS. Pat, who believed I could accomplish whatever I set out to do, who gave me support, encouragement and confidence to fly. Because he believed ... so did I. Sally, who shared with me her formula for utilizing SINS' opportunities to find the *perfect match* ... and so she did!

My heartfelt and deep thanks to E, one of my very first and lasting SINS introductions, who unknowingly inspired my search to understand and accept our human flaws and frailties. E stretched my boundaries of love and the meaning of love unconditional. I shall be eternally grateful you were in my life.

To Dr. Clarence W. Mixon, another exceptional SINS friend, who continually amazes me as to how he savors everything in his life. He has shown me the steady accumulation of years need not slow us down ... there is always something more to learn, experience ... and share. His smile is witness to the beauty and actualization of peace we can radiate because of the understandings each of us might draw out of a lifetime's worth of realizations, experiences, and accomplishments.

To Larry J Payne, met on SINS, who introduced me first hand to the wonderful and vibrant world of country music and the inner workings of the recording industry ... a galaxy of stars I had never dreamed of joining. You possess true talent, my friend. It was a joy being part of your journey.

To my ex-husband and father of our two wonderful daughters ... Thank you. Thank you for bringing me to Canada and sharing with me so much of a world I never would have known without you. I am forever grateful we heard the fire engine sirens so many years ago.

To Kelsey Collins, my laser technician and friend, who not only helps her clients address the visible signs of aging, but also eases their inner struggles. She has such great insights into life ... like a wise *old soul* owl. I often think she should be a pedicurist, as her clients' faces have to be still for her to work her magic ... very tough to do while sharing with her their life's latest trials and celebrations.

To marvelous Jutta and Dietmar Knauer, who taught me to always choose to focus on the positive side of every person and situation and to proceed accordingly. When you do, to no surprise ... you and your situation improve beyond what might be gained with a negative approach. Jutta and Dietmar are beautiful living examples of that philosophy. Jutta's wise counsel has helped shape my philosophy and so much of what I have written. She taught me *attitude* accounts for more than we realize in our lives. It can make the whole difference in what comes next *and* the ultimate outcome. I love you ... I admire you, my dearest Jutta and Dietmar.

To Randy Glasbergen, my fabulous cartoonist ... his interpretations of Mature Singles life communicated in a few strokes of the pen and accompanied by his sharp wit brought immense humor to Candyland S.I.N.S. He was an unexpected gift to help me tell my story. Thank you, Randy.

To Gordon McFarlane, RMT, my massage therapist who kept my body in working order during this sojourn ... he performed his magic on my wrists, neck, back, abdomen, etc. keeping them functioning while they endured grueling hours, weeks, months on my computers. Gord is the only reason I am at the finish line walking upright ... and able to hold my tennis racquet.

To Andrew of Andrew's Copy & Print Centre who showed *the big guys* how good taste, good business ethics and good attitude always outshine glitz and glowing promises. You got it!! You understood and executed my vision. You saved my sanity, Andrew, during those final days of steering this book to print. Thank you.

And, to so many who have made lasting imprints on my life, who gave, encouraged, shared, loved ... and remain (some sadly only in my heart). Solveiga and Gerry, Birte, Ursula and Charles, Sigrid and Dieter, Lis, Jacqui, Paula, Lucy, Janet, Karen and Michael, Tita and Paul, Loren and Norma, Zbigi and Barbara, Tony, Lene and Dave, Gary, my parents Dot and Ziggy who patiently nurtured my curious and passionate nature and so many more dear to me all of who provided a safe harbor in turbulent seas on moonless nights and shared calm, glistening waters on sunny days.

My love and thank you, all.

PEOPLE COME INTO YOUR LIFE FOR A REASON
Excerpt

People come into your life for a reason,
a season or a lifetime.
...
It is said that love is blind.
But friendship is clairvoyant.

Thank you for being a part of my life, whether you were
a reason, a season or a lifetime.

--Author Unknown--

Reader Reflection and Discussion Group Topics

Questions and thoughts to ponder and discuss:

Focus One: Suddenly Single

1. What emotions come to mind when you read or hear that phrase ... *suddenly single?*
2. Are/Were you *suddenly single?* Do you know someone who is/was?
3. Care to share a short version of your or that person's story?
4. How did character flaws play a part in the full story?
5. What half-aware suspicions did you, s/he have? RED FLAGS? If so, how did you, s/he handle them?
6. What was the decisive event and who took action?
7. What was the outcome of your or her/his choices? Any regrets?

8. After reading *Candyland S.I.N.S.*, what could/should you or s/he have done differently?
9. Might family responsibilities or age affect someone's decision? How?
10. How do you now feel about someone you know who is now *suddenly single*?

Focus Two: Mature At Last?

1. When did you realize you were a Mature Adult? The age? The event?
2. As a Mature Adult, what is one of your happiest memories from your younger years? If it involves romance, all the better.
3. What issues are you or someone you know facing as a Mature Single?
4. Relate the storyline of one of your favorite movies involving Mature romance.
5. Is there a topic you would like to bring up relevant to Mature Singles and dating or other challenges/adventures you'd like to discuss?

~~~~~~

Do you agree with the following statement? Why? Why not?

"People who live life in fear of taking risks die without living it."
-Fola, *The Seed*-

~~~~~~

Reader Notes

Reader Suggestion: For easy referring, first jot down the page number for the passage that prompted each note.

_____

_____

_____

_____

_____

_____

_____

_____

_____

_____

_____

_____

_____

_____

About the Author

Seasoned Single Joan Barrett has navigated the tricky, exciting and challenging Mature Singles lifestyle in her own *modus vivendi*, as can you. Joan's passion for **SINS** (her playful term for **S**ingles **In**ternet-dating **S**ervices) and its benefits for Mature Singles inspired her to create *Candyland S.I.N.S.* to support current members, especially newbies, and *not-yet* members who want to know more about this Candyland of tempting treats.

In her continuing journey, one punctuated with sugary highs and fall-back lows, she has savored many beautiful moments and endured disappointments and disillusionments but has always bounced back. Her experiences will ably help readers navigate the peaks, the valleys and ... the inevitable curves. She has maneuvered them all and has survived to tell about some of them with a smile.

Left Suddenly Single at 62, Joan began her new life in unfamiliar territory by facing it head-on. She opened a cooking school for 'Seasoned' Singles called Kiss the Cook xo. She saw the need to encourage interaction in the somewhat socially marginalized, at the time, Mature Singles segment of the population. This venture renewed her energy and love for life.

Joan then discovered the existence of SINS for Mature Singles. Her entrance into this new-to-her, exciting online dating world further invigorated her as she joined other like-minded Mature Singles who were not about out to roll over alone and sit out their remaining years. *Candyland S.I.N.S.* was written for those who have chosen, as Joan did, to do the same. Life loves people who live it with passion.

As a member of SINS, Joan has formed innumerable friendships and been blessed with two very deep relationships that morphed into enduring connections. Her exposure to the broad range of members in SINS has changed her life forever. She has actively participated in SINS over a fun-filled eight-year period, a deep enough engagement to know the game and how the game is being played ... and *how not to be played*!

Joan initially joined SINS with the intention to find that special one long-term relationship so many seek. At times she found it necessary after disappointing or failed attempts to connect with that exceptional match to pick herself up, dust herself off and start all over again. At other times she communicated and dated just for the sheer fun of it or to allow herself to heal, recharge and once again move forward. Joan discovered SINS is a world of continuous life and activity *if* you know how to present and conduct yourself.

This world is anything but dull; any member new to the scene may be *the one*.

Joan has created *Candyland S.I.N.S.* as a compilation of an in-depth guide and truthful first-hand and shared accounts of Mature Internet dating. Her intention helps readers to successfully navigate their ways practically and emotionally through the varied aspects of SINS. *Candyland S.I.N.S.* is based in her experiences and those of other members in these online communities, in topical resources and in statistically framed studies. Joan informs and entertains as she introduces you to this online world and presents insights ranging from light-hearted to serious but never dull. In each chapter she keeps you looking forward to what could be around the corner for you (and her) as you all seek your later-in-life and, possibly, *best hurrah*.

Contact Joan .... candylandsins@rogers.com

Visit Candyland S.I.N.S. .... www.candylandsins.com

Visit Candyland S.I.N.S. .... www.facebook.com/candylandsins

CPSIA information can be obtained at www.ICGtesting.com
Printed in the USA
LVOW07s0513131114

413374LV00002B/4/P